Girls and Women of Color in STEM

A volume in
Research on Women and Education
Beverly J. Irby and Julia Ballenger, *Series Editors*
Janice Koch, *Editor Emerita*

Girls and Women of Color in STEM

Navigating the Double Bind in K–12 Education

edited by

Barbara Polnick
Sam Houston State University

Julia Ballenger
A&M University–Commerce

Beverly J. Irby
Texas A&M University

Nahed Abdelrahman
Texas A&M University

INFORMATION AGE PUBLISHING, INC.
Charlotte, NC • www.infoagepub.com

Library of Congress Cataloging-in-Publication Data

A CIP record for this book is available from the Library of Congress
http://www.loc.gov

ISBN: 978-1-64802-097-1 (Paperback)
       978-1-64802-098-8 (Hardcover)
       978-1-64802-099-5 (E-Book)

Printed in the United States of America

CONTENTS

PART I

BUILDING CAPACITY OUTSIDE THE SCHOOL WALLS

v

PART II

BUILDING CAPACITY INSIDE THE SCHOOL WALLS

FOREWORD

So, I want all the girls watching here, now, to know that a new day is on the horizon!
And when that new day finally dawns, it will be because of a lot of magnificent
women, many of whom are right here in this room tonight, and some pretty phenom-
enal men, fighting hard to make sure that they become the leaders who take us to the
time when nobody ever has to say "Me too" again.

—Oprah Winfrey, Golden Globe Awards address, January 7, 2018

"Time is up!" is the current impassioned battle cry launched at this year's 2018 Golden Globe awards ceremony. Supporters dressed in black to raise awareness concerning the plight of women, issues of inequity and racial prejudice not just in the film industry; but in all aspects of the workforce, and as this book will elucidate, most especially in the areas of science, technology, engineering, and mathematics (STEM). At the forefront of this current and decidedly complicated sociocultural climate, is the imbalance of power, particularly for women of color, in these STEM fields. At present, and perhaps fortunately for STEM, there appears to be an apparent shift in the tide of White dominated male influences in all areas of the global work force and women seem to be gaining force and power.

In fact, for the first time in its 80 years in print, the December 4, 2017 issue of *Time* (Disis, 2017) magazine named the most influential force of this past year is not a single individual but a collective force—the underrepresented voice of women known as the, "Silence-breakers." It is a recognition of the cultural reckoning this year and the #MeToo movement, which represents the people, mostly women, who have fueled a worldwide discussion about sexual harassment, assault, and disparities in the workplace. "This reckoning appears to have sprung up overnight. But it has actually been simmering for years, decades, centuries" (Disis, 2017, n.p.), *Time*'s story said. The chief editor of *Time*, Rosenthal, claims, "This is the fastest-moving social change we've seen in decades, and it began with individual acts of courage by hundreds of women who came forward to tell their own stories of inequality" (Bromwich, 2017, para. 3). Now that the stories are being told and tales of gender inequity in the workforce have finally come to light, the time is right to ultimately welcome a new era of hope for these tenacious women of all colors to pursue, contribute, achieve, and thrive in STEM fields.

I have had the privilege of teaching in the STEM education realm for the past 4 decades as a science educator, Pre–K through graduate students. My early experiences with the reform movement, Project 2061, inaugurated by the American Association for the Advancement of Science (AAAS) and funded by the Carnegie Foundation in the late 80s afforded me the opportunity to work with diverse groups of scientists, mathematicians, engineers, and educators and helped to frame my understanding of the significance of STEM for *all* Americans—most especially women and underrepresented groups. It has always been my personal career goal to inspire girls to pursue their natural interests and develop the necessary habits of mind such as curiosity, creativity, informed skepticism, and openness to new ideas which are necessary to invent new things, solve problems, and create meaningful change—the very essence of STEM characteristics. As a co-author of a chapter in a previous volume of women of color in STEM, "Breaking Barriers: Inspiring Stories of NASA Women of Color" (Brown, Foster, & Polnick, 2017), I realized and better understood the struggle NASA women of color endured during the milieu of 1960's through today. The book and film "Hidden Figures" seemed very similar to the stories of the women we interviewed and researched for the series. "Their dark skin, their gender, their economic status—none of those were acceptable excuses for not giving the fullest rein to their imaginations and ambitions." (Shetterly, 2016). Persistence, perseverance, and opportunities for all girls to thrive in STEM fields are what make the difference.

This exceptional volume in Research on Women and Education, *Women of Color in STEM: The Double Bind in K–12 Schools*, offers thirteen critical stories of how the responsibility of strengthening the worlds' engines of discovery and innovation rest on nurturing the early interest and talents of girls of color in science, technology, engineering, and mathematics. The chapters offer a compilation of significant quantitative studies and qualitative stories about gender equity in the sciences, Black and Latina girls whose STEM ambitions are developed, researched, and nurtured. The authors in this series further our understanding of how providing opportunities and experiencing STEM ambitions of students in cultural, economic, and contemporary contexts is critical for changing larger societal patterns of inequality.

Nonetheless, despite a national focus on directing more students toward science, technology, engineering, and math fields—particularly women and minorities—the STEM workforce is no more diverse now than in 2001 (Bidwell, 2015). So, what are we doing and what can be done to promote and "charm" women and minority students who may represent overlooked talent in schools nationwide? The authors of these chapters skillfully provide insights, ideas, pedagogical strategies that support diverse communities of female learners to realize their STEM strengths, their vibrancy and the opportunities to break down those tough cultural and gender barriers. Although the overall face of the workforce throughout the country has changed—a higher representation of younger and minority individuals, the demographics in STEM fields have remained largely unchanged, until now. Time is up. Indeed, a new day is on the horizon—women of color in STEM are our future.

—**Andrea S. Foster**

REFERENCES

Bromwich, J. E. (December 6, 2017). "The Silence Breakers" named *Time*'s Person of the Year for 2017. *New York Times*. Retrieved from https://www.nytimes.com/2017/12/06/business/media/silence-breakers-time-person-of-the-year.html?searchResultPosition=2

Brown, L., Foster, A., & Polnick, B. (2017). Breaking barriers: Inspiring stories of NASA women of color. In J. Ballenger, B. Polnick, & B. Irby (Eds.), *Women of color navigating the double blind in the workforce* (pp. 57–77). Charlotte, NC: Information Age.

Bidwell, A. (2015, February 24). STEM workforce no more diverse than 14 years ago. *U.S. News*. Retrieved from https://www.usnews.com/news/stem-solutions/articles/2015/02/24/stem-workforce-no-more-diverse-than-14-years-ago

Disis, J. (2017, December 6). *Time*'s person of the year is "The Silence Breakers." *CNN*. Retrieved from http://money.cnn.com/2017/12/06/media/time-person-of-the-year-2017/index.html

Shetterly, M. L. (2016). *Hidden figures: The American dream and the untold story of Black women mathematicians who helped win the space race*. New York, NY: Harper Collins.

Winfrey, O. (2018, January 7). *Golden Globe Cecil B. Demille Award address*. Retrieved from https://www.goldenglobes.com/articles/oprah-winfrey-recipient-cecil-b-demille-award-2018

INTRODUCTION

AN OVERVIEW OF K–12 ISSUES RELATED WOMEN AND GIRLS OF COLOR IN STEM

At no time in our period in history is it more important for us to engage the untapped resource of women of color in today's workforce, specifically in the fields of science, technology, engineering, and mathematics (STEM). Girls and women of color bring culturally different understandings and experiences that can be leveraged to innovatively solve complex problems. It is both timely and imperative that education and career efforts work to build the capacity of girls and women of color to advance in STEM fields. This book is a culmination of research on the issues and challenges (and successes!) for girls and young women in the fields of STEM. Authors in these thirteen chapters share their research on the impact of current practices in schools and related educational settings, as well as effective interventions that illustrate ways to assist and promote girls and women of color to navigate the double bind in STEM fields today. The chapters address issues experienced across multiple ethnicities and races and span a broad range of settings from early childhood to high school to higher education. The book is organized around two parts: those studies which focused on partnerships and professional development outside the school walls and those studies of girls and young women of color within schools.

Girls and Women of Color In STEM, pages xiii–xvii
Copyright © 2020 by Information Age Publishing

PART I: BUILDING CAPACITY OUTSIDE THE SCHOOL WALLS

In our first chapter, Larke, Webb-Hasan, Jimarez, and Li illustrate how opportunities outside of the regular school day provide young Hispanic and African American girls with the tools for improving their own skills in reading, mathematics, and science. Through a grant from the National Science Foundation, the authors created a conference (CHARMS) that included public school leaders, parents, teachers, and students, all learning as a team that through the use of hands-on activities, positive support, encouragement, African American and Hispanic elementary girls can succeed in math and science.

In her description of a collaborative project between a university and an urban, underserved elementary school, Kelly-Jackson outlines ways to increase upper elementary girls' awareness and interest in STEM through Girls Engaged in Mathematics and Science (GEMS), a summer robotics program. In her chapter, "Plugging the Leaks in the Stem Pipeline: Nurturing Early Interest in Science, Technology, Engineering, and Mathematics Among Girls of Color," she highlights the curriculum, which was developed using a student-centered, engineering design and problem based approach inclusive of the sociocultural approach framed by Vygotsky's theories of learning. Results from the administration of multiple surveys reflected a positive change in students' perceptions and feelings toward STEM domains and careers, especially in the field of robotics.

Mitchell and Squires in their chapter, "Uno Eureka-Stem: Doing Something About the Double Bind," illustrate how a university and nonprofit agency partnership can impact the lives of middle school girls of color by increasing their interest, participation, and success in STEM-related activities. University of Nebraska–Omaha in collaboration with the Omaha Girls, Inc., included two groups of girls, new (Rookies) and returnees (Vets), in robotics, university faculty-taught STEM coursework in lab environments, personal development, and friendly swimming lessons and competition. The girls' perceptions of the experiences showed greatest gains in robotics and rocketry for the Rookies, while the Vets felt their knowledge increased the most in physics.

PART II: BUILDING CAPACITY INSIDE THE SCHOOL WALLS

In the chapter "We Stumble, Fall, Get up, and Continue Walking: Latina Students' Attitudes towards Science," Scantlebury and Wassell focus on the attitudes and experiences in science of 70 urban middle school Latina students. Interviews, field notes, observations, cogenerative dialogues, and videos of science classes were utilized to collect qualitative data, while quantitative data was collected from a science attitude survey which analyzed students' descriptions of (a) what I do in class, (b) what my teacher does, and (c) what my friends do. The authors highlight the impact that native language has on girls' attitudes toward science as well as those pedagogical practices that best support Latina girls, specifically in learning environments where the ongoing domination of teachers' attention to boys remains an issue.

Riegle-Crumb, Morton, and Blanchard explore the question "How do math and science grades, advanced coursework, and test scores predict the STEM expectations of Hispanic youth, and how do these differ by gender?" in their study of 4,000 ninth and tenth graders in a large urban predominantly Hispanic school district. In this chapter, "Developing STEM Ambitions: An Examination of Inequality by Gender and Race/Ethnicity," the authors offer us the challenge of finding solutions for encouraging the many young Hispanic women who have strong math and science credentials but who hold minimal expectations towards pursuing STEM fields.

In their study, "Black Women and Girls, Science Achievement, and Education Policy: Black Feminist and Critical Race Feminist Perspectives," Berry and Roby examine ways in which Black feminist thought and critical race feminism can be used to examine how science can be taught in a way that makes it more accessible to Black girls. By identifying the differences in which Black girls interact with one another, interact with teachers, and engage in learning, school leaders can more effectively select interventions that teach the ways in which Black girls learn. The authors conclude that changes in science education policies are needed to provide Black girls more opportunities to engage their unique voices and experiences in the context of science learning.

Young and Young in their chapter "African American Female Achievement in STEM: AP Courses Provide a Different Story?" illuminate African American female achievement—not the lack thereof, by adjusting the focus "Gap Gazing" to "Success Seeking." Using critical race feminism as a complementary framework to critical race theory, they analyze the intersection between race and gender as an essential element in the analysis of African American female achievement in Advanced Placement high school classes.

In their study, Shumow and Wasonga analyzed whether Kenyan secondary school students' motivation to learn science varied by gender and school type. Utilizing the elements of self-determination theory in their study the authors studied classroom processes and practices in classrooms serving mainstream (not wealthy or elite) students. While the authors found no gender differences in students' perceptions of their skill, interest, relevance, and cooperation in science class, female Kenyan secondary school students did report a lower sense of control, marginally less success, and more competitiveness than male students. However, in their chapter,

"Kenyon Secondary School Students' Perceptions of Their Science Classroom: Influence of Gender, School Type, and Instructional Context," the authors noted that female autonomy (control) ratings were dramatically higher than those reported by U.S. female secondary school students.

King, Pringle, Cordero, and Ridgewell illustrate how informal learning environments with culturally relevant instructional strategies, such as in the FOCUS program, can spark the interests of African American middle school girls from low SES backgrounds to participate in STEM-related activities. In their chapter, "Mining Rare Gems to Pursue STEM in African American Middle School Girls in a Community-based Informal Program," the authors make a case for providing girls from low SES backgrounds with rich experiences outside of school that facilitate these girls' abilities to see themselves as future mathematicians, scientists, and engineers in safe, supporting environments. The authors share six strategies learned from this informal environment that can be used by schools to encourage creative thinking and leverage their cultural strengths.

The authors of "Latina Parental Involvement: Contributions to Persistence in STEM Fields" utilized sociocultural theory to frame their case study of three Latina women (two high school and one college student). Brkich, Martinez, Stevenson, Bayne, Pitts, Wassell, Claeys, and Flores focused their interviews on five major strands of inquiry: (a) on what it means to be a girl, (b) on what it means to be Latin@, (c) on their educational and career aspirations, (d) on the obstacles they faced to their educational success, and (e) on the roles their parents played in their education. Results indicated that parents of these women utilized multiple interactions through the application of social capital, interactions not typically characterized by some White middle-class female teachers as "parental involvement."

In "Participation in the Advancing Out-of-School Learning in Mathematics and Engineering (Aolme) Project: Supporting Middle School Latinas' Bilingual and STEM Identities," authors LópezLeiva, Celedón-Pattichis, and Pattichis, describe how three bilingual Latina girls developed a sense of comfort, expertise, agency, and belonging for (STEM) fields by participating in an integrated curriculum involving mathematics and engineering activities through computer programming. The AOLME project included student-based storytelling processes in a collaborative setting. The girls described their experiences as both enjoyable and areas that they, as girls, would be interested in pursuing.

West-Olatunji drew our attention to the influence school counselors' have in making appropriate referrals regarding the pursuit of STEM fields for African American girls. In her study "Exploring How School Counselors Position Low-Income African American Girls as Mathematics and Science Learners: Findings From Year Two Data," the author provided evidence of the need for more comprehensive training for school counselors, specifically emphasis on multicultural competence with sustained supervision and the use of a master counselor model for ongoing development. In so doing, counselors can become agents of change for STEM, especially for culturally marginalized girls in low-resourced schools.

The authors of "STEM-ing the Tide: Women of Color Reimaging Their "Place" Through Sociocultural Action," offer us insight into the benefits of providing a long-term STEM professional development program (PROJECT) for women of color teachers working with English learners (ELs) in K–8 classrooms. Alkandari and Torres examined both ideological and identity challenges experienced by these teachers as they participated in the PROJECT program. Through their sociocultural embedded action research, they concluded that there was a need for engaging teachers in authentic, collaborative action research approaches when designing teacher professional development in STEM and to create spaces where issues of gender and race are critically discussed.

—**Barbara Polnick**
Beverly J. Irby
Julia Ballenger
Nahed Abdelrahman

PART I

BUILDING CAPACITY OUTSIDE THE SCHOOL WALLS

CHAPTER 1

CULTIVATING HISPANIC/ LATINA AND AFRICAN AMERICAN FEMALES IN READING, MATHEMATICS, AND SCIENCE (CHARMS) FOR STEM AT THE ELEMENTARY SCHOOL

Results of One Project

Patricia J. Larke
Gwendolyn Webb-Hasan
Teresa Jimarez
Yeping Li

There is a concern in science, technology, engineering, and mathematics (STEM) career fields to address the scarcity of diversity among our professionals relating to females of color, more specifically, African American and

Girls and Women of Color In STEM, pages 3–17
Copyright © 2020 by Information Age Publishing

Latina females (Alvarez & Harris, 2010; Espinosa, 2009; US Commission, 2010). There has been a plethora of research on the need to increase the number of females to select STEM academic majors that transforms into STEM careers (American Association of University Women, 2010; Bayer Cooperation Report, 2010; Beede et al., 2011; Tyler-Wood, Ellison, Lim, & Periathiruvadi, 2012). While such emphasis has been the pathway for career development of the 24% of females in STEM careers (Beede et al., 2011), the majority who are of European and Asian descent, there is a need to cultivate Latina and African American (LAA) females. They comprise 25% of the current school-age population who will be a major component of the future workforce (Espinosa, 2009). However, increasing the number of female professionals in STEM fields means starting at the elementary level (K–5) with an assessment of the academic achievement of LAA females in reading, mathematics, and science (Bianchini, 2011; O'Brien, 2010). The fundamental research question is: What is the academic achievement of LAA females at the elementary level in reading, mathematics, and science? As such, this research question served as an impetus to secure funding from the National Science Foundation (NSF) to develop a conference for teachers, administrators, and parents (TAP) entitled, Cultivating Hispanics and African Americans' Reading, Math, Science (CHARMS) in Elementary Schools for Girls Conference: Project CHARMS for Elementary School Girls (NSF #1048544). Based on the results of this project, we (a) discuss an analysis of selected state accountability scores from the 2007 and 2011 Texas Assessment of Knowledge and Skills (TAKS) data for females in mathematics and science at the third and fifth grade level, (b) provide an overview of the CHARMS conference and share the results of the CHARMS conference evaluation, and (c) discuss the findings as related to LAA elementary girls and STEM.

ANALYSIS OF FEMALE STATE ACCOUNTABILITY MEAN SCORES FOR THIRD GRADE MATHEMATICS AND FIFTH GRADE SCIENCE, 2007 AND 2011

For LAA girls to seek STEM careers, they must have appropriate skills in subjects such as mathematics and science. Further, they must demonstrate their knowledge of those skills by making appropriate scores on state and national assessments. The assessment of their competency in mathematics and science skill development begins in elementary school. Often, students' competencies on state and national assessments are reported by passing and failure rates or by ethnicity and gender without the disaggregation of the data by subject matter objectives. To get a deeper understanding of the level of competency that LAAs exhibit on the mathematics and science assessments, it is necessary to disaggregate the data by subject matter objectives and gender. In Texas, the state assessments (TAKS) for reading and mathematics begin at third grade and science assessments begin at the fifth grade. This section provides a brief discussion of the TAKS and an analysis of TAKS data at the third grade in mathematics and fifth grade in science TAKS among females for the years 2007 and 2011.

TAKS

The TAKS stemmed from the state legislature in 1999 to create a more rigorous assessment program while also eliminating social promotion. The 1999 law mandated that students meet certain criteria to exit certain grade levels. Students must pass TAKS Grade 3 reading assessment as well as receive passing grades to be promoted to the fourth grade. In Grades 5 and 8, students must meet state requirements on TAKS mathematics and reading assessments while maintaining passing grades. In the eleventh grade, students must pass TAKS reading, mathematics, science, social studies, and writing while earning enough high school credits to be eligible to receive a high school diploma. The TAKS assessment program began testing in 2003 and continued till 2011. However in 2012 Texas implemented a new assessment entitled, State of Texas Assessments of Academic Readiness (STAAR).[1]

Third Grade Female TAKS Mean Scores for Mathematics, 2007 and 2011

The mathematics TAKS test for both third and fifth grade has six objectives. In Grade 3, there are 40 test items and 44 test items in Grade 5. There was an increase in the number of items in five of the objectives with only probability and statistics remaining with four test items (see Table 1.1). Objective 1 is

TABLE 1.1   TAKS Mathematics Objectives for Grades 3 and 5

Math Obj. #	Description	3rd Grade Items	5th Grade Items
1	Numbers, Operations, Quantitative Reasoning	10	11
2	Patterns, Relationships, & Algebraic Expressions	6	7
3	Geometry and Spatial Reasoning	6	7
4	Measurement	6	7
5	Probability and Statistics	4	4
6	Mathematical Processes and Tools	8	8
Total Items		**40**	**44**

comprised of Numbers, Operations, and Quantitative Reasoning. Objective 2 includes Patterns, Relationships, and Algebraic Expressions. Objective 3 is concerned with Geometry and Spatial Reasoning. Objective 4 addresses Geometry, while Objective 5 relates to Probability and Statistics. Objective 6 is the final objective and focuses on Mathematical Processes and Tools. For the purpose of this article, the third grade mathematics results will be presented.

In Grade 3, LAA females continue to score below Native, European, and Asian Americans in all six objectives. In Objective 1, Numbers, Operations, and Quantitative Reasoning with 10 items, the 2011 mean scores showed an increase over the 2007 mean scores for all females (see Figure 1.1). Latina ($M = 8.29$) and African American ($M = 7.88$) females had the lowest means while Asian Americans had the highest means ($M = 9.1$). However, African Americans represented the greatest gains between 2007 and 2011 from 7.92 to 8.29.

For Objective 2, Patterns, Relationships, and Algebraic Expressions, which includes 6 items, three groups showed an increase (African American, $M = 4.59$; Latina, $M = 4.76$; and Asian American, $M = 5.39$) in the 2011 means scores, while two groups (European and Native American) had their highest mean scores in 2007. As in Objective 1, LAAs have the lowest mean scores (see Tables 1.2 and 1.3).

Geometry and Spatial Reasoning included 6 items in Objective 3. Like Objective 2, three groups showed gains from 2007 to 2011 (European, Latina, and African American) while Native Americans showed no changes in the mean score during the same period. Asian Americans showed a decrease in the mean score. African American females showed the greatest mean increase; yet, they still had the lowest mean score overall for females.

There was a similar pattern with Objective 4 (measurement with 6 items) in comparison to Objective 1. All groups showed an increase in the mean scores between 2007 and 2011. Both European and African Americans had the greatest mean score gains (.22) and Asian Americans continued to have

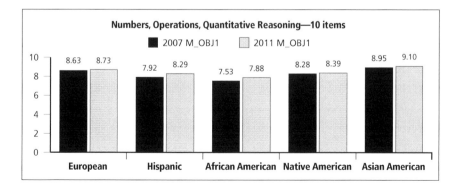

Figure 1.1 Math Objective 1, 3rd Grade Females Mean Scores, 2007, 2011

TABLE 1.2   Third Grade Female TAKS Mathematics Mean Scores, 2007

Ethnicity	N	O1 = 10 M(SD)	O2 = 6 M(SD)	O3 = 6 M(SD)	O4 = 6 M(SD)	O5 = 4 M(SD)	O6 = 8 M(SD)
NA	546	8.28(1.91)	4.87(1.21)	5.08(1.07)	4.85(1.10)	3.42(0.82)	5.68(1.92)
AS	5,570	8.95(1.48)	5.33(0.95)	5.48(0.86)	5.27(0.96)	3.67(0.64)	6.48(1.68)
AFA	22,368	7.53(2.15)	4.51(1.34)	4.70(1.30)	4.33(1.36)	3.23(0.93)	4.93(2.03)
L	64,407	7.92(1.99)	4.73(1.22)	4.98(1.71)	4.71(1.19)	3.32(0.88)	5.14(1.98)
EA	55,440	8.63(1.66)	5.02(1.09)	5.29(0.97)	5.01(1.04)	3.59(0.70)	6.05(1.81)

TABLE 1.3   Third Grade Female TAKS Mathematics Mean Scores, 2011

Ethnicity	N	O1 = 10 M(SD)	O2 = 6 M(SD)	O3 = 6 M(SD)	O4 = 6 M(SD)	O5 = 4 M(SD)	O6 = 8 M(SD)
NA	730	8.39(1.81)	4.79(1.20)	5.08(1.04)	5.04(1.20)	3.38(0.81)	5.75(1.83)
AS	6,541	9.10(1.52)	5.39(0.96)	5.47(0.89)	5.36(0.97)	3.66(0.67)	6.69(1.65)
AFA	21,872	7.88(2.09)	4.59(1.33)	4.86(1.22)	4.55(1.46)	3.20(0.92)	5.22(2.01)
L	81,170	8.29(1.89)	4.76(1.24)	5.09(1.08)	4.92(1.24)	3.32(0.83)	5.46(1.94)
EA	53,585	8.73(1.61)	5.01(1.13)	5.24(0.98)	5.23(1.06)	3.57(0.70)	6.25(1.73)

the highest means while African Americans had the lowest means. The pattern was very different for Objective 5 (Probability and Statistics—4 items). All groups except Latinas had higher means in 2007 than in 2011. The means of Latina remain the same for both years. Objective 6 (Mathematical Process and Tools—8 items), presented had the most difficulty for all students. While the mean scores ranged from 4.93 to 6.48 in 2007, and 5.22 to 6.69 in 2011, all subgroups showed an increase similar to Objectives 1, 3, and 6.

In summary, African American and Latina third grade females had the lowest means in all six objectives. Latina and African American third grade females showed gains in the same five of the six objectives for the years 2007 and 2011. Therefore, according to these results, more effective instruction is needed in all six mathematics objectives. This instruction must occur in kindergarten through second grade classrooms, since third grade builds on the skills learned in previous years. Skills such as the application of many mathematics concepts (e.g., place values, use fractions names and symbols, addition and subtraction of whole numbers to 999).

Fifth Grade Female TAKS Mean Scores for Science, 2011 and 2007

In science, the TAKS test is given at the fifth grade level. Four objectives are noted in Table 1.3. Objective 1 focuses on understanding the scientific processes. This includes the design of investigations, accurate data collection, use of models to represent the natural world, and data analysis. There are 13 items in this assessment, since this knowledge is critical to understanding the nature of science. Objectives 2, 3, and 4 include the primary content strands of science: life, earth, and physical. These objectives are given equal emphasis (9 items each) on the assessment. This fifth grade science assessment has a total of 40 items.

Tables 1.4 and 1.5 provide the mean scores for fifth grade science scores among females for the years, 2011 and 2007 in the four objectives. In Objective 1 (Nature of Science—13 items), the mean scores for African Americans fifth grade females ranged from 9.71 in 2007 to 10.78 in 2011. For Latina fifth grade females, the mean scores spanned from 10.05 in 2007 to 10.93 in 2011. Again, Asian American fifth grade females had the highest means—11.25 in 2007 and 11.83 in 2011. In 2011, Objective 2 (Life Science), African American females did not have the lowest mean score for the first time. Latina females had the lowest mean score as noted in Table 1.6.

On Objective 3 (Physical Science—9 items), LAAs continued to have the lowest mean scores for 2011, but made the greatest gains from 2007 to 2011 as revealed in Tables 1.4 and 1.5. Objective 4 (Earth Science—9 items) showed the greatest gains for both Latinas ($M = 5.67$; $M = 7.34$) and African Americans ($M = 5.42$; $M = 7.01$) during the years 2007 and 2011. The greatest challenges were found in earth science.

TABLE 1.4 Fifth Grade Female TAKS Science Mean Scores, 2007

Ethnicity	N	O1 = 13 M(SD)	O2 = 9 M(SD)	O3 = 9 M(SD)	O4 = 9 M(SD)
NA	534	10.68(2.54)	7.41(1.95)	7.35(1.84)	6.26(2.08)
AS	5,483	11.25(2.84)	7.71(2.06)	7.75(1.99)	6.79(2.18)
AFA	23,282	9.71(2.96)	6.81(2.21)	6.74(2.10)	5.42(2.23)
L	74,117	10.05(2.95)	6.84(2.21)	6.91(2.10)	5.67(2.25)
EA	54,522	11.22(2.46)	7.76(1.81)	7.61(1.79)	6.64(2.06)

TABLE 1.5 Fifth Grade Female TAKS Science Mean Scores, 2011

Ethnicity	N	O1 = 13 M(SD)	O2 = 9 M(SD)	O3 = 9 M(SD)	O4 = 9 M(SD)
NA	618	11.26(2.09)	7.89(1.45)	7.69(1.49)	7.57(1.67)
AS	6,560	11.83(1.99)	8.11(1.43)	8.06(1.40)	8.00(1.55)
AFA	21,834	10.78(2.20)	7.60(1.45)	7.47(1.49)	7.01(1.77)
L	87,182	10.93(2.13)	7.59(1.47)	7.54(1.46)	7.34(1.65)
EA	54,522	11.77(1.79)	8.14(1.25)	7.97(1.31)	7.79(1.50)

TABLE 1.6 Conference Participants						
Ethnicity	N	Gender		Parent	Teacher Parent	Administrator
African American	22	3 M	19 F	8	10	4
Hispanic/Latino/a	15	2 M	13 F	4	7	4
European American	19	3 M	16 F	0	16	3
Mixed Race	2		2 F		2	
Total	58	8 M	49 F	12	35	11

In summary, for all groups, the greatest improvement was in 2011. The mean scores increased on all of the objectives. Since the science assessment was administered for the first time in fifth grade, more instructional emphasis on science must begin in kindergarten through fourth grade, especially for LAA females. The analysis of the third grade reading and fifth grade TAKS for LAA females indicate that more effective instruction in these subjects is critical. On every assessment, they scored the lowest in comparison to their European and Asian American peers on all objectives of the math and science TAKS during 2007 and 2011. While both groups made gains from 2007 to 2011, these gains continue to indicate the need for more effective teaching and learning of both math and science concepts. As mathematics and science skills become more complex in more advanced grades, it is imperative that they develop a deeper understanding of their skills in the earlier years to learn more complex skills at the third and fifth grade levels.

CHARMS CONFERENCE

The CHARMS conference was held on September 10, 2011 on the campus of Texas A&M University. The purpose of the CHARMS conference was to provide a venue for teachers, administrators and parents to share information about the academic achievement of girls in Grades 3, 4, and 5 and to learn about STEM. The four objectives of the conference were to

1. share baseline data on national and state assessments by gender and subject matter content;
2. provide culturally responsive instructional strategies for teaching, reading, math, and science;
3. examine test data trends within their local school; and
4. provide information about STEM careers for conference participants to share with African American and Latina elementary girls in their respective schools and/or communities.

To participate in the CHARMS conference, school districts had to bring a team of five (5) that included two parents, two teachers, and one administrator. In addition, teams were required to bring copies of their TAKS data for the last 3 years. Due to the vast geographical regions of the state, each participant was given a $100 to $200 stipend (the amount varied by distance traveled) to defray travel expenses. Stipends were awarded at the end of the conference. There were 58 participants who attended the CHARMS 2011 Conference.

CHARMS Conference Activities

The activities for the CHARMS Conference were divided into four sections. Section 1 of the conference provided information on STEM careers as well as national and state assessments results for LAA girls, and culturally responsive teaching. Participants also received a booklet, developed by the STEM university team (Webb-Hasan, Zannou, & Larke, 2011). The booklet provided examples of culturally responsive teaching in reading, mathematics, and science. In the second section, conference participants were divided into breakout sessions in which they had to analyze their test data by gender and subject matter objectives and develop action plans for increasing the achievement of LAA girls in their respective schools. The plans were shared in section four of the conference. The third section included a working lunch in which Dr. Trina Davis, past president of the International Society for Technology in Education, spoke on the topic: "Encouraging African American and Hispanic Girls to Seek STEM Careers: The Role of Educators and Parents." Dr. Davis shared information about what teachers, administrators, and parents can do to increase the number of Latina and African females in STEM careers and provided websites where parents and teachers could go to assist LAA girls with mathematics and science learning. Their respective plans were shared in the fourth section of the conference. In the fourth section, teams had to present their action plans to the entire conference and the strategies they would implement to improve reading, mathematics, and science for girls in their respective schools during the 2011–2012 school year. Additionally, during the fourth section each of the participants were given CHARMS information (CHARMS activity booklet, STEM Career booklet) to share with African American and Latina girls at their respective schools. All materials were placed in a CHARMS bag that was developed by the STEM university team.

Conference Evaluation

At the close of the conference the participants were asked to complete an Institutional Review Board (IRB) approved conference evaluation survey.

The survey had three parts: background information (gender, race/ethnicity, education level, age, years of teaching and administrative experience); conference feedback with nine (9) questions with Likert-type scales that ranged from *strongly disagree* (1) to *strongly agree* (5); and five open-ended questions.

Demographics of CHARMS Conference Participants

Fifty-eight (58) participants attended the conference; however, only 57 completed the conference evaluation summary. Each school district had to bring a team of at least five members that included at least one administrator, two teachers, and two parents. There were 49 females and 8 males (African Americans (N = 22), Latino/as (N = 15), and 19 European Americans (N = 19) and two who identified themselves as biracial (see Table 1.6). There were 12 who identified themselves as parents only, while 35 teachers identified themselves as teachers and parents. Of the 11 administrators, four identified themselves as African Americans and four as Hispanics/Latinas while three identified themselves as European Americans. The participants came from urban, suburban areas across the state (East, West, North, South, Central Texas).

Responses to Survey Questions

The mean scores on the nine questions ranged from a mean score of 4.89 to 4.62 out of 5 as noted in Table 1.7. The participants agreed that

TABLE 1.7   Mean Scores of CHARMS Conference Evaluation

STEM	Mean (5)
Conference is helpful to provide achievement information H/LAA girls.	4.67
Conference provided great opportunity for us to share and discuss issues related to H/LAA girls.	4.81
Quality of invited speaker.	4.85
H/LAA girls are capable of doing well in math and science in the elem. schools.	4.89
Encouraging H/LAA girls to lean math and science in elem. school is important.	4.87
Learning math and science is mostly due to efforts and not students' own intelligence.	4.62
To engage H/LAA girls to learn well in math and science, everybody (parents, teachers, and students) need to help.	4.85
Want future information related to how H/LAA girls learn in elementary school.	4.83
Conference is well planned and organized.	4.83

Note: N = 57

the conference provided helpful information about the achievement of LAA girls ($M = 4.67$) and the conference was well planned and organized ($M = 4.83$). They also liked the talk given by the invited speaker ($M = 4.89$). Participants felt that the entire learning community was needed to help LAAs to do well in math and science ($M = 4.85$).

The highest mean score ($M = 4.89$) was in response to their belief that AAL girls are capable of doing well in math and science. The lowest mean score was in response to their belief that learning math and science mostly reflects the individual's efforts and not to a student's own intelligence ($M = 4.62$). They wanted more information in the future on how LAAs learn in elementary school ($M = 4.83$). Participants felt that the conference provided an opportunity to share information with other educators and parents ($M = 4.81$).

Open-Ended Questions

The analysis of three of the five open ended questions revealed specific information about how parents and educators felt about the conference and what was critical to helping students learn math and science. When asked what they gained most from the conference, the participants indicated that they never looked at gender in their test scores and that parent challenges were the same throughout the state. Further, they felt that they received many ideas to promote academic achievement for LAA females. When asked what was critical to helping LAA girls learn math and science, they felt that the use of hands-on activities, positive support, encouragement, and continued support throughout the school years as critical. They stated that the girls need more female role models. They also shared that educators and parents needed to convince girls that they could be great achievers in math and science. They also felt that more parents should be involved and there was a need for good teachers. When asked what they would do to engage LAA girls in learning math and science, they suggested (a) relating the subject to their lives, (b) searching for role models talk to LAA females about the benefits of STEM, and (c) getting more parents/family members involved. In addition, many of the parents noted that they were unaware of STEM until the conference.

DISCUSSION OF TAKS TEST, CONFERENCE FINDINGS, AND IMPLICATIONS FOR LAA GIRLS AND STEM

Having a conference that involved three critical stakeholders—teachers, administrators, and parents—who discussed STEM information and presented test data about the academic achievement of LAA girls can serve as a venue to address how the pipeline of LAA girls can obtain the reading, math, and science skills necessary to be able to select and participate in a pathway to STEM careers. Studies support our belief that to increase the STEM participation, academic preparation is pivotal (Hubbard & Stage, 2010). While this study used data from Texas' state assessment, it is important to note that Texas represents a microcosm of the demographics of the United States. In that, Texas has the second largest number of African American and Latina students in its K–12 in comparison to any other state in the United States (Texas Education Agency [TEA], 2012). It is important to note that while the percentages are higher in other states, the numbers are greater in Texas (TEA, 2012).

From the analysis of the TAKS data, the mean scores of LAA girls are lowest in math at the third grade level and science at the fifth grade level. While this represents findings in the literature, this study identified the subject matter objectives that accounted for differences of mean scores and by the female gender. When assessments are disaggregated by gender and ethnicity, it can assist stakeholders in identifying specific objectives for targeted instruction. For example, within this study, probability and statistics (Objective 5) showed the greatest difficulty. Helping students learn how to solve problems with graphs, tables, and probability is important in STEM careers. Developing foundational math skills at the third grade level can provide LAA girls both the confidence and academic background needed for higher level math courses. Higher level math courses serve as pathways to STEM careers.

The CHARMS conference evaluation supported many issues related to LAAs and STEM. The issues included strengthening LAA girls' skills in math and science, helping teachers and parents in developing culturally responsive math and science skills to assist student learning and deepen exposure to STEM information and STEM careers. The following recommendations are a result of the analysis.

1. *Increasing the participation pipeline.* The participation of LAAs in STEM fields cannot be increased until LAA students develop more strategic and critical math, science, and reading skills at the elementary level. Studies show that LAA girls score lower on state and national assessment than Native, European, and Asian American girls (AAUW, 2010; Darling-Hammond, 2010; Delpit, 2012). Texas' TAKS results show similar patterns. To help Africa American and Latina girls improve their math, reading, and science skills, elementary level educators must acquire a repertoire of culturally responsive teaching and learning skills in areas of reading, mathematics, and science (Gay, 2010).

2. *Teachers, Parents, and Administrators Teams.* The composition of the teams was intentional as research indicates that all stakeholders must be involved in the academic success of LAA girls (Gay, 2010; Kendricks & Arment, 2011). These are the key stakeholders who can impact the academic achievement of LAA girls. Most conferences do not require these stakeholders to attend as a team. As the evaluation revealed, teachers, parents, and administers had to develop and share strategies to increase the academic achievement of LAA girls and many of the strategies they shared are well documented in the literature (Atwater, 2010a, 2010b; Gay, 2009). The conference provided information about culturally responsive strategies for participants. Many of them used the strategies in the breakout session to develop action plans for their respective schools.

3. *STEM Information.* It was not surprising that many parents and teachers were unaware of STEM. Research supports that mothers/parents are instrumental in the career decisions of their daughters (AAUW, 2010; Shome, 1997). Therefore, the conference staff developed booklets to provide parents/educators information about STEM. For example, parents, teachers, and administrators were given booklets (Young & Larke, 2011) to disseminate to LAA girls in their respective schools as well as to share with their daughters.

4. *Analyzing Test Data.* Having a team of parents, teachers, and administrators critically analyze test data by gender and subject matter content is beneficial to all. Such information can assist with professional development as well as curriculum alignment. The team approach to this process can empower parents who often do not participate in test data analysis, yet are instrumental in the factors associated in children's educational attainment (Malcom, 2010).

Implications for LAA Girls and STEM

To increase the number of LAA girls in STEM careers, more programs must be developed and implemented at the elementary level to target girls, families, and educators. While most STEM programs and activities target females at the secondary level and in higher education (Fadigan & Hammrich, 2004; North & Jobs, 2011), there are few STEM programs at the elementary level. Elementary STEM programs for girls can create a ripple effect, thus, increasing the pool of students at the secondary and collegiate level. The NSF in its DR-K12 initiative has provided funds for the elementary level, however, few proposals have actually been funded.

For many parents and teachers, the CHARMS conference provided useful information about STEM. Such information included an explanation of what STEM is to the various types of STEM careers. The STEM community tends to assume that everyone knows the meaning of STEM; however, STEM is not a topic of common discussion among LAA communities. Parents and teachers are vital players in increasing the awareness of LAA girls about STEM.

In summary, the impact of increasing the number of LAA girls in the STEM field has many benefits. The career decisions of LAA girls can impact the quality of life of not only for themselves but for the next generation as well. The research continues to support that women of color are underrepresented in the STEM fields (Bayer, 2010; North & Jobs, 2011; Business-Higher Education Forum, 2011). This article responds to the findings of the 2010 Bayer Facts of Science Education XIV report that states that one of the reasons for the underrepresentation of women of color in STEM is because they were not identified, encouraged, or nurtured to pursue STEM early. Project CHARMS shared information on how teachers, administrators, and parents could identify, encourage, and nurture LAA girls to seek careers in STEM while sharing data about the academic achievement of LAA girls at the elementary level. If the pool is not increased at the elementary level, then the saga of underrepresentation of women of color in STEM will continue to be rhetoric for LAA females who constitute more than 25% of the school-age population.

NOTE

1. While Texas no longer uses the TAKS but the STAAR test, our findings from the analysis of the 2013–2015 STAAR data indicate similar findings for LAA girls.

REFERENCES

Alvarez, C. A., Edwards, D., & Harris, B. (2010). *STEM specialty programs: A pathway for underrepresented students into STEM fields. NCSSSMST Journal, 16*(1), 27–29.

American Association of University Women. (2010). *2010 AAUW annual report.* Washington, DC: Author.

Atwater, M. M. (2010a). Dr. Geneva Gay: Multicultural education for all disciplines. *Science Activities: Classroom Projects and Curriculum Ideas, 47*(4), 160–162.

Atwater, M. M. (2010b). Multicultural science education and curriculum materials. *Science Activities: Classroom Projects and Curriculum Ideas, 47*(4), 103–108.

Bayer Corporation. (2010). *Bayer facts of science education XIV: Females and minority chemist and chemical engineers speak about diversity and underrepresentation in STEM.* Retrieved from http://www.igert.org/system/content_item_assets/files/579/Bayer_Facts_of_Science_Education_Executive_Summary.pdf

Beede, D., Julian, T., Langdon, D., McKittrick, G. Khan, B., & Doms, M. (2011). *Women in STEM: A gender gap to innovation.* Washington, DC: U.S. Department of Commerce Economics and Statistics Administration. Retrieved from https://files.eric.ed.gov/fulltext/ED523766.pdf

Bianchini, J. A. (2011). How to foster student-student learning of science? The student, the teacher and the subject Matter. *Cultural Studies of Science Education, 6*(4), 871–882.

Business-Higher Education Forum. (2011, August). *Creating the workforce of the future: The STEM interest and proficiency challenge* (BHEF Research Brief). Retrieved from https://www.bhef.com/sites/default/files/BHEF_2011_stem_increst_proficiency.pdf

Darling-Hammond, L. (2010). *The flat world and education: How America's commitment to equity will determine our future.* New York, NY: Teachers College Press.

Delpit, L. D. (2012*). "Multiplication is for White people": Raising expectations for other people's children.* New York, NY: The New Press.

Gay, G. (2010). *Culturally responsive teaching: Theory, research and practice* (2nd ed.). New York, NY: Teachers College Press.

Espinosa, L. L. (2009). *Pipelines and pathways: Women of color in STEM majors and the experiences that shape their persistence* (Unpublished doctoral dissertation). University of California, Los Angees, California. Retrieved from ERIC Database. (ED513969)

Fadigan, K. A., & Hammrich, P. L. (2004). A longitudinal study of the educational and career trajectories of female participants of an urban informal science education program. *Journal of Research in Science Teaching, 41*(8), 835–860.

Hubbard, S. M., & Stage, F. K. (2010). Identifying comprehensive public institutions that develop minority scientists. *New Directions for Institutional Research, 2010*(148), 53–62.

Jimarez, T., Zannou, Y., Larke, P., Webb-Hasan, G., Li, Y., & Fox, B. (2011). *Science, technology, engineering, mathematics: Cultivating, Hispanics and African Americans girls for STEM careers* (Funded by NSF Grant-DRL 1048544). Unpublished document.

Kendricks, K., & Arment, A. (2011). Adopting a K–12 family model with undergraduate research to enhance STEM persistence and achievement in under-represented minority students. *Journal of College Science Teaching, 41*(2), 22–27.

Malcom, L. E. (2010). Charting the pathways to STEM for Latina/o students: The role of community colleges. *New Directions for Institutional Research, 2010*(148), 29–40.

North, C., & Jobs, T. (2011). *Designing STEM pathways through early college: Ohio's metro early college high school.* Retrieved from https://jfforg-prod-prime.s3.amazonaws.com/media/documents/ECDS_DesigningSTEMPathways_081511.pdf

O'Brien, S. (2010). Characterization of a unique undergraduate multidisciplinary STEM K–5 teacher preparation program. *Journal of Technology Education, 21*(2), 35–51.

Shome, S. (1997). *The influence of feminist mothers on their adolescent daughters' career aspirations.* (Unpublished doctoral dissertation). Virginia Polytechnic Institute

and State University, Blacksburg, VA. Retrieved from https://pdfs.semantic
scholar.org/51a6/f81f4a0af5a769584981b11c8b2bd0c77c44.pdf

Texas Education Agency. (2012). *Academic excellence indicator system report.* Retrieved
from https://rptsvr1.tea.texas.gov/perfreport/aeis/index.html

Tyler-Wood, T., Ellison, A., Lim, O., & Periathiruvadi, S. (2012). Bringing up girls in
science (BUGS): The effectiveness of an afterschool environmental science
program for increasing female students' interest in science careers. *Journal of
Science Education and Technology, 21*(1), 46–55.

US Commission on Civil Rights. (2010). *Encouraging minority students to pursue sci-
ence, technology, engineering and math careers. A briefing before the United States
Commission on Civil Rights held in Washington, D.C. briefing report.* Washington,
DC: Author.

Webb-Hasan, G., Zannou, Y., & Larke, P. (2011). *Culturally responsive teaching strategies: Examples of facilitating brilliance* (Funded by NSF Grant-DRL 1048544).
Retrieved from http://charms.tamu.edu/

Young, J., & Larke, P. (2011). *CHARMS activity book* (Funded by NSF Grant-DRL
1048544). Unpublished document.

CHAPTER 2

PLUGGING THE LEAKS IN THE STEM PIPELINE

Nurturing Early Interest in Science, Technology, Engineering, and Mathematics Among Girls of Color

Charlease Kelly-Jackson

> *Our success as a nation depends on strengthening America's role as the world's engine of discovery and innovation.*
> —Former President Barak Obama (Obama, 2010)

The nation is experiencing a shortage in the science, technology, engineering, and mathematics (STEM) workforce (Drew, 2011; Hill, Corrbett, & Rose, 2010; National Academies, 2007; National Science Board, 2006; Ong, Wright, Espinosa, & Orfield, 2011). This deficiency impacts national security, Americans' quality of life, and the ability to remain competitive in the increasingly globalized economy (American Association of University Women[AAUW], 2010; Maltese & Tai, 2011; National Research Council, 2011). The above quote from President Obama's "Educate to Innovate" campaign (2010) speaks to the importance and urgency of improving STEM achievement in the United States. Hence, policymakers have made

Girls and Women of Color In STEM, pages 19–34
Copyright © 2020 by Information Age Publishing

building a robust STEM workforce a top priority (AAUW, 2010; Maltese & Tai, 2011; National Academies, 2010; National Research Council, 2011).

One major factor that contributes to the shortage of STEM professionals is the historical underrepresentation of women and racial/ethnic minorities in STEM disciplines (Drew, 2011; Margolis & Fisher, 2002; National Academies, 2010; President's Council of Advisors on Science and Technology, 2010). When compared to other groups, women of color—African Americans, Asian American/Pacific Islander, Chicana/Latina, and Native American groups are considered untapped resources (Burrelli, 2009; National Academies, 2010; Perna, Gasman, Gary, Lundy-Wagner, & Drezner, 2010) and are less likely to complete a STEM major (Jones, Howe, & Rua, 2000; National Academies, 2010; National Science Board, 2007). Women of color account for 34% of female undergraduates (National Science Foundation, 2011). Surprisingly, these women make up two-thirds of the population, but represent only one-quarter or less of STEM professionals in the workforce (Lucore, 2011). According to the National Science Foundation (NSF; 2013) report, *Women, Minorities, and Persons with Disabilities in Science and Engineering: 2013*, one in ten employed scientists and engineers are minority women. These demographics clearly suggest that the infrastructures set in place to educate and utilize women of color have failed (Ong, Wright, Espinosa, & Orfield, 2011). "It is timely, and perhaps imperative, that education and career efforts work to build the capacity of women of color to assume advanced STEM positions" (Ong, 2010, p. 8).

Researchers have developed a learning pathway known as the STEM pipeline model that is used to understand and address the underrepresentation of people of color and women in the workforce (Level Playing Field Institute, 2005). This model represents the "long-standing logical framework describing how trainees advance through the scientific educational and training process, with success measured by movement from the precollege levels to more advanced postgraduate levels" (Allen-Ramdial & Campbell, 2014, p. 612). The pipeline analogy has been long recognized and described as "leaky"—a term used to illustrate the unintended loss of trainees from the field (Allen-Ramdial & Campbell, 2014; Level Playing Field Institute, 2005). Researchers are examining each stage of the pipeline in efforts to "plug" the leaks (Level Playing Field Institute, 2005). Focusing on this issue is critical to the recruitment and retention of STEM trainees in addition to improving diversity in the STEM pipeline (Allen-Ramdial & Campbell, 2014) especially as it relates to women of color in STEM.

Even though the STEM pipeline illustrates the flow of trainees from the precollege levels to more advanced postgraduate levels, researchers' analyses of the pipeline tend to focus on recruitment and retention at the undergraduate level (Allen-Ramdial & Campbell, 2014). One intervention strategy to addressing the "leaks" in the pipeline and building the capacity of women of color in the STEM workforce is focusing on the precollege level of the pipeline as early as the elementary level.

According to the Congressional Commission on the Advancement of Women and Minorities in Science, Engineering, and Technology Development (2000), students, especially girls, tend to lose interest in STEM disciplines by middle school. To address this issue, numerous efforts have been made to incorporate STEM into elementary classrooms, especially as it relates to the integration of mathematics and science. More and more teachers are moving toward robotics as an educational tool because it allows students to experience designing and building (Matson, DeLoach, & Pauly, 2004; Rogers & Portsmore, 2004) and test the results of abstract design concepts through concrete, hands-on robotic manipulatives (Druin & Hendler, 2000). For all students to be prepared for life in the 21st century, it is critical to cultivate their interest in STEM at a younger age (Varney, Janoudi, & Graham, 2011), especially girls of color.

To that end, this chapter will focus on a collaborative project between a university and an urban, underserved elementary school to increase upper elementary girls' awareness and interest in STEM through a robotics summer program entitled, *Girls Engaged in Mathematics and Science* (GEMS). The author will highlight how the summer program served as an impetus to increasing girls' of color awareness and interest in STEM. The article will also provide qualitative and quantitative data that illustrate students' overall summer experience.

PURPOSE OF THE STUDY

About four decades ago, a report entitled, *The Double Bind: The Price of Being a Minority Woman in Science* (Malcom, Hall, & Brown, 1976), illuminated the disparity of underrepresented minority women who pursued education and careers in STEM fields (Malcom & Malcom, 2011). Since this publication, STEM fields have continued to be overwhelmingly composed of Whites and men; however, the pathway to understanding the STEM pipeline for minority women has changed (Malcom & Malcom, 2011).

There is a greater emphasis from community colleges, master's degree granting colleges, universities, and minority serving institutions, and for-profit institutions to be more of a recognizable entity in the collegiate experiences of individuals holding a STEM degree (Malcom & Malcom, 2011). Research shows that undergraduate women of color showed greater intentions to major in STEM during their freshman year of college than White women. However, in 2008, women earned 38% of the STEM baccalaureate degrees in the United States, while women of color earned only 6.1% of all the degrees that year. Women of color ranked significantly lower in the number of STEM masters and doctorates conferred in 2008 (National Science Foundation, 2011). With these data, it is no surprise that researchers are continuing to analyze the STEM pipeline and search for multiple pathways rather than the single route to a STEM degree.

There is a plethora of literature around women of color in STEM tends to focus on the undergraduate, graduate, and/or the workforce entry points of the pipeline (Brown, 2008; Chinn, 2002; Espinosa, 2011; Holmegaard, Madsen, & Ulriksen, 2012; Malcom & Malcom, 2011; Perna et al., 2010). However, the body of research that focuses on girls of color in STEM, specifically at the precollege stage, is limited. Studies, on girls specifically, show that parents' and teachers' expectations of boys and girls, learning styles by gender, and different profession choices contribute to the lack of girls in STEM (Bamberger, 2014; Osborne, Simon, & Collins, 2003; Zohar & Sela, 2002). We examined the impact a summer robotics program had on elementary girls' of color awareness and interest in STEM. The following research question guided this study: What coherent set of experiences effectively and efficiently increase girls' awareness and interest in STEM and cognate careers?

THEORETICAL FRAMEWORK

For years, there has been concern about the disproportionate number of girls who choose science and technology in high school and STEM related majors in college (Bamberger, 2014; Holmegaard et al., 2012). The gender gap in these fields has been well documented (Bamberger, 2014; Jones et al., 2000; National Science Foundation, 2002, 2011; Margolis & Fisher, 2002). This study's theoretical underpinnings are drawn from the sociocultural approach framed by Vygotsky's theories of learning (1978), which focuses on how school aged children learn and develop through social interactions that may vary from culture to culture (Bamberger, 2014; Mahn, 1999). Vygotsky (1978; as cited in Bamberger, 2014) "asserts that social interactions and cultural symbols provide essential opportunities for constructing meanings, with the cultural context influencing one's perception of professions" (p. 550). Girls may choose not to pursue STEM degrees/ careers because of their dispositions toward the national culture of professions, gender identity, and community values (Bamberger, 2014).

The importance of STEM degrees and cognate careers varies among countries. Researchers assert that American and European students' job pursuits mimic that of the traditional employment patterns of men and women (Archer et al., 2012; Bamberger, 2014; Murphy & Whitelegg, 2006). However, girls in Kenya tend to favor science and STEM careers (Bamberger, 2014; Chetcuti & Kioko, 2012). These data show that nationality should be considered when discussing girls' pursuit of STEM degrees/careers (Bamberger, 2014).

Gender difference has been recognized in the literature as a reason why girls avoid STEM degrees/careers (Bamberger, 2014; Jones et al., 2000). Researchers suggest that girls view science and its relevance to their lives less favorably than boys (Bamberger, 2014; Chetcuti & Kioko, 2012; Zohar & Sela, 2002). As a matter of fact, girls do not see themselves as future STEM professionals in the future (Bamberger, 2014; Murphy & Whitelegg, 2006). Shaped by culture, gender identity begins to register in students' minds around middle school. This is when students typically begin to connect professions to gender (Bamberger, 2014; Fung, 2002). The sciences are generally identified as a White, male dominated field (Farenga & Joyce, 1999; Johnson, 2007; Johnson, Brown, Carlone, & Cuevas, 2011; Seymour & Hewitt, 1997) and students, for years, drew scientists as male (Bamberger, 2014; Boylan, Hill, & Wallace, 1992; Chambers, 1983; Finson, 2003). This shows how some markers of culture can impact girls' dispositions and pursuit of STEM careers.

Another cultural marker that may influence girls' decisions to avoid STEM fields is community values (Bamberger, 2014).

> The socio-cultural perspective deals with the ways cultural values, concepts and methods are being transferred … The socio-cultural perspective highlights that formal as well as informal learning accrues in a social context, where students interact with each other and influence each other's ideas" (pp. 550–551). Children look to parents and teachers for guidance and acceptance and as messengers of the culture, these social agents have the tendency of demonstrating cultural biases and varying expectations between girls and boys when it comes to STEM (Archer et al., 2012; Bamberger, 2014; Mujtaba & Reiss, 2012). Not only do parents and teachers transfer specific perceptions about STEM to girls, their peers do as well. (Bamberger, 2014)

We highlight the GEMS program, a university-funded project designed to increase upper elementary girls' awareness and interest in STEM and cognate careers and nurture a lifelong interest in STEM subjects. The objectives included: (a) 75% of the participating girls will increase their *awareness* of STEM careers in broad science areas as measured by the Career Interest Questionnaire, (b) 75% of the participants will increase their *interest* in STEM and careers as measured by the STEM Semantics Surveys, and (c) 100% of the participants will work in collaborative teams to design and construct robots using the LEGO WeDo Construction Kit (Kelly-Jackson, 2015). The next few sections will illustrate evaluative data that confirms the importance of STEM related summer programs for elementary girls of color.

RESEARCH METHODS

Context of the Program

The GEMS program began as a collaborative project between a large, public university and an urban, underserved elementary school in the Southeastern region of the United States. Supported by grant funds, the 5-day summer robotics program targeted 4th and 5th grade girls, specifically girls of color. The program instructors included a science education professor, a public school STEM lab teacher, and a preservice teacher from an elementary and early childhood department. The program's curriculum was developed using a student-centered, engineering design and problem based approach. This approach emphasized the engineering design process and allowed the girls to participate in a series of team building activities. LEGO robotics teams were created based on the girls' familiarity with LEGO robotics. Each team had at least one member with LEGO experience (Kelly-Jackson, 2015).

The GEMS program allowed girls to work collaboratively to solve problems and interact with women in STEM careers (Kelly-Jackson, 2015). As the literature suggests, people are more likely to choose a profession when they can associate a familiar person or role model to the profession (Bamberger, 2014; Lent, Brown, & Hackett, 1994; Zirkel, 2002). These female role models represented each of the STEM disciplines and served as mentors throughout the summer program. The women speakers connected real-life situations to their specific career, created STEM design challenges that focused on their STEM career, and helped the girls conceptualize their LEGO robot designs (Kelly-Jackson, 2015).

Each day, the girls were presented with an engineering design challenge where they were reminded of the engineering design process and charged with solving a problem. The program explored the use of motors, motion sensors, LEGO bricks, and gear mechanisms. Additionally, the curriculum paired the STEM activities with programming software where students created their own robot that combined LEGO construction with computer animation.

STEM journal writing was a huge emphasis of the program and the girls individually recorded their ideas and designed sketches. The program's culminating activity consisted of each team participating in a poster session displaying their LEGO robot design and describing their weekly STEM challenges and activities. University faculty, school administrators and teachers, parents, and community stakeholders were invited to the event (Kelly-Jackson, 2015).

Setting and Participants

The GEMS program took place at an urban, Title I elementary school located approximately 20 miles from one of the largest cities in the Southeastern region of the United States. The school had a very diverse population of 750 students: 47% African American, 30% Hispanic, 18% Caucasian, 4% Asian, and 1% Native American. Approximately 30% of the student body receive special education through special needs inclusion or programs for Pre–K, visually impaired, and mildly intellectually disabled. The school is known as one of the few elementary schools that house an authentic space team program in which elementary students compete for 36 positions to plan and execute a 27-hour simulated space launch.

Twenty-one fourth and fifth grade girls between the ages of 8–10 were selected using purposeful and convenience sampling (Patton, 2002). The participants, ten fourth graders and eleven fifth graders, were selected based on their involvement with the school's robotics club and/or performance in STEM related after school programs advised by the STEM lab teacher and school principal. Based on demographic data provided by parents, the girls consisted of 14 African Americans, 3 Hispanics, 3 Whites, and 1 Indian; all of whom identified as economically disadvantaged (Kelly-Jackson, 2015).

Instruments

Pre and post instruments were administered by an external evaluator: The STEM Semantics Survey developed by Tyler-Wood, Knezek, and Christensen (2010) and the Career Interest Questionnaire modified from Knezek and Christensen's (1998) Teacher's Attitudes toward Information Technology Questionnaire (TAT). The STEM Semantics Survey is a five-part questionnaire that measures perceptions of science, technology, engineering, and mathematics and interest in STEM careers (Kelly-Jackson, 2015; Tyler-Wood, Knezek, & Christensen, 2010). The Career Interest Questionnaire is composed of three parts that measure "perception of supportive environment for pursuing a career in science, interest in pursuing educational opportunities that would lead to a career in science, and perceived importance of a career in science" (Tyler-Wood, Knezek, & Christensen, 2010, p. 348). It is a 12-item, Likert-type (1—*strongly disagree* to 5—*strongly agree*) survey that measures interest in careers in broad science areas. Both instruments are valid and reliable and capable of measuring the intended constructs (Kelly-Jackson, 2015).

DATA COLLECTION AND ANALYSIS

In seeking to understand what coherent set of experiences effectively and efficiently increase girls' awareness and interest in STEM and cognate careers, quantitative and qualitative research measures were employed. Evaluators collected quantitative data from the STEM Semantics Survey and the Career Interest Questionnaire. Qualitative data was comprised of direct observations and focus group interviews. A final program evaluation survey was administered to assess the overall program effectiveness. All assessments except the observations and focus group interviews were completed digitally using Google Docs. Focus group interviews were conducted on-site in two small groups with ten or less participants (Glesne, 2006). The results from all assessments are reported at the group level (Kelly-Jackson, 2015).

Quantitative data were collected at the beginning and end of the summer program. Instructors were responsible for collecting direct observations throughout the study; while focus group interview data and the program evaluation survey data were collected on the last day of the program. Open coding (Cortazzi, 2001) was used to identify themes from the focus group interview data. As data were chunked into smaller units, critical themes emerged (Patton, 2002). After codes were added to each unit, they were grouped into categories. More themes were defined to express the content of each group and checked for external and internal homogeneity (Strauss & Corbin, 1990, 1998).

RESULTS

Based on the data, Objective 1 (75% of the participating girls will increase their awareness of STEM careers in broad science areas) and Objective 2 (75% of the participating students will increase their interest in STEM and careers) were met. Evaluators used the pre and post Career Interest Questionnaire, completed at the beginning and the end of the program, to measure Objective 1. To complete the questionnaire, participants had to choose between a series of adjectives to describe STEM domains. Each domain contained five positive adjectives and five negative. The change in the percentage of students selecting the positive adjective for each domain is illustrated in Table 2.1. One student's response was equivalent to 5.3; therefore, a change of 5.3 illustrates that one more student chose the positive adjective on the posttest than did on the pretest. A negative change is represented by the number in parenthesis (Kelly-Jackson, 2015).

The domain of science had the greatest change with four adjectives representing double-digit support. Although, engineering also had four adjectives with double-digit growth, the average was slightly lower than

TABLE 2.1 Change in Students' Selections on STEM Semantics Survey

	To Me Science is:	To Me Math is:	To Me Engineering is:	To Me Technology is:
Fascinating	+21.1	(5.3)	+21.1	+21.2
Appealing	+26.3	10.5	+15.8	NC
Exciting	+15.8	36.8	+15.8	+5.3
Means a Lot	+31.6	(5.3)	NC	+5.3
Interesting	NC	NC	+10.5	+5.3

for science. Technology was the domain with the least amount of positive change in student feedback (Kelly-Jackson, 2015).

The pre and post STEM Semantics survey data were used to measure Objective 2. Similar to the Career Interest Questionnaire, participants were given an opportunity to choose between a series of adjectives to describe STEM domains. Table 2.2 shows the change in the percentage of students selecting the positive adjective for each statement. Here again, one student's response equals 5.3 and the change of 5.3 shows one more student chose the positive adjective on the posttest (Kelly-Jackson, 2015).

There was no change in the number of students who thought a career in STEM would be *exciting*; however, positive change occurred in the number of students who viewed a career in STEM as *meaningful, interesting, fascinating,* and *appealing*. Student data showed a positive change in the number of girls who agreed they would like to have a career in science, enjoy a career in science, and get a job in a science related field. Six students responded positively from the pre to post assessment to the statement, "I would enjoy a career in science," while 11 students showed no change and two showed a decrease in interest in a science career (Kelly-Jackson, 2015).

TABLE 2.2 Change in Students' Selections on STEM Semantics Survey and Career Interest Questionnaire

Statement	Change
To me, a CAREER in science, technology, engineering, or mathematics means a lot.	+5.3
To me, a CAREER in science, technology, engineering, or mathematics is interesting.	+10.5
To me, a CAREER in science, technology, engineering, or mathematics is exciting.	NC
To me, a CAREER in science, technology, engineering, or mathematics is fascinating.	+15.8
To me, a CAREER in science, technology, engineering, or mathematics is appealing.	+21.1
I would like to have a career in science.	+15.8
I would enjoy a career in science.	+5.3
I will get a job in a science-related area.	+10.5

Objective 3, (100% of the participating girls will work in collaborative teams to design and construct robots using the LEGO WeDo Construction kit), was measured using direct classroom observations by the instructors. Each instructor conducted observations daily. Two girls were absent on the day these observations were completed resulting in 90% of the program participants working collaboratively to complete the activities (Kelly-Jackson, 2015).

The external evaluators collected focus group interview data from 19 out of the 21 participants. The girls described their summer learning experience as appealing, fascinating, fun, exciting, and expanding. Seven of the 19 girls liked math best, six liked science best, five liked technology best, and one student liked engineering the best (Kelly-Jackson, 2015). When asked why they prefer one subject versus another, students' responses included:

> I like math more than the others because almost everything you do involves math.

> I like science better than any other subject because when I grow up I want to be a vet and that has more to do with science than any other subject.

> I like engineering the most because I can be creative and I can build robots and stuff and I can be creative with the engineering and design and stuff.

> I like science best because I think that it's a lot of fun and I can be creative and make new worlds and just investigate what you like. (p. 788)

An overwhelming majority (17 girls) reported that the program enhanced their knowledge/awareness of STEM fields/careers. Eighteen of the 19 girls said that they would enjoy attending another workshop like GEMS in the future (Kelly-Jackson, 2015).

To capture the program's effectiveness, a program's evaluation survey was administered. The survey asked students to rank their favorite to least favorite GEMS program activity on a scale of 1 to 6 with 1 being their most favorite activity to 6 being their least favorite activity. The Robotics Field Trip was rated as the first most favorite activity from 11 girls. Six students ranked the LEGO WeDo kits as their second favorite activity while 9 rated the invitations STEM Challenge as their third favorite activity. Seven girls rated the LEGO WeDo kits as their fourth favorite activity and 9 ranked the Silly Straws STEM Challenge as their fifth favorite activity. It was no surprise that 14 girls rated the STEM journal reflections as their sixth least favorite activity. Table 2.3 shows students' ratings of program activities (Kelly-Jackson, 2015).

TABLE 2.3 Students Rating Program Activities						
Rating Scale	1	2	3	4	5	6
STEM Challenge—Angry Bird Display	4	5	3	2	3	2
STEM Challenge—Invitations	2	2	9	6	0	0
STEM Challenge—Silly Straws	1	3	4	1	9	1
LEGO WeDo Construction Kits	4	6	0	7	2	0
Journal Reflections	0	1	0	1	3	14
Robotics Facility-Field Trip	11	1	2	2	1	2

DISCUSSION

Arne Duncan, former U.S. Secretary of Education, said,

> Everyone has a stake in improving STEM education. Inspiring all our students to be capable in math and science will help them contribute in an increasingly technology-based economy, and will also help America prepare the next generation of STEM professionals—scientists, engineers, architects, and technology professionals—to ensure our competitiveness. (U.S. Department of Education, 2010)

Unfortunately, the disproportionate number of women of color in STEM fields continues to show the nations' failure to "plug" the leaks in the STEM pipeline. Are we turning a blind eye? Will women in STEM overcome this notion of a *double bind* (Malcom, Hall, & Brown, 1976)? Until the nation recognizes the urgency to populate the STEM pipeline with women of color, we will continue to fall behind others in science, technology, engineering, and mathematics.

The data from this study show the impact of introducing girls of color to STEM at an early age. A coherent set of experiences such as hands-on, problem-based experiences, STEM related field trips, women of STEM as role models and mentors, effectively and efficiently increase girls' awareness and interest in STEM and cognate careers. Data showed a positive change in students' perceptions and feelings toward STEM domains and careers. One of most significant findings from the data is the overwhelming majority of girls that rated the robotics field trip as their first most favorite activity. This response rating is contributed to the hands-on and problem based approach of the experience. Participants were allowed to test drive robots, work in collaborative teams to build a robot using scrap materials, and interact with high school females who are members of their school's robotics team. In addition, they were able to observe, on a larger scale, how larger and more sophisticated robots are designed and programmed. The robotics field trip was embedded in the program to expose students to robotics in every day, realistic situation and to "give students something to do…and the doing is of such a nature as to demand thinking or intentional connections" (Dewey, 1944, p. 154).

Overall, the participants and instructors were satisfied with the implementation of the program (Kelly-Jackson, 2015). However, areas of improvement include: (a) modifying the schedule to incorporate more team building activities on the first two days, (b) allowing the girls to select a partner to encourage a richer bonding experience, and (c) modifying the journal writing component to make it more hands on and relevant to the programs' objectives. Fourteen of the 19 girls rated the journal writing as their least favorite activity. Because communication (written and oral) is a vital component of the program, instructors suggested keeping the written component but also embedding an oral component. This modification would still allow the researcher to capture students' voices in addition to building communication skills.

The GEMS program has the potential to impact many students' awareness and interest in STEM careers especially elementary aged girls of color. The next steps of this program are to expand to other elementary schools and embed a mentoring component that involves middle and high school girls. Teachers and curriculum specialists are encouraged to use these findings to structure similar summer programs or in school collaborative robotics projects. Elementary level STEM programs, like GEMS, is necessary to build and nurture the STEM pipeline, a pipeline where girls and women of color are underrepresented. GEMS serves a model program that has only touched the surface toward helping underserved girls of color increase their awareness of and interest in STEM careers at an early age.

REFERENCES

American Association of University Women. (2010). *Improve girls' and women's opportunities in science, technology, engineering, and mathematics.* Retrieved from http://www.aauwaction.org/wp-content/uploads/2012/02/2010_0505_STEMrecs.pdf

Allen-Ramdial, S., & Campbell, A. (2014). Reimagining the pipeline: Advancing STEM diversity, persistence, and success. *BioScience, 64*(7), 612–618.

Archer, L., Dewitt, J., Osborne, L., Dillion, J., Willis, B., & Wong, B. (2012). "Balancing acts": Elementary school girls' negotiations of femininity, achievement, and science. *Science Education, 96*(6), 967–989.

Bamberger, Y. (2014). Encouraging girls into science and technology with feminine role models: Does this work? *Journal of Science Education and Technology, 23*(4), 549–561.

Boylan, C., Hill, D., & Wallace, A. (1992). Beyond stereotypes. *Science Education,* *76*(5), 465–476.

Brown, S. (2008). The gender differences: Hispanic females and males majoring in science or engineering. *Journal of Women and Minorities in Science and Engineering, 14*(2), 205–223.

Burrelli, J. (2009, October). *Women of color in STEM education and employment.* Paper presented at the Mini-Symposium on Women of Color in STEM, Arlington, VA.

Chambers, D. (1983). Stereotype images of the scientist: The draw-a-scientist test. *Science Education, 67*(2), 255–265.

Chetcuti, D., & Kioko, B. (2012). Girls' attitudes towards science in Kenya. *International Journal of Science Education, 34*(10), 1571–1589.

Chinn, P. (2002). Asian and pacific islander women scientist and engineers: A narrative exploration of model minority, gender, and racial stereotypes. *Journal of Research in Science Teaching, 39*(4), 302–323.

Congressional Commission on the Advancement of Women and Minorities in Science, Engineering and Technology Development. (2000). *Land of plenty: Diversity as America's competitive edge in science, engineering and technology.* Retrieved from http://www.nsf.gov/pubs/2000/cawmset0409/cawmset_0409.pdf

Cortazzi, M. (2001). Narrative analysis in ethnography. In P. Atkinson (Ed.), *Handbook of ethnography* (pp. 384–394). London, England: SAGE.

Dewey, J. (1944). *Democracy and education.* New York, NY: Free Press.

Drew, D. (2011). *STEM the tide: Reforming science, technology, engineering, and mathematics education in America.* Baltimore, MD: The Johns Hopkins University Press.

Druin, A., & Hendler, J. (2000). *Robots for kids: Exploring new technologies for learning.* San Diego, CA: Academic Press.

Espinosa, L. (2011). Pipelines and pathways: Women of color in undergraduate STEM majors and the college experiences that contribute to persistence. *Harvard Educational Review, 81*(2), 209–241.

Farenga, S., & Joyce, B. (1999). Intentions of young students to enroll in science courses in the future: An examination of gender differences. *Science Education, 83*(1), 55–75.

Finson, K. (2003). Applicability of the DAST-C to the images of scientists drawn by students of different racial groups. *Journal of Elementary Science Education, 15*(1), 15–26.

Fung, Y. (2002). A comparative study of primary and secondary school students' images of scientists. *Research in Science & Technological Education, 20*(2), 199–213.

Glesne, C. (2006). *Becoming qualitative researchers* (3rd ed.). New York, NY: Pearson.

Hill, C., Corrbett, C., & Rose, A. (2010). *Why so few? Women in science, technology, engineering, and mathematics.* Washington, DC: American Association for University Women.

Holmegaard, H., Madsen, L., & Ulriksen, L. (2012). To choose or not to choose science: Constructions of desirable identities among young people considering a STEM higher education programme. *International Journal of Science Education, 36*(2), 186–215.

Johnson, A. (2007). Unintended consequences: How science professors discourage women of color. *Science Education, 91*(5), 805–821.

Johnson, A., Brown, J., Carlone, H., & Cuevas, A. K. (2011). Authoring identity amidst the treacherous terrain of science: A multiracial feminist examination of the journeys of three women of color in science. *Journal of Research in Science Teaching, 48*(4), 339–366.

Jones, M., Howe, A., & Rua, M. (2000). Gender differences in students' experiences, interests, and attitudes toward science and scientists. *Science Education, 84*(2), 180–192.

Kelly-Jackson, C. (2015). Girls engaged in mathematics and science (GEMS): Building awareness and interest in STEM careers through robotics. *Journal of Multidisciplinary Engineering Science and Technology, 2*(4), 785–792.

Knezek, G., & Christensen, R. (1998, March). Internal consistency reliability for the teachers' attitudes toward information technology (TAT) questionnaire. In S. McNeil, J. Price, S. Boger-Mehall, B. Robin, & J. Willis (Eds.), *Proceedings of the society for information technology in teacher education annual conference* (pp. 831–836). Bethesda, MD: Society for Information Technology in Teacher Education.

Lent, R., Brown, S., & Hackett, G. (1994). Toward a unifying social cognitive theory of career and academic interest, choice, and performance. *Journal of Vocational Behavior, 45*(1), 79–122.

Lucore, R. (2011). American women more than ready to take their place at the nation's STEM table. In E. Fraser & L. S. Fimbers (Eds.), *100 women leaders in STEM* (pp. 10–12). Retrieved from http://education.ti.com/images/in-the-news/pdf/100-Women-Leaders-in-STEM.pdf.

Mahn, H. (1999). Vygotsky's methodological contribution to sociocultural theory. *Remedial and Special Education, 20*(6), 341–350.

Malcom, L., & Malcom, S. (2011). The double bind: The next generation. *Harvard Educational Review, 81*(2), 162–171.

Malcom, S., Hall, P., & Brown, J. (1976). *The double bind: The price of being a minority woman in science.* Washington, DC: American Association for the Advancement of Science.

Maltese, A., & Tai, R. (2011). Pipeline persistence: Examining the association of educational experiences with earned degrees in STEM among U.S. students. *Science Education, 95*(5), 877–907.

Margolis, J., & Fisher, A. (2002). *Unlocking the clubhouse: Women in computing.* Cambridge, MA: MIT Press.

Matson, E., DeLoach, S., & Pauly, R. (2004). Building interest in math and science for rural and underserved elementary school children using robots. *Journal of STEM Education, 3*(4), 35–46.

Mujtaba, T., & Reiss, M. J. (2012). *Factors affecting whether students in England choose to study physics once the subject is optional.* London, England: Institute of Education.

Murphy, P., & Whitelegg, E. (2006). *Girls in the physics classroom: A review of the research on the participation of girls in physics.* London, England: Institute of Physics.

National Academies. (2007). *Rising above the gathering storm: Energizing and employing America for a brighter economic future.* Washington, DC: The National Academies Press.

National Academies. (2010). *Rising above the gathering storm, revisited: Rapidly approaching category 5.* Washington, DC: National Academies Press.

National Research Council. (2011). *Successful K–12 STEM education: Identifying effective approaches in science, technology, engineering, and mathematics.* Washington, DC: National Academies Press.

National Science Board. (2006). *America's pressing challenge-building a stronger foundation: A companion to science and engineering indicators 2006.* Washington, DC: National Science Foundation.

National Science Board. (2007). *A national action plan for addressing the critical needs of the U.S. science, technology, engineering, and mathematics education system.* Arlington, VA: National Science Foundation.

National Science Foundation. (2002). *Women, minorities, and persons with disabilities in science and engineering.* Arlington, VA: NSF, Division of Science Resources Statistics.

National Science Foundation. (2011). *Women, minorities, and persons with disabilities in science and engineering.* Arlington, VA: NSF, Division of Science Resources Statistics.

National Science Foundation, National Center for Science and Engineering Statistics. (2013). *Women, minorities, and persons with disabilities in science and engineering: 2013* (Special Report NSF 13-304). Arlington, VA. Retrieved from http://www.nsf.gov/statistics/wmpd/

Obama, B. (2010). *Press release: Obama to announce major expansion of "Educate to Innovate" campaign to improve STEM Education.* Retrieved from https://obama whitehouse.archives.gov/the-press-office/2010/09/16/president-obama -announce-major-expansion-educate-innovate-campaign-impro

Ong, M. (2010). *The mini-symposium on women of color in science, technology, engineering, and mathematics (STEM): A Summary of events, findings, and suggestions* (p. 8). Cambridge, MA: TERC.

Ong, M., Wright, C., Espinosa, L., & Orfield, G. (2011), Inside the double bind: A synthesis of empirical research on undergraduate and graduate women of color in science, technology, engineering, and mathematics. *Harvard Educational Review, 81*(2), 172–208.

Osborne, J., Simon, S., & Collins, S. (2003). Attitudes towards science: A review of literature and its implications. *International Journal of Science Education, 25*(9), 1049–1079.

Patton, M. (2002). *Qualitative research and evaluation methods* (3rd ed.). London, England: SAGE.

Perna, L., Gasman, M., Gary, S., Lundy-Wagner, V., & Drezner, N. (2010). Identifying strategies for increasing degree attainment in STEM: Lessons from minority-serving institutions. *New Directions for Institutional Research, 2010*(148), 41–51.

President's Council of Advisors on Science and Technology—PCAST. (2010). *Designing a digital future: Federally funded research and development in networking and information technology.* Retrieved from https://obamawhitehouse.archives .gov/sites/default/files/microsites/ostp/pcast-nitrd-report-2010.pdf

Rogers, C., & Portsmore, M. (2004). Bringing engineering to elementary school. *Journal of STEM Education, 5*(4), 17–28.

Seymour, E., & Hewitt, N. (1997). *Talking about leaving: Why undergraduates leave the sciences*. Boulder, CO: Westview Press.

Strauss, A., & Corbin, J. (1990). *Basics of qualitative research: Grounded theory procedures and techniques*. Newbury Park, CA: SAGE.

Strauss, A., & Corbin, J. (1998). *Basics of qualitative research: Techniques and procedures for developing grounded theory*. Thousand Oaks, CA: SAGE.

Tyler-Wood, T., Knezek, G., & Christensen, R. (2010). Instruments for assessing interest in STEM content and careers. *Journal of Technology and Teacher Education, 18*(2), 341–363.

U.S. Department of Education. (2010). *U.S. Education secretary Arne Duncan issues statement on the release of the president's council of advisors on science and technology (PCAST) K–12 STEM education report*. Retrieved from https://www.ed.gov/news/press-releases/us-education-secretary-arne-duncan-issues-statement-release-presidents-council-advisors-science-and-technology-pcast-k-12-stem-education-report

Varney, M., Janoudi, A., & Graham, D. (2011). Building young engineers: TASEM for third graders in Woodcreek Magnet Elementary School. *IEEE Transactions on Education, 55*(1), 78–82.

Vygotsky, L. (1978). *Mind in society: The development of higher psychological processes*. Cambridge, MA: Harvard University Press.

Zirkel, S. (2002). Is there a place for me? Role models and academic identity among White students and students of color. *Teacher College Record, 104*(2), 357–376.

Zohar, A., & Sela, D. (2002). Her physics, his physics: Gender issues in Israeli advanced placement physics classes. *International Journal of Science Education, 25*(2), 245–268.

CHAPTER 3

UNO EUREKA!-STEM

Doing Something About the Double Bind

Carol T. Mitchell
Amelia Tangeman

There are few women of color in STEM fields because there are few women of color in science, technology, engineering, and mathematics (STEM) classes other than those courses required by schools and districts for graduation. There are few women in STEM classes, because there are few girls encouraged and invited into science and math coursework. We are not surprised now that we are involved in and promoting STEM that the faces of women and women of color are still unseen and unheard. So while the research is going on . . . when do we move to action? When do we begin doing something about the *double bind?* These are the questions the authors wrestled with before beginning the UNO EUREKA!-STEM program, a program that focused on "doing something" about the double bind and realize the possibility that truly "the sky's the limit!"

Girls and Women of Color In STEM, pages 35–47
Copyright © 2020 by Information Age Publishing

UNO EUREKA!-STEM PROGRAM DESCRIPTION

A metropolitan university in Omaha, Nebraska, the University of Nebraska Omaha (UNO) in collaboration with the Omaha Girls, Inc., a nonprofit agency that serves girls in the metro area and whose partnership with UNO spans more than fifteen years, has focused on a UNO EUREKA!-STEM summer engagement. The goal was to increase the interest, participation, and success of girls of color in STEM. The majority of the girls in this program were girls of color. The work, a 3 year commitment, began with seventh grade girls who matriculated on campus at the University of Nebraska and who returned to the campus a second summer as eighth graders. During the third summer the girls were assigned internships in the Omaha community. Two of the internships recently included working with a local veterinarian and working in a college biochemistry lab. Girls who participated were required to be members of Omaha Girls, Inc. Parental permission was required and parents were a part of the program. The first cohort began in June 2011. Omaha Girls, Inc. staff and the University of Nebraska faculty from the arts and sciences and the teacher education departments worked collaboratively.

We describe in this chapter the actions that were implemented during the 4 weeks of work with the girls. A description of the 4 week program is given as well as data that has been collected and analyzed during the early part of this program. Through this discourse we hope to share why we believe that the UNO EUREKA!-STEM program addresses the double bind in a proactive way.

Reasons for the Success of EUREKA!-STEM

Opportunity and commitment—these two words sum up the reasons why the UNO is an ideal place for Omaha's EUREKA!-STEM camp for girls. The University of Nebraska Omaha, and in particular the leadership team, has a strong commitment to both STEM education and the promotion of equity in the STEM disciplines. In fact, UNO has explicitly made a commitment to STEM by identifying this commitment as one of the top five campus priorities. The University of Nebraska Omaha is committed also to the community at large, as it has served the Omaha Metropolitan area for the past 100 years. In particular, UNO has served the urban community through student camps, outreach to schools, service learning projects in the community and in schools, as well as forming partnerships with agencies in the Omaha area. The opportunity to work with Girls, Inc. in STEM-related projects, along with recreation and personal growth for young women, further increases UNO's community collaborations.

Qualitative and quantitative research was found to be the best measure of this program (McLeod, 2008) and was conducted since year one. Girls completed surveys, our evaluators made observations during the engagements, and the Girls, Inc. staff followed the girls during the school year. Some of this ongoing research is shared in this chapter.

Content and Pedagogy

Advancing girls of color in STEM is what the EUREKA!-STEM program is all about. For 4 weeks girls of color are engaged in STEM activities including: robotics, programming, aerospace and aeronautics, life science, mathematics, and field trips that are related to the topics during the week. The core program and curriculum, including strategies used, are outlined below.

Core Program
EUREKA!-STEM follows the standard core program suggested by Girls, Inc. for EUREKA! programs. We focus our academic program on STEM courses which were taught by a combination of lead faculty and guest teachers/speakers. The courses have undergraduate education majors as helpers to further engage the girls. Our sports/recreation has a daily swimming component taught by Red Cross certified instructors. Yoga, running, Tae Kwon Do, personal defense, weight lifting, group fitness classes, and so forth were other options provided at UNO's facilities with access to fitness instructors.

Curriculum
In an effort to give the Girls, Inc. participants an experience that is STEM-based, EUREKA!-STEM focused on an integrated approach of mathematics, science, engineering and technology. Girls, Inc. curriculum was used and supplemented with units that had proven to be successful at UNO and/or are linked directly to field experiences. Specifically, each week of the camp focused on a STEM theme. For example, biomechanics, aviation, life sciences, mathematics, energy and robotics were all themes. Each of these were connected to an appropriate field experience: Strategic Air and Space Museum, Henry Doorly Zoo, OPPD, and IS&T Engineering.

Inquiry Strategies
Inquiry strategies included a hands-on approach to learning STEM. Girls learned to pose questions about phenomena, develop experiments to test questions, collect data, ask more questions, and come to some conclusions about the data collected. The participating girls worked collaboratively in all of these investigations. Asking questions and developing conceptual understandings were critical to students successfully engaging in STEM.

Friendly Competition

At the end of the first and second years, a competition was held among the girls to continue to emphasize and promote the competition that they will face outside of the camp environment. They were mentored and supported in this competition experience. Girls were prepared to face and engage successfully in competitions in the schools and in extracurricular activities related to STEM.

Certificate of Completion

In order that the girls recognize the importance of STEM and continue to be motivated in STEM experiences, UNO awarded the girls an official and personalized letter from the university at the end of the 2 year participation, acknowledging the importance of the EUREKA! experience, and encouraging them to someday enroll in college.

Working on the Double Bind—A Close-Up Look at UNO EUREKA!-STEM

As after-school and summer enrichment programs become increasingly more prevalent and STEM focused, it is necessary that these programs ensure that participants engage in the learning processes of each STEM activity, rather than just the completion of a single STEM activity before moving to the next. In the UNO EUREKA!-STEM program, faculty, staff, and certified teachers with expertise in their STEM fields exposed the 50–60 seventh and eighth grade Girls Inc. members involved with the EUREKA! program to STEM content and hands-on activities, from start to finish. Students were not just told that they were going to make paper rockets; they were instructed on the science behind propulsion and flight, the engineering design process, and explanations of which careers are related to rocketry and how what they just learned may help them in those careers. According to the National Research Council (2009), "There is mounting evidence that structured, nonschool science programs can feed or stimulate the science-specific interests of adults and children, may positively influence academic achievement for students, and may expand participants' sense of future science career options" (pp. 2–3). It is the goal of the EUREKA!-STEM program that the girls who participated in the program continue to pursue their education in a STEM field, eventually graduating and working within the STEM career of their choosing.

It was also critical that students had access to an out-of-school time program that was, "intentionally inclusive, multicultural, and systematically nondiscriminatory" (Nicholson, Collins, & Holmer, 2004, p. 55). We felt that students must feel that the program they were participating in was conducted in a safe space, with opportunities for personal growth, positive interactions with adult staff, and instances of empowerment. Through EUREKA!-STEM Personal Development hour, the girls participated in a workshop, which allowed personal reflection and inspiration, and included topics such as personal health and hygiene, the dangers of drugs and alcohol, and career talks by local women in STEM. The goal for this time period was to empower the girls to make the best choices for their health and safety, while also allowing time for inward reflection and relaxation, supporting mental health and the development of each girl as a whole person.

In addition to STEM content delivery with related activities and the personal development hour, the girls also participated in physical fitness every day of the program. Fitness faculty and students at UNO's Health and Physical Education and Recreation (HPER) center led the girls in swimming instruction, as well as activities such as yoga, cardio dancing, rock wall climbing, wheelchair basketball, group aerobics, and outdoor sports. Instructors felt that the swimming component was critical because research has proven that the drowning rates of African American children are three times as high as Caucasian children within the same age groups. As Irwin, Irwin, Ryan, and Drayer wrote, "Adequate swimming skills are considered a protective agent toward the prevention of drowning, but marginalized youth report limited swimming ability" (2011, p. 561). It is important to note that not all of the girls who participated in the UNO EUREKA!-STEM program were considered disadvantaged, but they did belong to underrepresented groups. All but one of the girls in the 2014 program had competed on a swim team, and over half of the rest of the girls reported that they did not know how to swim. The students were given a progress report at the conclusion of the summer program, in which 95% of the previous year's girls completed a swimming checklist which assessed whether they could complete basic swimming skills tests independently. Fitness instructors also taught the girls about the health benefits of daily physical activity, promoting healthy lifestyles with an emphasis on nutrition.

The UNO EUREKA!-STEM program was facilitated throughout the month of June, with programming held on campus, lending an authentic learning environment to the students as sessions were held in real university classrooms, labs, and recreational facilities. Because of these environments, students used the same tools and resources that scientists, engineers, and mathematicians on campus use. Friday field trip destinations throughout the program occurred off campus. Locations were chosen by how well the facility and its activities aligned with the program curriculum the students participated in throughout the week. Program curriculum was selected in collaboration with Girls Inc. EUREKA! staff and the UNO faculty, staff, and certified teachers leading each activity. Student workers hired through the university were also an integral part of the program, as they were undergraduate students majoring in either STEM or education fields. These student workers essentially filled the role of a camp counselor. They ate lunch with the girls, participated in the fitness activities with them, assisted the instructor in each session, and lent help to the girls during the sessions as needed. The relationship building between the participants and the student workers was a necessary component of the program.

A EUREKA! participant stays in the program for 5 years. The first and second year they attend the UNO EUREKA!-STEM camp. Following the first 2 years, participants are given an internship and paired with businesses and community partners who serve as mentors. The goal is that these girls major in a STEM field in college, and hopefully then work for one of the STEM businesses in the community, thus fortifying the STEM pipeline in Omaha.

During the third year of the UNO EUREKA!-STEM program, 30 seventh grade girls and 23 eighth grade girls attend camp. At camp, seventh grade students in the program are referred to as "Rookies," while the eighth grade students are referred to as "Vets." The transition from Rookie to Vet and Vet to graduation is a huge accomplishment for the girls. The Rookies look up to the Vets, and are motivated to stay in the program because they get to see what they will be able to do in their second year. For the Vets, graduation means that the following year they will be interning and shadowing in various STEM career fields. Multiple scholarships are also available to EUREKA!-STEM alumni, motivating the students to apply what they have learned through the program during the school year, receiving good grades and participating in extracurricular activities. In order to provide better insight into the themes and daily activities of the 4-week UNO EUREKA!-STEM program described in this chapter, a daily schedule with explanation is included below with an explanation of the STEM concepts covered throughout the camp, field trip learning experiences, and the importance of STEM learning.

Every day of the UNO EUREKA!-STEM program, excluding Friday field trip days, participants followed a tight schedule. The girls were on campus from the time the bus arrived at 9:00 a.m. until they departed at 4:00 p.m. Following a personal development hour, the Rookies and Vets were separated into different sessions for the STEM sessions in order to differentiate instruction. As STEM is the overarching theme of the UNO EUREKA!-STEM program, each week of the sessions related to STEM in some way. Week 1's theme, Robotics and Technology, was the same for both the Rookies and the Vets. The Rookies first session of the day used hands-on STEM kits to teach concepts such as circuitry, electronics, and robotic design through Snap Circuit, Solar Robot, and Hovercraft kits. Again, it is important to note that the girls were not just handed the kits and told to construct. Each session began with a mini-lesson covering the specific objective for the day, and the girls were given an explanation of how the kit they were using for the day addressed that objective before they began with the project. Programming was taught using Pico Boards and Makey kits. Each girl worked on a laptop for these activities. These sessions were co-taught by local certified elementary school technology specialists.

In Week 1 there was an introduction to the CEENBoT for the Rookies, and the creation of a "ME-UREKA" movie for the Vets. The CEENBoT is an educational robotics platform created by the University of Nebraska at Lincoln's Computer and Electrical Engineering department at the Peter Kiewit Institute, in collaboration with the University of Nebraska at Omaha's College of Education. This video was an important activity for the Vets, as it allowed them time for reflection, and to add their personality to the project to create something that really represented who they are, using the technology provided to them.

In Week 2, the Rookies designed and launched straw, paper, water, and Estes® rockets. Vets created their own simple machines that would carry out a task, such as Rube Goldberg machines, using recycled materials, cardboard boxes, and household items. Allowing the girls to work as real engineers do, they had to have a plan with step-by-step instructions, "blueprint" drawings of their models, and time for redesign and testing was also incorporated into each session. An engineering education faculty member led the week's sessions on these concepts. Many of the girls expressed that the robotics sessions were among their favorites.

In Week 3, Rookies enjoyed science and "Mathemagic" with science and Biomechanics for the Vets. Rookie sessions included learning math magic games to perform for parents and staff on the Friday of the week. These activities moved basic arithmetic to a higher level of thinking, as the girls then had to figure out why a certain trick works for solving a problem, and then be able to teach the trick to another person. A mathematics education professor taught the girls the math tricks and the processes for solving them. The Rookies also participated in Chemistry and Life Sciences sessions that were held in a chemistry lab facilitated by a chemistry professor on campus. Many girls commented about the fact that they were conducting experiments that college students do, and that they felt accomplished and confident that they could participate in chemistry coursework in college because of the experiences they gained through these sessions. During life sciences sessions, the Rookies were paired with undergraduate education majors in a science methods class, to conduct hands-on activities and experiments at various stations the instructor and students had previously selected and set up for the EUREKA! participants. Girls reported that they liked working with the undergraduate students because they were not far away from the age of the girls themselves. The Vets also participated in chemistry sessions this week, with the same professor who taught the Rookies. Labs in these sessions were similar to those the Rookies did, but were differentiated by allowing more independence in conducting the labs, such as examining the effects of smoking on the lungs. The authentic learning environment of the lab, and the use of freshmen level chemistry experiments, offered the Vets a more advanced chemistry experience than they had been exposed to during the formal school year. The Vets also spent the week visiting and working with students and researchers in the Biomechanics Research Building and touring a variety of labs such as the Motor Development Lab and Robotic Surgery Lab. The girls' participation in the activities in the Biomechanics Research Building was an extremely unique and unforgettable opportunity.

Week 4 for the Rookies consisted of High Altitude Ballooning and Financial Literacy, while the Vets participated in Mathematics and Health and Nutrition sessions. The High Altitude Ballooning sessions were co-taught by a faculty member on campus, as well as a local astronomer and expert in the field. The girls learned about the equipment and processes associated with a high altitude balloon launch (HABL), as well as created experiments to fly as payload on the balloon's tethers as it was launched into near space. As mentioned earlier, because of the mathematics connection associated with financial literacy, the Rookies participated in sessions with real world activities such as budgeting for a party and creating a savings plan. This week included hands-on stations for the Rookie's Life Sciences instruction led by the Vets' Health and Nutrition sessions. The same format was presented to the Vets, but with activities that related to Health and Nutrition instead of Life Sciences. Throughout the program, the Vets seemed appreciative that they didn't have to do the same activities as the previous year, and the Rookies could see what they would be doing in their Vet year.

UNO EUREKA!-STEM Field Trips

Each Friday of the program, the Rookies and Vets participated in separate field trips, which aligned to the activities and themes of each week of the program. Although logistically harder to coordinate, it was important to split the girls into separate field trips, so that the field trip appropriately tied in to what the girls learned in their different STEM sessions. Field trip sites included the Strategic Air and Space Museum, Peter Kiewit Institute, the Durham Western Heritage Museum (which had a traveling Design Zone exhibit related to engineering at the time), as well as a tour of campus, including the residence halls. The Vets field trips included visits to Acieta, an industrial robotics automation facility, City Sprouts (a community garden complex), and Adventureland amusement park. It was important that field trips not only align to the curriculum, but were also fun. Because the Vets continued with the program after their Rookie year, and participated in physics and simple machine activities during the week, they were rewarded with the trip to Adventureland. It was also imperative that the Rookies saw the Vets going to Adventureland, as they knew that they would get to go the next year if they stayed in the program.

FINDINGS

Does the Work Make a Difference? Survey Data from the Voices of the Girls

Participants in the UNO EUREKA!-STEM program completed a pre- and post-survey, composed of 21 questions that addressed attitudes regarding STEM content areas, STEM careers, future plans, and favorite aspects of the EUREKA! program. The pretest was given on the first day of the camp, with the posttest occurring on the last day before the graduation ceremony, with 30 Rookies and 23 Vets taking the survey. The students' names were coded by whether they were a Vet (V), or a Rookie (R), and given a random number for an identifier.

Attitudes Regarding STEM

The following four questions of the survey assessed the participants' attitudes toward STEM. A Likert scale from 1–5 was used for assessment, with an answer of 1 = *Strongly Disagree*, 2 = *Disagree*, 3 = *Neutral*, 4 = *Agree*, and 5 = *Strongly Agree*. Table 3.1 displays the average responses for both the Rookies and the Vets from the pre- and post-survey questions.

The data reflect that the strongest gains in positive attitudes toward STEM from the Rookies occurred in technology, while the strongest gains toward positive attitudes in STEM for the Vets occurred in mathematics. There was no change in the Rookies' attitudes towards mathematics, nor the Vets' attitudes toward technology. The Vets' recorded higher scores in positive attitudes in both the pre- and post-survey questions, likely because

TABLE 3.1   Participant Attitudes Toward STEM

Questions	I Like Doing Science Activities	I Like Doing Technology Activities	I Like Doing Engineering Activities	I Like Doing Mathematics Activities
Pre-Survey				
Average Rookie Response	3.7	3.6	3.5	3.3
Average Vet Response	3.9	4.1	3.6	3.4
Post-Survey				
Average Rookie Response	3.8(+0.1)	4.0(+0.4)	3.6(+0.1)	3.3(+0.0)
Average Vet Response	4.2(+0.3)	4.1(+0.0)	3.8(+0.2)	3.8(+0.4)

of their previous attendance and additional year of schooling. The changes show us that the girls already had high interest in STEM when they entered the program, but after the program they reported liking STEM even more.

Content Knowledge

The following five questions assessed the degree to which the participants believed they knew about each of the topics surveyed: robotics, rockets, chemistry, physics, and life science, and how they are used in real life. A Likert scale from 1–5 was used for assessment, with an answer of 1 = *Strongly Disagree*, 2 = *Disagree*, 3 = *Neutral*, 4 = *Agree*, and 5 = *Strongly Agree*. Table 3.2 displays the average responses for both the Rookies and the Vets from the pre- and post-survey questions.

The data indicates that the Rookies gained the most in knowledge covering the topics of robotics and rocketry, while the Vets felt their knowledge increased the most in physics. The Rookies received extensive robotics and rocketry lessons, so it is likely that this is the cause for gains in content knowledge for the Rookies. The Vets reported increase in physics is likely due to the week of intensive physics instruction that was given before their field trip to Adventureland. The data infers that the content presented in the program increased student knowledge.

Careers

The following four questions of the survey assessed the participants' attitudes toward STEM Careers. A Likert scale from 1–5 was used for assessment, with an answer of 1 = *Strongly Disagree*, 2 = *Disagree*, 3 = *Neutral*, 4 = *Agree*, and 5 = *Strongly Agree*. Table 3.3 displays the average responses for both the Rookies and the Vets from the pre- and post-survey questions.

As evidenced by the data, both groups' interest in STEM careers increased by the end of the program. The Rookies' largest increase was in engineering, while the Vets' largest increase was in technology. It is interesting to note the change in engineering career interest for the Rookies. Many

TABLE 3.2 Participants' Knowledge of Topics					
Questions	I Know About Robots	I Know About Rockets	I Know About Chemistry	I Know About Physics	I Know About Life Science
Pre-Survey					
Average Rookie Response	2.4	2.4	2.8	2.8	3.6
Average Vet Response	3.2	3.6	3.4	3.2	3.6
Post-Survey					
Average Rookie Response	3.6(+1.2)	3.6(+1.2)	3.4(+0.6)	3.6(+0.8)	3.7(+0.1)
Average Vet Response	4.2(+1.0)	3.9(+0.3)	4.0(+0.6)	3.9(+0.7)	4.2(+0.6)

TABLE 3.3 Participants' Attitudes Toward STEM Careers

Questions	I Might Want a Career in Science	I Might Want a Career in Technology	I Might Want a Career in Engineering	I Might Want a Career in Mathematics
Pre-survey				
Average Rookie Response	2.9	3.1	2.4	2.9
Average Vet Response	3.4	3.1	3.1	3.2
Post-Survey				
Average Rookie Response	3.1(+0.2)	3.3(+0.2)	3.1(+0.7)	3.1(+0.2)
Average Vet Response	3.9(+0.5)	3.8(+0.7)	3.3(+0.2)	3.3(+0.1)

of the Rookies indicated on their pre-survey that they were least looking forward to the engineering sessions of the camp. However, the Rookies responded that one of the sessions they enjoyed most was the engineering sessions in the post-survey. As engineering is a STEM field that has historically been driven by White males, this is an inspiring outcome of the program. One participant said this about the subject in her post-survey, "I think more girls should become engineers because that's a more man-dominated job." The girls realized where the needs were, and saw how they could fill those needs in the future.

Open Response Questions

The post-survey also asked the girls to answer some open-ended questions about their future and what they liked the most or least about EUREKA! When asked what they wanted to do after they graduated high school, an overwhelming majority of the girls responded they wanted to go to college. Only four responded that they were unsure, two responded that they wanted to go into the military before college, and three said they wanted to get their PhD. When asked what they thought girls could contribute to careers in STEM, many girls responded that girls could bring a different perspective to STEM careers. One participant noted that girls can "Use different ideas and show that girls are smart too."

When asked what they liked most about the program, a few of the girls mentioned swimming, but a few more responded that they enjoyed the engineering activities, mentioning the professor who taught by name. One of the Vets noticed the changes in the program from the year before and noted that she liked, "the way they took our recommendations and made the program better." When asked what they liked least about the program, many girls responded that they didn't like all the walking, or when other girls caused "drama" during the month. These were minimal issues, and while there were some instances of drama, the EUREKA! coordinators handled each situation individually, and the girls were given three chances before they were no longer able to return to the program. This was a rare occurrence, as the girls were handpicked to be in the EUREKA! program, and were among the most well behaved and motivated at Girls, Inc.

Another survey question asked the girls how well they thought they performed on the STEM content during the camp. The majority of the responses were positive. The girls felt proud of how they did and that they did a good job. One girl responded, "I think I did really good. I even impressed some people." Another participant commented, "I thought that STEM was going to be hard but they make it easy to understand." These responses were very positive, and lent the program facilitators and coordinators an idea of how the program was received in the eyes of the girls.

The responses to the survey helped the program coordinators and facilitators reflect on how to continue improving the programming. The girls took the survey seriously, as evidenced in their thoughtful answers, and the information gathered was extremely telling of the efficacy of the UNO EUREKA!-STEM program.

CONCLUSIONS

The UNO EUREKA!-STEM program at UNO is taking action to do something about the double bind. While this 5 year program is still in operation and the research continues, the evidence of positive effects can be seen in the sustained interest and involvement in STEM by the girls. The Girls, Inc. organization follows up with the girls during the school year where STEM is a part of the regular programming. The work at the university during the summer is an extension of what the girls do during the school year. Parent understanding of the importance of the double bind also helps as girls enroll in courses that are STEM related. EUREKA!-STEM girls understand that even if you are not invited or encouraged to be a part of the STEM scene, they can "choose" to participate and feel confident in their contributions because of their EUREKA!-STEM experiences. Finally, the pride and confidence that the girls exhibit at the end of the second year speaks volumes about their desire to move on a positive trajectory towards a career in STEM.

REFERENCES

Irwin, C., Irwin, R., Ryan, T., & Drayer, J. (2011). The legacy of fear: Is fear impacting fatal and non-fatal drowning of African American children? *Journal of Black Studies, 42*(4), 561–576.

McLeod, S. A. (2008). *Qualitative vs. quantitative*. Retrieved from www.simply psychology.org/qualitative-quantitative.html

National Research Council. (2009). *Learning science in informal environments: People, places, and pursuits.* Washington, DC: National Academies Press.

Nicholson, H. J., Collins, C., & Holmer, H. (2004). Youth as people: The protective aspects of youth development in after-school settings. *Annals of the American Academy of Political and Social Science, 591*(1), 55–71.

PART II

BUILDING CAPACITY INSIDE THE SCHOOL WALLS

CHAPTER 4

"WE STUMBLE, FALL, GET UP, AND CONTINUE WALKING"

Latina Students' Attitudes Towards Science

Kathryn Scantlebury
Beth Wassell

Since 2000, the number of Latin@[1] has increased to 16% of the population in the United States of America and represent an increasing segment in U.S. schools (United States Census Bureau, 2011), yet the numbers of Latin@ pursuing STEM degrees and careers has not increased (Peralta, Caspary, & Boothe, 2013). Many Latin@ students are often ill-prepared in science and mathematics, have underdeveloped critical thinking and communication skills, and poor study habits, which makes pursuing a degree in STEM particularly challenging (Peralta et al., 2013). Some of these issues are particularly salient for Latinas.

While there is a growing body of work examining both the impact of policy and testing practices on English language learner (ELL) immigrant students in school science (Fine, Jaffe-Walter, Pedraza, Futch, & Stoudt,

Girls and Women of Color In STEM, pages 51–67
51

2007; Short & Fitzsimmons, 2007) and there are some new trends in collaborative research involving teachers, administrators, and parents of Latin@ students in school and science (Carreón, Drake, & Barton, 2005; Hagiwara, Calabrese Barton, & Contento, 2007) more research needs to be conducted within these diverse communities of ELL immigrant students to better appreciate the challenges faced by their science teachers, parents, schools, and the communities where this growing population of girls are being educated. Although there have been some advances in our understanding of girls' experiences in school, much of the research on girls has failed to examine the educational experiences of females who speak another language at home or females from different racial groups than African American and White. An American Association of University Women (AAUW) study noted that only 1% of over 400 gender and science projects included ELL students (AAUW, 2004). Given the increasing numbers of Latinas in K–12 schools, identifying the issues that may positively impact their involvement in science and their learning in science is crucial. Specifically, there is a need for examining the experiences of these learners while they are still adolescents and still have some opportunities for positively connecting to school and science in ways, which may help to sustain these girls' interest in STEM education in the high school.

Recent research by Peralta et al. (2013) used LatCrit and critical race theory to reframe studies of Latin@ youth in terms of community cultural wealth which defines capital associated as aspirational, linguistic, social, navigational, familial, and resistant. Aspirational capital is one's ability to maintain hopes and dreams, while linguistic capital gives credit for one's ability to communicate in more than one language and/or style. Latin@ STEM students in this research reported that professionals were unwilling to work with ELL students and that language challenges were an impediment to their progress and success. But several students in the study noted how they applied their skills related to learning a new language to learning science terminology and vocabulary. This research also noted that Latin@ parents employed as manual laborers encouraged their children to advance their education. Families often wanted to preserve their Spanish linguistic abilities and students spoke their native language with their parents at home.

Middle school, especially for girls, is a critical point in students' learning trajectory. Over a decade ago, the AAUW documented that girls' achievement and attitude towards schooling declined in middle school (AAUW, 1998; Cohen & Blanc, 1996). While some recent research has noted how Latina girls in urban middle schools make hybrid spaces to engage with their science learning and developing their science practices (Calabrese Barton & Tan, 2008). Two Latina girls viewed biology as a pathway to study medicine, a career trajectory where they could "give back" to their communities.

Garcia (2013) confirmed that we know little about the educational needs, achievements, or problems of Latin@ students in science. Nor do we know how the needs of Latina students may differ from their male peers in learning and doing science. Thus, a particular focus on adolescent Latina students and science *through the lens of gender* is absent in the literature.

The term Latin@ refers to a diverse group of individuals in terms of race, ethnicity, culture, and language. Although many educators assume that Latin@s speak Spanish or come from homes where Spanish is spoken, their native language (L1) could be English, an indigenous language (e.g., Nahuatl, Mayan), or another language based on a variety of factors. However, for many linguistically diverse students in the United States who have experienced another home or native language is a lack of access to and proficiency in, English, the dominant language in the United States and the language used in school. While learning English, ELL students must also master the content area learning outcomes. Thus, ELL students are forced to do "double the work" as they simultaneously seek language proficiency and academic content knowledge (Short & Fitzsimmons, 2007). This is particularly problematic when students come to the United States during the middle and high school years, and have six or fewer years of formal schooling to gain enough proficiency in English to meet all of the requisite standards in science to graduate high school. Estimates for acquiring the academic English range from 4 to 7 years (Butler, Hakuta, & Witt, 2000) to 10 years for students with weak native language literacy levels (Collier, 1987).

Many linguistically diverse students attend segregated schools and live in linguistically isolated families. Fewer than 3% of teachers instructing ELL students have a degree in teaching English as a second language (ESL) or bilingual education and many teachers hold deficit views of linguistically diverse students' learning abilities. Dropout rates for Latin@ students in the United States are high compared to other ethnic groups. Immigrant Mexican youth between the ages of 16 and 19 have the largest dropout rates (40%) in the United States. For Latin@ youth who have attended U.S. schools for longer periods, the dropout rate is approximately 20%, compared to 8% for non-Hispanic White students (Morse, 2005).

Science practices can be defined as investigative, communicative, and epistemic, but this perspective can be expanded to include the example of science from sociocultural perspectives, such as classroom interactions and exchanges between students and their peers and teachers. Several studies have findings related to gender and ethnicity (Ayala, 2006; Lopez, 2006; Parker, 2014) with Latin@ students and other studies have briefly mentioned secondary findings discussing school practices that could improve ELL girls' experiences in STEM education as part of larger investigations about school experiences (Guzmán & Denner, 2006). Recent research has documented how teachers do not view Latinas as capable in science, which reflects in the teaching the girls receive. Latinas and their teachers discussed students low level cognitive engagement with science concepts, the experience of repetitive exercises and worksheets that reflect busy work rather than assisting students in developing their understanding of science and a lack of advocacy or recommendations from teachers to support or promote academic talented Latina students into higher level science courses leading to what Richardson (2013) has described as a spiral of (mis)education in science (Parker, 2014; Richardson, 2013).

We also acknowledge the complicated and complex social categories that influence students' learning, and planned the data analysis using intersectionality as a framework for analyzing the data and understanding the outcomes (McCall, 2005). Intersectionality examines how multiple social categories (e.g., gender, social class, native language) are interdependent and mutually constitutive which can manifest in different ways, producing a variety of power relationships. Researchers have used intersectionality to examine the micro and macro structures that impact individual's identities and lives (Bowleg, 2008). In this study we focused on students' gender, ethnicity, and native language as categories that may impact their science experiences and learning. By using quantitative and qualitative data we attempted to problematize the assumption that social categories are independent and contribute to layers of disenfranchisement that can lead to a "ranking." That is, being Latina, from a low socioeconomic background with Spanish as a first language generates more challenges for a student to pursue science than being a Latino from a middle level socioeconomic background.

At a macro level science is viewed as masculine, thus Latino boys may have more interest in the subject than their female peers and the potential to pursue science. However, Latina girls often have higher verbal and literacy skills and are less likely to drop out of school compared to boys. Literacy and positive attitudes towards school and valuing formal education are key for students' persistence in school, along with parental support and encouragement. Latin@ students in other studies have reported that their teachers often did not have academic expectations of ELL students and teachers noted that they have no or little preparation or knowledge in how to assist ELL students in learning science (Parker, 2014; Peralta et al., 2013).

This chapter focuses on 12- and 13-year old Latina students' experiences and attitudes towards science and the teaching practices that supported their science studies in a U.S. urban middle school. This research uses gender as an analytical category and focuses on factors that impacted Latin@ students' attitudes towards science such as teachers' practices, parental support, students' language acquisition, their perceptions of home, and peer support for science participation and achievement. The research question that guided the study was: Do Latina middle school students have the same attitudes towards science, experiences in science classes, and support from family and peers regardless of their native or home language (i.e., Spanish or English)?

METHODS

The data analyzed for this chapter is part of a larger, longitudinal, mixed-method study that utilized qualitative and quantitative data from students, teachers, and parents to examine the teaching and learning of ELL students in an urban, charter, middle school. Researchers have found that using a combination of qualitative and quantitative data strengthen the study by providing evidence for research claims from multiple sources (Tobin & Fraser, 1998). Qualitative data can offset the tendency for quantitative data to produce additive results from social categories rather than showing how the interdependence of social categories produce different power hierarchies (Bowleg, 2008).

Context and Participants

Honor Charter is a public charter school in a medium-sized city in the Northeast United States located in a poor neighborhood. The school includes Grades 5–8 and is affiliated with a K–4 school and a high school, which are located in adjacent school buildings. At the time of data collection, Honor had nearly 400 students over the four grade levels, 28% who self-identified as Black/Non-Hispanic, and 72% who identified as Hispanic. Ninety percent of the school population was eligible for free or reduced lunch.

Six science teachers and one administrator (an assistant principal who was the science department supervisor) participated in the study. All but one of the teachers entered the profession through either Teach for America or the state's alternate route program. The teacher who had completed a traditional teacher education program was certified in special education and was teaching science out-of-field. Teachers were interviewed twice formally during the academic year: once, in December and once, in June. The interviews lasted between 30 and 45 minutes and were semi-structured. Teachers also allowed researchers to video science lessons.

Data Sources

Qualitative data sources for the study included student, teacher, and parent/guardian interviews; field notes; observations; cogenerative dialogues;

and videos of science classes. One hundred and forty-two Latin@ students answered a survey focused on their attitudes towards science and in and out of school science experiences to produce the quantitative data. Seventy-four students self-identified as Latin@ reported English as their "native language" and 68 Latin@ students reported Spanish as their native language. The data sample included nearly equal numbers of females ($n = 70$) and males ($n = 72$).

Cogenerative Dialogues, Interviews, and Meetings

During the spring semester, selected students from each class were engaged in structured discourse on teaching and learning science in conversations called cogenerative dialogues. Cogenerative dialogues (cogens) have various structures and goals that are established by the participants. A common theme is for participants (i.e., students and teachers) to focus on the characteristics of the classroom environment or other sociocultural phenomena that would enhance and promote student learning (Wassell, Martin, & Scantlebury, 2013). Previous research has documented that cogens have provided teachers and researchers unique insights into students' views of the science classroom and suggestions for improving student learning (2013).

At Honor, groups of girls participated in several cogenerative dialogues to discuss and share their perspectives, preferences, and observations of science teaching and learning. The cogenerative dialogues were videotaped and transcribed. In addition, students were also interviewed about their science learning experiences, their beliefs about school, their practices in class, and their understanding of the role of gender and language in teaching and learning. The research team also held 1-hour teacher meetings once a week from January–June, during which field notes were taken and informal interview questions were asked. Parents/guardians of students involved with the cogens were invited to an interview. Interviews were conducted in either English or Spanish, whichever language the parents/guardians chose and conducted by bilingual researchers. These interviews were about an hour with informal interview questions.

Instruments

The science attitude survey[2] has questions related to student demographics such as sex, age, grade level, languages spoken at home; and questions about students' science practices in and out of school and their friends' science interests; teachers' practices in the science class; and parents/guardians' practices. The data for this study was collected from responses to the following subscales: (a) What I do in class, (b) What my teacher does, and (c) What my friends do. The subscale *What I do in class* had 17 items, which asked the students to describe how often they participate in activities such as talking with classmates about science, using information to support science answers, and using worksheets. *What my teacher does* has 5 items and asks students to indicate how often teachers ask questions, checks homework, or uses inquiry as a pedagogical approach. The scale, *What my friends do*, has 8 items that focus on whether a student's friends enjoy and engage in science activities outside of the class. Items were answered using Likert-type scales that indicated frequency of use—*almost never* to *very often*. The survey is a well-established instrument with the subscales' reliability ranging from 0.65 to 0.87 (Scantlebury, Boone, Fraser, & Kahle, 2001).

RESULTS AND DISCUSSION

This section presents the student survey results. The students' comments about science learning, teaching, and support from home shared during cogenerative dialogues and interviews and teachers' perspectives on students' engagement with science are incorporated into the section to expand upon the survey results.

The initial analysis showed there were no gender differences on the survey. Then, the dataset was analyzed using a one-way ANOVA comparing Latin@ students who identified English as their native language with Latin@ students who identified Spanish as their native language (L1). There were no interaction effects between students' gender and L1. As depicted in Table 4.1, for both groups, there were significant differences on all of

TABLE 4.1   Latin@ Students' Mean Subscale Scores by First Language

Subscales		n	M	SD	F	Sig.
What I do	English	73	3.65	0.80	13.903	0.000
	Spanish	64	3.05	0.49		
	Total/Average	**137**	**3.37**	**0.74**		
What my teacher does	English	74	3.11	0.60	22.934	0.000
	Spanish	67	3.79	0.57		
	Total/Average	**141**	**3.43**	**0.68**		
What my friends do	English	73	3.11	0.71	46.103	0.000
	Spanish	68	2.10	0.55		
	Total/Average	**141**	**2.63**	**0.81**		
What parents/adults do	English	74	3.20	1.20	0.844	0.432
	Spanish	67	3.18	1.19		
	Total/Average	**141**	**3.19**	**1.19**		

Note: 1 = *Almost Never*, 2 = *Seldom*, 3 = *Sometimes*, 4 = *Often*, 5 = *Very Often*

the subscales, except *What adults do.* The students who indicated English as their L1 had a higher mean score ($M = 3.65$) on the *What I do* item compared to the Spanish speaking Latin@ students ($M = 3.05$). A response of 3 indicated *sometimes* and thus the mean score of 3.65 is closer to *often.*

The students who indicated Spanish as their L1 had a significantly higher mean score ($M = 3.79$) on the *What teachers do* item compared to the English-speaking Latin@ students ($M = 3.11$). That is, students perceived that their teachers used more standards-based reform practices[3] compared to English speaking Latin@ students. There were no differences between the students' perception of adult support for their academic efforts, but there was a significant difference on the *What my friends do* between the two groups. The mean score for Latin@ students who identified English as their L1 ($M = 3.11$) was significantly higher than for the Latin@ students who identified Spanish as their L1 ($M = 2.10$).

Table 4.2 shows the mean scores and significant differences between English and Spanish L1 students by gender on the *What I do* subscale. For Latinas, the mean for English L1 ($M = 3.71$) and Spanish L1 ($M = 3.01$) were significantly different. There was also a significant difference for Latinos with English as their L1 ($M = 3.60$) and Spanish as their L1 ($M = 3.09$).

Table 4.3 shows the mean scores and significant differences between English L1 and Spanish L1 students within gender on the *What teachers do*

TABLE 4.2 Latin@ Students' Mean Subscale Scores on What I Do subscale by Student Gender and First Language

Sex	L1	*M*	*SD*	*n*	*F*	Sig.
Female	English	3.71	.81	32	20.338	.000
	Spanish	3.01	.45	37		
Male	English	3.60	.81	41	7.974	.006
	Spanish	3.09	.55	27		

Note: 1 = *Almost Never*, 2 = *Seldom*, 3 = *Sometimes*, 4 = *Often*, 5 = *Very Often*

TABLE 4.3 Latin@ Students' Mean Subscale Scores on What Teachers Do subscale by Student Gender and First Language

Sex	L1	*M*	*SD*	*n*	*F*	Sig.
Female	English	3.02	.47	32	32.661	.000
	Spanish	3.78	.63	37		
	Mean	**3.45**	**.68**	**69**		
Male	English	3.18	.69	41	15.721	.000
	Spanish	3.79	.48	27		
	Mean	**3.42**	**.68**	**68**		

TABLE 4.4 Latin@ Students' Mean Subscale Scores on What Friends Do subscale by Student Gender and First Language

Sex	L1	M	SD	n	F	Sig
Female	English	3.11	.58	32	78.20	.000
	Spanish	2.04	.45	37		
	Mean/Total	2.51	.74	69		
Male	English	3.11	.79	41	24.958	.000
	Spanish	2.20	.67	27		
	Mean/Total	2.74	.87	68		

subscale. For Latinas, the mean for English L1 ($M = 3.02$) and Spanish L1 ($M = 3.78$) were significantly different. There was also a significant difference for Latino English L1 students ($M = 3.18$) and Spanish L1 students ($M = 3.79$). Students whose L1 was Spanish reported that their teachers had higher occurrences of standards-based teaching practices compared to students who spoke English at home.

Table 4.4 shows the mean scores and significant differences between English and Spanish L1 students within gender on the *What friends do* subscale. For girls, the mean for English L1 ($M = 3.11$) and Spanish L1 ($M = 2.04$) students were significantly different. There was also a significant difference for the male English L1 students ($M = 3.11$) and Spanish L1 students ($M = 2.20$).

Students' Engagement in Class

Researchers used interviews and cogens with students about their preferences for pedagogical practices in science. The students noted that experiments, projects, supplementary materials, and group work helped their science learning. During cogenerative dialogues the students offered teachers suggestions for teaching practices that included use of laboratory stations and supportive reading strategies to learn science concepts. The Latinas liked their science teacher but gave the following comments: "He takes time to explain it and everything...kind of but he kind of talks too fast" (Cogen, February 2012). The girls were comfortable asking their teacher for further assistance and he would show them pictures to help them make connections between the science content and concepts and the language.

Teachers reported students' different attitudes towards their engagement in science classes. For example, one teacher, Amy described girls' and boys' different attitudes towards assignments that may improve their English and science literacy. Amy detailed:

The boys really disengage if we're reading out of the book or taking notes. Even if I let them do it in a group so that they can goof off and get it done, they don't learn any of it. They need you to talk it over with them out loud, and they need to be able to vocalize it before they get it, whereas the girls, if I hand them the book and say, "Read this section and take notes" the next day they know it. (Amy, January 2011)

Although teachers reported that Latinas were developing the language skills needed to succeed in science, they were often focused on managing boys' behavior. For instance, another teacher noted:

The guys are the . . . loud ones, and [the females] will volunteer every now and then, but they kind of tend to keep to themselves unless you bring a little extra attention to them specifically. I definitely do see where the males are more dominant, confident, and outgoing. Where the girls are more meek and mild. (Yamilla, March 2011)

However, girls were more likely than boys to show an interest in science and value academic success in school. As with previous gender research in a wide variety of classrooms and contexts, and spanning over decades, boys continue to dominate the physical (i.e., the laboratory equipment) and human resources (i.e., teachers and support staff). Because Latinas do not disrupt the classroom learning environment, they did not garner their teachers' attention which may have truncated their opportunities to learn science.

Some girls, such as Leanne enjoyed laboratory work but her teacher noted that he used her to modify boys' behavior. This is a common management strategy by teachers where they include high functioning and well behaved girls into groups of boys with the expectation that the girls will moderate the boys' behavior by focusing the group on the tasks. Leanne was interested in completing the experiments, so she assigned tasks to the boys and the group completed laboratory assignments. The boys in Leanne's group "behaved" and the teacher achieved her goal of ensuring they did not disrupt other students. As noted here, Leanne's teacher, Amy, also used her to explain science to her peers:

Leanne is a really great science student. She catches onto things really quickly, and she's really good at helping Arial, which I think is a great skill. She can really explain it to him on a different level using words that I never said to her about a topic to make him understand, which is pretty impressive. (Amy, January 2011)

Leanne helped male students focus on conducting experiments and her teacher asked her to explain science concepts to other (male) students. As discussed in other studies (Scantlebury, 2014), these common approaches that teachers use girls for, to modify boys' behavior and or explaining concepts to their peers can mean that girls are expected to assume a nurturing, caring role within the science class rather than assume the mantle of "science student." Latinas, such as Leanne, are asked to put other people's needs before their own and could have limited opportunities to extend and expand their own learning. Girls in other settings have voiced their frustration at teacher's expectations that they will "catch boys up" on material they have missed through being absent from class (Scantlebury, 2014).

The Latinas with Spanish as their L1 had lower scores on *What I do* in class compared to their English speaking peers. This in part is also due to teachers using strategies that would help improve the students language acquisition. One of the science teachers purchased wireless headphones so ELL students could listen to the audio on the class's digital textbooks while other students worked in laboratory groups. This allowed him to have students improving their language skills, fewer students involved in lab and then he could focus on assisting the students during lab. He rotated the groups increasing the time in class that ELL students spent on language and lab work. During the study, this teacher, Matt, became more aware of the impact the resources he was using could influence students' learning. For example, he commented that he was "staying away with custom-made worksheets because [they are] just loaded with background experience that you assume that [the students] know" (Matt, January 2011). On reflection of his ELL students' learning needs, this teacher had lobbied to purchase textbooks that had a digital version and was also planning to change his class to reintroduce a *Word Wall* and include a science word written in Spanish each day to help the students make connections between words and science concepts.

The science teachers at Honor used various strategies to engage the students. Yamila was the only teacher who spoke Spanish, she had trained in special education and had a limited science background but her ability to help the students, connect between the language of science, Spanish, and English, placed her as a role model for the students and her fellow teachers. Her colleagues were receptive to learning and implementing strategies to support ELLs' science learning.

What My Friends Do

When asked about friends, the students who identified Spanish as their L1 reported playing with siblings rather than friends, while English L1 students spent time with friends from school and their neighborhood. But their personal safety was a concern for their parents and girls reported that parents confined students to the house for their safety, as Ana explained:

"Sometimes my mom doesn't let me outside because people...some people with drugs they deal across from my moms" (Ana, December 2011).

Teachers also noted that girls whose first language was Spanish preferred to communicate with their friends in Spanish, and they were more likely to talk in Spanish than the boys. Yamilia shared:

> Isabel is a little more shy because of the language barrier, so she hasn't built up the confidence. But when they're speaking Spanish and they're kind of going back and forth, they're their own—When they're in their own group, at recess, she will often walk through the yard and through the blacktop outside, you can hear them speaking Spanish. (Yamilia, January 2011)

> Amy elaborated with: "I've noticed is that our girl ELLs tend to speak Spanish a lot more to each other than our males do. (Amy, January 2011)

The Spanish-speaking girls also were less likely to meet friends outside of school, their families preferring them to remain at home. Latinas are often expected to do domestic chores such as caring for younger siblings or relatives, helping with cleaning, laundry, or cooking. One mother noted that her daughter "likes to clean and helps others, helps me with the kids, I have four children. She bathes the baby, She watches her" (Interview, Spring 2011).

While speaking Spanish provided students time to develop their linguistic skills in their first language, this prevented the girls from developing their linguistic capital in English and/or science. Serendipitously, during a science teacher interview—with Yamilia, about the arrangement of learning pairs, a strategy for improving ELL students' English that could be used in the future emerged. Yamilia explains:

> "[Pairs assignment], it's at random, sometimes they're paired with non—Isabel was very lucky this year to befriend Brianna, who doesn't speak a lick of Spanish, so they've kind of helped each other out, she's taught Brianna some Spanish words, and Brianna's helped her with her English. (Yamilia, January 2011)

For Latinas in urban settings, school is often the place where they can socialize with friends. The science teachers had discussed introducing after-school activities in science that could stimulate students' interest. However, they had limited time and no or little fiscal resources to support these opportunities.

Support from Family and Community

Yamilia, the fluent Spanish-speaking science teacher was particularly insightful regarding her students and their families, in part because she called, texted, and connected with her students' parents. Yamilia jokingly labeled herself the "Teacher Stalker" but parents who were monitoring their children's academic progress appreciated her texts and messages. She was aware that parents with good English literacy skills could be in a better position to assist their children with homework and also more confident in asking teachers about students' progress in school compared to Spanish speaking parents.

Yamilia was empathetic to the challenges the girls' parents faced in helping their children learn science. Yamilia voiced:

> I feel that with sciences a lot of times parents' lack of knowledge stops them from asking questions or maybe they see science and they become intimidated, they see these books and they're like "whoa, I never learned that." I know one of my students mentioned that Mom said, "Oh I learned this in college," and she's English speaking, I could only imagine how the Spanish speaking parents feel. I don't know if there's that initial "oh maybe I'll look dumb" or not educated if I ask her what they're doing or if I don't understand. (Interview, January 2011)

Gender role stereotypes from family and culture also appeared in the science classroom, as Yamilia noted:

> With our backgrounds, and I say our because myself being brought up in that kind of home (Latin@), the moms tend to be the caretakers, and they nourish their children and make sure they're safe, and I feel like that's passed on to the girls, where they're always taking care of a younger sibling, or a pet, or even a friend they take care of or look out for. The males are more like[ly] to be working ... you know traditionally ... in school you see the males and the females taking those roles. (Interview, January 2011)

LatCrit values language and culture, however, the challenge for Latinas is that cultural values prioritize their nurturing and caring skills over the development of their aspirational and academic capital which is necessary to pursue higher education, especially in science. Further, the resistant cultural wealth is produced by a resistance to inequality, but Yosse (2005) did not take into account gender inequality within the Latin@ culture in the LatCrit framework. Replicate of many other classrooms where gender researchers have noted how boys dominate the physical and human resources of the class (Scantlebury, 2014).

Parents/guardians were supportive of their children's studies. Yamilia described the efforts of one mother:

> Last year there was a student whose mom's English was limited [but] she would sit and translate every direction and every word, and she ... stays up to 11:00 at night and does homework with her girls. She was a lawyer in Santo

> Domingo and moved here for a better life, and lives in Camden and has a low
> paying job, but she does things like that to help her kids. (Yamilia, Interview,
> January 2011)

During an interview with one of the girls' mother, Manuela explained how
she helped Andrea with her school work, and if she was unable to, how she
would ask the teachers for their assistance.

> I try. If I don't understand what . . . then she calls her friend. Her friend comes.
> If together they don't understand, then I call the teacher in the morning and
> explain why she didn't do it, and ask her if they can give her a little more help
> and explain it to her. Because she, since it's too late for her to get herself
> together, then I call and her teacher helps her. (Manuela, Honor student's
> mother, May 2012)

When asked about her aspirations for her daughter, Manuela offered the
following, which highlights the importance of education:

> To continue the way she is doing, she is intelligent. We have, had some little
> problems with her sometimes . . . but I tell her that she has to . . . has to come
> to school to be someone in the future, because there is nothing out there.
> (Manuela, Honor student's mother, May 2012)

CONCLUSION

The research connects to the book's theme in highlighting the pedagogical
practices that support Latina girls and it also shows that native language has
an impact on students' attitudes towards science. Teachers and schools may
need to explore different strategies to connect Spanish speaking Latina girls
to science. Moreover, the ongoing domination of teachers' attention to boys
remains an issue. While the teachers reported that Latino boys would engage in labs, they often refused to provide written answers and explanations.
Teachers will need to intervene during laboratory activities to ensure that
the "quiet Latina," is provided the opportunity to use science equipment.

The Next Generation Science Standards (NGSS) has further challenges
for science teachers of ELL students. The NGSS (2012) outlines scientific
practices, some of which offer particular challenges to ELL students such as
(a) asking questions and defining problems; (b) constructing explanations
and designing solutions; (c) engaging in argument from evidence; and (d)
obtaining, evaluating, and communicating information. For ELL students'
aspects of these 21st century scientific practices may offer particular challenges, as they work to acquire the language skills to successfully engage
in arguments and construct explanations. With increasing diversity in the

K–12 population and emphasis on language skills such as argumentation, science educators need to explore the different learning needs for Latin@ students in connection with their home languages and current proficiency levels in English.

Latin@ culture values community cultural wealth, and in particular the connection to family. However, women and girls are expected to assume nurturing and caring roles to establish the community and maintain networks. For Latinas to continue in science they may have to challenge these family and community values. Moreover, for ELL Latinas, they face the added challenge of learning science's language and vocabulary that can be difficult to understand (Peralta et al., 2013). In general, few teachers have expertise in working with ELL students, but science teachers can provide Latinas the opportunities to learn and develop their language skills through various pedagogical practices (Stevenson, 2013). Schools and teachers can engage Latin@ community members, particularly parents, in the decision making process of choosing courses for their daughters that can lead to higher education, and provide information as to why Latinas are qualified for these career paths and how such careers may provide Latinas opportunities to give back to their communities (Licona, 2013).

However, schools need to provide language support for non-Spanish speaking teachers, so they can connect into the community and with the Latinas families. This outreach could help parents understand the value of their daughters studying science. Parents interviewed in the study had high expectations for their children, they had taken the necessary steps to enroll them in a charter school and attended school events. A grandfather was interviewed as he was assisting his son parent the children. The grandfather explained that education was important, and it was a journey to obtain an education and he was there to support his grandchildren because on the journey "we stumble, fall, get up, and continue walking" (Pedro, Honor student's grandfather, Interview, May 2011).

NOTES

1. Latin@ is preferred over Latino/a.
2. A Spanish version of the survey was available for students.
3. Standards-based teaching practices include using inquiry approaches to teaching science, engaging students in discussion and writing about science, using a variety of formative and summative assessments to ascertain students' science knowledge and understanding.

66 ■ K. SCANTLEBURY and B. WASSELL

REFERENCES

American Association of University Women Educational Foundation. (1998). *Gender gaps: Where schools still fail our children*. Washington, DC: Author.

American Association of University Women Educational Foundation. (2004). *Under the microscope: A decade of gender equity projects in the sciences*. Washington DC: Author.

Ayala, J. (2006). Confianza, consejos, and contradictions: Gender and sexuality lessons between Latina adolescent daughters and mothers. In J. Denner & B. L. Guzmán (Eds.), *Latina girls: Voices of adolescent strength in the United States* (pp. 29–43). New York, NY: New York University Press.

Bowleg, L. (2008). When Black + lesbian + woman ≠ Black lesbian woman: The methodological challenges of qualitative and quantitative intersectionality research. *Sex Roles, 59*(5/6), 312–325. https://doi.org/10.1007/s11199-008-9400-z

Butler, Y. G., Hakuta, K., & Witt, D. (2000). *How long does it take English learners to attain proficiency* (Policy Report 2000-1; pp. 1–28). Santa Barbara: The University of California Linguistic Minority Research Institute.

Calabrese Barton A., & Tan, E. (2008). Funds of knowledge, discourses and hybrid space. *Journal of Research in Science Teaching, 46*(1), 50–73.

Carreón, G. P., Drake, C., & Barton, A. C. (2005). The importance of presence: Immigrant parents' school engagement experiences. *American Educational Research Journal, 42*(3), 465–498. https://doi.org/10.3102/00028312042003465

Collier, V. (1987). Age and rate of acquisition of second language for academic purposes. *TESOL Quarterly, 21*(4), 617–641.

Cohen, J., & Blanc, S. (1996). *Girls in the middle: Working to succeed in school*. Washington DC: American Association of University Women Educational Foundation.

Fine, M., Jaffe-Walter, R., Pedraza, P., Futch, V., & Stoudt, B. (2007). Swimming: On oxygen, resistance, and possibility for immigrant youth under siege. *Anthropology & Education Quarterly, 38*(1), 7–96.

García, Y. V. (2013). When preparation meets opportunity: A case study exploring the feasibility of pursuing a career in biology for two Latina high school girls. *Cultural Studies of Science Education, 8*(4), 935–951. https://doi.org/10.1007/s11422-013-9519-2

Guzmán, B. L., & Denner, J. (2006). Conclusion: Latina girls, social science, and transformation. In J. Denner & B. L. Guzmán (Eds.), *Latina girls: Voices of adolescent strength in the United States.* (pp. 226–238.) New York, NY: New York University Press.

Hagiwara, S., Calabrese Barton, A., & Contento, I. (2007). Culture, food, and language: Perspectives from immigrant mothers in school science. *Cultural Studies of Science Education, 2*(2), 475–515.

Licona, M. (2013). Mexican and Mexican-American children's funds of knowledge as interventions into deficit thinking: Opportunities for praxis in science education. *Cultural Studies of Science Education, 8*(4), 859–872. https://doi.org/10.1007/s11422-013-9515-6

Lopez, N. (2006). Resistance to race and gender oppression: Dominican high school girls in New York City. In J. Denner & B. L. Guzmán (Eds.), *Latina girls:*

Voices of adolescent strength in the United States (pp. 79–92.) New York, NY: New York University Press.

McCall, L. (2005). The complexity of intersectionality. *Signs: Journal of Women in Culture and Society, 30*(3), 1771–1800. http://dx.doi.org/10.1086/426800

Morse, A. (2005). *A look at immigrant youth: Prospects and promising practices.*Washington, DC: National Conference of State Legislatures.

Next Generation Science Standards Lead States. (2012). *Next generation science standards: For states, by States.* Washington, DC: The National Academies Press.

Parker, C. (2014). Multiple influences: Latinas, middle-level science, and school. *Cultural Studies of Science Education, 9*(2), 317–334.

Peralta, C., Caspary, M., & Boothe, D. (2013). Success factors impacting Latina/o persistence in higher education leading to STEM opportunities. *Cultural Studies of Science Education, 8*(4), 905–918. https://doi.org/10.1007/s11422-013-9520-9

Richardson, B. K. (2013). The spiral of science (mis)education, Parker's "multiple influences," and missed opportunities. *Cultural Studies of Science Education, 9*(2), 335–342. https://doi.org/10.1007/s11422-013-9506-7

Scantlebury, K., Boone, W. J., Fraser, B. J., & Kahle, J. B. (2001). Design, validation, and use of an evaluation instrument for monitoring systemic reform. *Journal of Research in Science Teaching, 38*(6), 646–662. https://doi.org/10.1002/tea.1024

Scantlebury, K., (2014). Promoting girls' voices: Using cogernative dialogues (cogen)s in science. *Biology International, 54*(2), 198–207. Retrieved from http://www.iubs.org/fileadmin/user_upload/Biology-International/BI/BI_Numero_54.pdf

Short, D., & Fitzsimmons, S. (2007). Double the work: Challenges and solutions to acquiring language and academic literacy for adolescent English language learners—A report to Carnegie Corporation of New York. Washington, DC: Alliance for Excellent Education.

Stevenson, A. R. (2013). How fifth grade Latino/a bilingual students use their linguistic resources in the classroom and laboratory during science instruction. *Cultural Studies of Science Education, 8*(4), 973–989. https://doi.org/10.1007/s11422-013-9522-7

Tobin, K., & Fraser, B. J. (1998). Qualitative and quantitative landscapes of classroom learning environments. In B. J. Fraser & K. Tobin (Eds.), *International handbook of science education.* (pp. 623–640). Dordrecht, The Netherlands: Kluwer.

United States Census Bureau. (2011). *Newsroom archive: Profile America facts for features.* Retrieved from https://www.census.gov/newsroom/releases/archives/facts_for_features_special_editions/cb11-ff18.html

Wassell, B., Martin, S., & Scantlebury, K. (2013). Using cogenerative dialogues to foster community and support English language learner students' language and science learning. *TESOL Journal, 4*(4), 759–771. https://doi.org/10.1002/tesj.109

CHAPTER 5

DEVELOPING STEM AMBITIONS

An Examination of Inequality by Gender and Race/Ethnicity

Catherine Riegle-Crumb
Karisma Morton
Sarah Blanchard

In the last few decades, women have surpassed men in rates of college attendance and graduation (Diprete & Buchmann, 2013), as well as made some notable strides towards greater parity in income (Bobbitt-Zeher, 2007). Yet despite this notable progress, women remain underrepresented in many science, technology, engineering, and math (STEM) majors in college, and likewise underrepresented in STEM-related occupations, which are comparatively high-status and high-earning fields. (England, 2010; National Academy of Sciences, 2007). For instance, within the U.S. workforce today, women represent just 13% of engineers (Landivar, 2013). Further, although jobs in computer science will likely continue to offer greater opportunities for future workers, women's participation in computer science

Girls and Women of Color In STEM, pages 69–90
Copyright © 2020 by Information Age Publishing
All rights of reproduction in any form reserved.

has declined since the 1990's (Landivar, 2013). These examples illustrate persistent gender segregation within some of the most advantaged sectors of the U.S. economy.

Recent research provides strong empirical evidence that the most proximate source of this inequality is the gender gap in STEM expectations and aspirations that emerges during adolescence (Legewie & Diprete, 2014b; Morgan, Leeman, Todd, & Weeden, 2013; Xie & Shauman, 2003). Specifically, the underrepresentation of adult women in STEM postsecondary and occupational fields is not due to females' relative lack of skills or perseverance, but rather that many females have decided not to pursue STEM fields long before they enter college (Riegle-Crumb, King, Grodsky, & Muller, 2012; Xie & Shauman, 2003). Therefore, this study focuses on the critical period of adolescence to examine the emergence of gender differences in future expectations of pursuing STEM fields. Importantly, it explicitly focuses on the patterns and predictors of STEM expectations for minority youth, as the large extant body of quantitative research on gender inequality in STEM tends to focus on aggregate differences between males and females (Blickenstaff, 2005; Xie & Shauman, 2003), thereby obscuring the experiences of females and males from different racial/ethnic backgrounds (Andersen, 2005; Browne & Misra, 2003).

RESEARCH DESIGN

Specifically, we utilize a new dataset collected from a predominantly minority school district to address two related research questions. First, *to what extent are there gender and racial/ethnic differences in the expectations of pursuing STEM fields in college among young high school students in an urban, predominantly minority district?* After examining differences between groups with regard to STEM expectations, we subsequently turn to an in-depth investigation of Hispanic youth. The composition of our sample (65% Hispanic), as well as the rich information from administrative records available in our dataset, presents a rare opportunity to examine how academic factors shape the expectations of this critically important and growing population that is typically understudied (National Research Council, 2011; Pew Research Center, 2012). Therefore, our second research question is: *How do prior math and science grades, advanced course-taking, and test scores predict the STEM expectations of Hispanic youth, and does this differ by gender?*

In addressing these questions, our study relies on a more detailed and comprehensive account of the future plans of adolescent youth than is currently available in the literature. The "STEM" acronym, while convenient to use and pronounce, is comprised of many distinct fields, some of which are considerably more gender equitable than others (Landivar, 2013).

Thus we empirically measured students' intentions to pursue each of five separate fields (biological sciences, physical sciences, mathematics, computer science, and engineering), and empirically assessed whether students hold clear preferences for specific fields (e.g., engineering) or instead are inclined (or disinclined) towards all STEM fields at this point in their lives. In sum, our study will contribute new knowledge about adolescents' early plans to pursue STEM fields among a sample of diverse youth.

Examining Gendered Expectations for STEM: Considering Race/Ethnicity

In early adolescence, individuals start actively contemplating their future adult lives (Greenfield, 1997; Sorge, 2007). As mentioned above, this is the critical period where adolescents decide whether they want to pursue future education and occupations in STEM fields (Eccles, 2009). A wealth of prior literature reveals that on average, female youth are much less likely to harbor future STEM educational and occupational ambitions than their male peers. While most studies measure future plans towards the end of high school (Legewie & Diprete, 2014b; Morgan, Gelbgser, & Weeden, 2013; Xie & Shauman, 2003), some have documented gender disparities in future STEM plans as early as middle school or the beginning of high school (Barton, Tan, & Rivet, 2008; Sadler, Sonnert, Hazari, & Tai, 2012). For example, in their analyses of national data from the high school class of 1992, Xie and Shauman (2003) found that among high school seniors who expected to major in STEM, boys outnumbered girls 2 to 1. Similarly, a study by Sadler and colleagues found that at the beginning of high school, 40% of male students in their sample reported future plans to pursue a STEM occupation compared to only 15% of female students (Sadler et al., 2012).

While the gender gap in early STEM plans is firmly well-established in the empirical literature, there are relatively few studies that explicitly consider the plans of minority youth. As national studies are comprised mostly of White students, the gendered patterns reported generally reflect the experiences of the dominant group (Maltese & Tai, 2011; Riegle-Crumb et al., 2012; Xie & Shauman, 2003). Gender theories of intersectionality argue that this is highly problematic, as it obscures the experiences and obstacles experienced by members of different racial/ethnic groups (Andersen, 2005; Browne & Misra, 2003). Prior research points to the potential complexity of this intersection; some studies suggest that as members of two traditionally disadvantaged groups, Black and Hispanic girls experience a "double jeopardy" which may deter them for aspiring to STEM fields as traditionally White male domains (Archer-Banks & Behar-Horenstein, 2012). Yet still others point to the potential for resiliency against gender stereotypes, and the higher utility value that minority females may place on STEM fields as venues of upward mobility and status (Hanson, 2006). Indeed, some studies find that Black females exhibit signs of stronger interest and affect towards STEM fields than their White female peers (Hanson, 2006; Riegle-Crumb, Moore, & Ramos-Wada, 2011), and suggest that Black females may be more likely to reject gender stereotypes of STEM fields as masculine.

This study builds on the currently limited research on intersectionality in STEM fields by focusing not only on differences across racial/ethnic groups, but also specifically focusing on Hispanic youth. Despite the growing representation of Hispanic individuals in the U.S. population and among the school-age population in particular (Dondero & Muller, 2012; Pew Research Center, 2012), the literature on inequality has paid little attention to STEM ambitions of female (as well as male) Hispanic youth.

Given the salience of traditional gender-role attitudes among Hispanic populations (Kane, 2000; Ovink, 2014), one might expect that Hispanic females would be even less likely to intend to pursue male-dominated STEM fields than their White female peers particularly if doing so requires postsecondary study away from home (Turley, 2009). Yet such an assumption may be far too simplistic, as it overlooks diversity and heterogeneity within the Hispanic population (Kane, 2000; Montoya, 1996). Additionally, while there is certainly evidence of the endorsement of traditional or conservative gender roles among Hispanics (i.e., importance of family and domestic responsibilities for women), such views do not necessarily translate to lack of educational and occupational ambition among Hispanic females or familial support for postsecondary attainment (Harklau, 2013; Kane, 2000; Ovink, 2014). Therefore, with particular attention to Hispanic youth, this study examines differences in students' expectations to major in STEM fields at the beginning of high school.

Shaping STEM Expectations: The Role of Academic Achievement

As young people contemplate what kinds of jobs and future courses of study to undertake, they logically consider the areas in which they excel or have the strongest skills. Indicators such as grades and test scores can function as feedback from presumed experts (i.e., teachers) not only about students' current aptitude in a field, but also the probability that they will be successful in future endeavors in related fields (Schneider & Stevenson, 1999). Not surprisingly then, prior research shows that students' achievement in math and science is related to their intentions to pursue a STEM major or career (Correll, 2001; Riegle-Crumb & King, 2010; Tai, Lui, Maltese, & Fan, 2006; Xie & Shauman, 2003).

Beyond this general trend, our study seeks to provide new insights into the extent to which academic factors, including grades, test scores, and exposure to rigorous curriculum, shape the future STEM ambitions of minority students, as well as whether this differs by gender. Our focus is motivated in part by research that provides some evidence that the aspirations of minority youth are not necessarily strongly tied to academic feedback. Specifically, some studies suggest that Black high school youth do not view low levels of performance as a deterrent against high aspirations (Mickelson, 1990; Morgan & Mehta, 2004). Indeed there is evidence that minority youth exhibit strong interest in STEM fields despite comparatively low levels of achievement (Riegle-Crumb et al., 2011). Although informative, the research in this area is currently limited in scope, particularly regarding the patterns between academic achievement and STEM expectations for Hispanic youth.

Additionally, the extant literature tells us virtually nothing about whether academic achievement works differently to shape the STEM expectations of minority females compared to their male peers. The literature that considers aggregate gender differences across all racial/ethnic groups in the salience of performance feedback has mixed results. For example, Katz, Allbritton, Aronis, Wilson, and Soffa (2006) and Ost (2010) both found that females' interest in pursuing STEM was more negatively influenced by earning a "B" when compared to their male peers. Such results are consistent with the idea that females are more responsive to signals and feedback about their academic performance (Riegle-Crumb, Farka, & Muller, 2006; Seymour & Hewitt, 1997). Yet other studies find an opposite pattern; a recent study by Griffith (2010) using two nationally representative datasets found that the effect of grades was stronger for male students, suggesting that perhaps males are more responsive to grades than females when making decisions about persisting in STEM.

One possibility for the inconsistencies in this literature is that observing gender differences in the aggregate may obscure important variation by race/ethnicity. Specifically, the role of grades in STEM persistence may be different for certain groups. Ideally, research should consider how academic achievement shapes the STEM expectations of all students, with attention to differences across multiple racial/ethnic and gender subgroups. The data used in this study (described below), however, is best suited to an in-depth examination of how academic factors shape the STEM expectations of Hispanic students in particular, and whether and how this differs by gender. By addressing this topic we will contribute new information to the limited extant research, particularly for this minority population.

DISAGGREGATING THE ACRONYM:
LOOKING WITHIN "STEM"

Before turning towards our empirical investigation of inequality in STEM expectations among high school students in a primarily Hispanic school district, it is important to discuss substantive and empirical issues in defining "STEM." The fields that are typically subsumed under the category of STEM share a disciplinary focus on numeracy and empirical proof and emphasize the importance of physical observations, objective measurement, and replication. However, the broad umbrella of STEM extends over many distinct fields, each with their own substantive emphasis as well as their own norms and cultures. Importantly from the perspective of equity, some STEM fields have fared better than others. At the collegiate level as well as the occupational level, gender disparities are largest in engineering and computer science (Landivar, 2013; National Science Board, 2014). For example, among the graduating class of 2011, men earned the vast majority of bachelor's degrees in engineering, computer science, and physics, but women earned more degrees in the biological sciences (National Science Board, 2014).

Consequently, some recent research on the gender gap in entry into STEM college majors has treated the biological sciences separately from other STEM fields (Riegle-Crumb et al., 2012), yet the bulk of research on higher education and occupational disparities continue to model individuals' decisions to enter STEM in the aggregate (Glass, Sassler, Levitte, & Michelmore, 2013; Legewie & Diprete, 2014a; Mann & Diprete, 2013; Morgan, Gelgsber et al., 2013; Xie & Shauman, 2003).

Research on the development of STEM expectations at the secondary level follows the same trend, with most studies treating STEM as a monolithic whole (for exceptions see Riegle-Crumb et al., 2011; Sadler et al., 2012) or alternatively focusing exclusively on a single, particular STEM field such as engineering (Constentino de Cohen & Deterding, 2009; Zarrett & Malanchuk, 2005). The focus on STEM in the aggregate is often the result of data limitations, as large national datasets typically include only categories of response that capture students' general aspirations towards STEM. But this approach loses the ability to discern the extent to which gaps in adolescence mirror those observed later. For example, is girls' interest in computer science at the beginning of high school consistent with their underrepresentation among college graduates with degrees in computer science? Or is there evidence that the gender gap in adolescents' interest in computer science is quite small, suggesting that factors that dissuade girls from this field operate more powerfully at a later point in time?

Perhaps even more importantly, the extant empirical literature measures students' ambitions as a set of mutually exclusive choices. For example, a study by Sadler et al. (2012) asked participants to indicate their intended field of study when they were beginning high school, and although categories of response included separate categories for engineering and other sciences in addition to non-STEM fields, students could only select one. At face value this might appear as a trivial issue relating to choice of measurement, but in fact it reflects an assumption (perhaps implicit) that students at this age have a starkly defined preference. Put differently, while college students are eventually forced to pick a major (or perhaps as many as two if they double major), there is no reason that adolescents' plans have to be so clearly defined. In fact, sociological and social-psychological perspectives on the development of expectations suggest that students consider a range of options concurrently as they make plans for the future during adolescence (Eccles, 2005; Morgan, Gelbgser et. al, 2013).

To summarize, we argue that how we measure students' future STEM plans has important consequences. If we ask students only to report their interest in STEM as an aggregate category, we risk missing important differences across fields. Yet if we instead ask students to choose their favorite among a list of different STEM fields, we risk missing critical insights into the degree to which their preferences are (or are not) clearly defined at this point. Therefore in this study, we rely on newly collected data that enables us to measure students' intentions to pursue each of five separate fields (biological sciences, physical sciences, mathematics, computer science, and engineering), as well as consider the relationship between them to assess whether some students harbor strong preferences for specific fields (e.g., engineering) or are alternatively favorably inclined (or disinclined) towards all STEM fields. Only when we gain more insight into how adolescents view STEM fields can we work effectively to counter negative perceptions and cultivate the interest of all students, particularly female and minority youth who have been traditionally underrepresented.

DATA COLLECTION AND ANALYSIS

In Spring 2014, our research team collected data from a very large urban school district in the Southwest. Its diversity (approximately 65% Hispanic and 25% Black) makes it an ideal location to investigate the experiences of minority youth. The district profile is consistent with high-minority districts across the country, as a very high percentage of students come from economically disadvantaged backgrounds. Specifically, more than 75% of students in the district qualify for free or reduced lunch.

The team collected survey data from approximately 4,000 ninth and tenth graders attending 11 public comprehensive high schools. Additionally, the team collected extensive administrative data from students' middle school years (2011–2013) that included detailed information on courses taken, grades, and statewide test scores. We know of no other large-scale dataset that tracks students over time across these critical formative years of STEM pathways, nor that have such a strong representation of minority youth, particularly Hispanic youth who are too often overlooked in research on gender inequality.

Dependent Variable

The high school survey was specifically designed to measure students' expectations to major in different STEM fields, which serves as the dependent variable of interest in this study. Students were asked how likely it is that if they attend college they will major in (a) biological sciences, (b) physical sciences, (c) math, (d) computer science or technology, and (e) engineering. Categories of response for each question included: 1 (*very unlikely*), 2 (*unlikely*), 3 (*neutral*), 4 (*likely*), and 5 (*very likely*). In order to describe meaningful patterns of student responses on these survey items, we utilized latent profile analyses (LPA) using Mplus Version 7.2. Unlike factor analysis, which is variable-centered, LPA is person-centered and, as such, focuses on the profiles of individuals instead of the structure of variables and how they correlate. It uses continuous variables to identify discrete latent variables that best categorize people based on their responses from two or more variables and uses probabilities to perform such categorization. LPA, in essence, provides a representation of data through the classification of people into meaningful categories based on similarities in responses.

The following is an example to demonstrate how and why LPA is useful. Suppose a researcher has data on different high school activities of adolescents (e.g., playing football, swimming, singing in the choir, performing in plays, reading comic books, playing video games). A factor analysis would seek to categorize these activities to create a smaller number of new variables based on how they generally relate to one another. In this example, football and swimming might be collapsed into a measure for athletics, whereas, singing in the choir and performing in plays could be categorized under the performing arts.

With LPA, on the other hand, responses to questions related to these activities would result in a categorization of people into different latent classes based on their similarities on their responses about their level of engagement in all of these activities. So, it might distinguish between three different classes of students based on what kind of activity they specialized in (jocks, geeks, or thespians) *as well as* identify two additional classes of students—one class that has a high score on all activities (well-rounded or over-achieving students), and yet another class of students who participated in no activities (slackers). Therefore the number of classes LPA identifies might not be that much lower than the number of variables used to identify the classes, but the result is a series of different profiles or classes of students that takes into account all of their activities (or lack thereof).

Results of LPA indicated that a four-class solution was the best fit for our data on STEM expectations, based on the values of the AIC, BIC, and the Vuong-Lo-Mendell-Rubin indicators produced by the Mplus output. Based on inspection of the means on the five different STEM fields for each of the four classes, we observed that there were two classes of students that held similar expectations of majoring in all STEM fields. We characterize the first class as having *Low STEM Expectations*. Students in this class have average scores on each of the five STEM categories ranging from 1.2–1.8, indicating that they reported that it was unlikely that they would pursue any STEM major in college. This class captured 34% of students. The second class is characterized by having *Neutral STEM Expectations*. The average scores on each of the five STEM categories ranged from 2.1–3.0 for students in this class, indicating that they were generally neutral or in the midpoint of the 5 point likelihood scale. This class captured 33% of students.

We identified two remaining classes of students that exhibited a strong preference for one or more STEM fields. The first of these we characterized as a *Physical Science Preference*. Students in this class had an average score of 4.4 on a 5 point scale for expecting a physical science major, while scores on the other four STEM majors were neutral (ranging from 3.3–3.5). This class represented 17% of students in the sample. Finally, the last class exhibited a *Computer Science and Engineering Preference (CS/E)*. Average scores were highest for engineering (3.9) and computer science (3.6). This group was neutral on math (3.0), but disinclined towards either biology (1.6) or physical science (1.3). This last class captured just 15% of students. In the next section we will model membership in these four different categories of STEM expectations as the dependent variables in our analyses.

Independent Variables

All independent variables come from administrative data collected and maintained by the school district. This includes students' gender and their racial/ethnic classification. The latter distinguishes between the following categories: White, Hispanic, Black, Asian, and other ethnicity. Due to the very small numbers of students in the latter two categories, we do not include them in the analyses presented here. Our final analytic sample is 72% Hispanic, 21% Black, and 7% White. Students' limited English proficiency (LEP) status is an additional indicator used as a control variable in the second part of our analyses. Students were coded as LEP if their transcripts indicated LEP status for any of the middle school years. Approximately 40% of Hispanic students were coded as LEP in our sample.

The independent variables in our study also represent a comprehensive description of students' middle school academic profile in math and science. For grades we include the average of students' sixth, seventh, and eigth grade math and science courses, respectively. Also included are two indicators for whether a student was ever in a math honors or science honors course in middle school. Students taking Science 6, Science 7, and Science 8 courses labeled "Pre-AP" and those taking Math 6, Math 7, or Math 8 Pre-AP courses or Algebra I were assigned an honors distinction in science and math, respectively. The final two independent variables, math and science test score, represent the average of standardized math and science tests (represented as z-scores) taken in middle school.

We calculated correlation coefficients between our independent variables and determined that students' math grades and science grades were highly correlated (0.73), as was their advanced course-taking in science and math (0.64). Math and science test scores were more moderately correlated (0.43). There were weaker correlations among our math indicators (i.e., math grades, math honors, and math test score) and our science indicators (i.e., science grades, science honors, and science test score) suggesting that each of our subject indicators contribute individually to a more comprehensive math and science student achievement profile.

Analyses and Results Examining Gender and Racial/Ethnic Differences in STEM Expectations

Our first research question addresses whether there are gender and racial/ethnic differences in expectations to pursue STEM fields in college. To address this question, we look at the distribution of different gender and racial/ethnic groups in the four classes of STEM expectations discussed above, and note differences that are statistically significant.[1]

Starting with aggregate differences by gender, as seen in Figure 5.1, we find that females are significantly more likely to be in the low STEM expectation group than males. Specifically, almost half of all females in the sample (44%) have low expectations of majoring in any of the five STEM fields; this is compared to only 25% of male students. Female students are significantly less likely to be in the neutral category than their male peers (30% vs. 37%). While there are no significant gender differences in the physical science preference group, with about 17% of male and female students in this category, female students are underrepresented in the CS/E preference group. Only 9% of females compared to 21% of males are in this group.

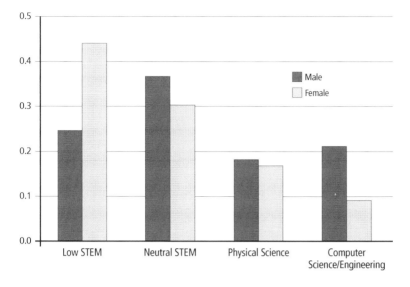

Figure 5.1 Gender differences in STEM expectations.

Turning to aggregate differences by race (see Figure 5.2), White students are significantly more likely to be in the low STEM preference group (43%) compared to both Hispanic (33%) and Black students (38%). White students are less likely to be in the neutral group (27%) compared to Hispanic youth (34%). We observe no statistically significant differences between

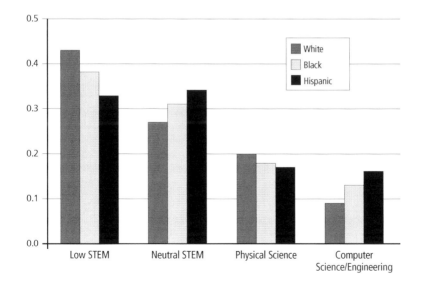

Figure 5.2 Racial/ethnic differences in STEM expectations.

racial/ethnic groups in membership in the physical science preference group. Yet regarding membership in the CS/E preference group, Hispanic students are significantly more likely to be in this group (16%) compared to both Black (13%) and White youth (5%).

Finally, we also examined differences across racial/ethnic and gender subgroups (not shown). We note that due to small cell sizes in some categories (i.e., of the 130 White females in the sample, only 10 are in the CS/E category) not all differences are statistically significant. Yet in general we see parallel patterns to those discussed in the previous two paragraphs, such that gender differences in representation in STEM categories are similar across the three different racial/ethnic groups, and racial/ethnic differences in STEM categories are similar across gender groups.

Stepping back, although data limitations prevent us from drawing conclusions about particular racial/ethnic and gender subgroups, there is nevertheless clear evidence that Hispanic youth in this district exhibit different STEM expectations than their White and Black peers. Contrary to some notions of a presumed disadvantage or lack of interest in STEM fields among minority youth in general, we find that compared to both White and Black students, Hispanic students have the lowest likelihood of being in the low STEM group and the highest likelihood of being in the CS/E group.

Keeping this finding in mind, we now turn to a closer examination of the STEM expectations of Hispanic high school youth, to assess how academic performance in math and science during middle school predicts such expectations, and whether and how this differs by gender.

Examining the Role of Academic Performance for Hispanic Male and Females Students

To address our second research question, we conduct a series of multinomial logistic regressions predicting membership in the different STEM expectation categories for Hispanic youth. All results in the tables are displayed as odds ratios, indicating the effect of each independent variable on the likelihood that a student is in one category vs. the contrast category. As we have four different categories, there are six possible comparisons between two single categories. However, we posit that the four following comparisons are the most relevant and interesting to consider:

1. *Low STEM vs. Neutral STEM*: a comparison of two groups whose expectation levels are consistent across all five STEM fields.
2. *Computer Science/Engineering vs. Neutral STEM*: a comparison between a group with a strong preference for a particular field(s) vs. a group that has neutral expectations across all STEM fields.

3. *Physical Science vs. Neutral STEM*: another comparison between a group with a strong preference for a particular field vs. a group that has neutral expectations across STEM fields.
4. *Physical Science vs. Computer Science/Engineering*: a comparison between two groups with a strong preference for particular STEM fields.

Our independent variables in all models are the indicators of math and science grades, test scores, and course-taking discussed earlier. We also include a measure of LEP status to capture heterogeneity within our Hispanic sample. Importantly, because we are interested in whether and how academic performance predicts STEM expectations differently for male and female students, we reran all models with interaction terms between gender and each measure of grades, advanced course-taking, and test scores. For each of the four comparisons listed above, we first discuss the results of pooled models and then move on to discuss significant gender interactions.

Predicting Low STEM vs. Neutral STEM

Our first model predicts the likelihood that students are in the low STEM vs. the neutral STEM category. As seen in Table 5.1 and consistent with previously mentioned descriptive results, the significant odds ratio of 2.082

TABLE 5.1 Multinomial Logistic Regression Results Predicting Low STEM vs. Neutral STEM Among Hispanic Early High School Students

	OR	Model 1 (SE) Sig	OR	Model 2 (SE) Sig
Female	2.082	$(0.193)^{***}$	14.610	$(13.730)^{***}$
LEP Status	0.812	$(0.062)^{***}$	0.817	$(0.062)^{***}$
Middle School Academic Profile Math Grade	0.992	$(0.004)^{**}$	0.991	$(0.004)^{**}$
Science Grade	0.993	(0.007)	1.006	(0.011)
Math Honors Placement	1.142	(0.216)	1.141	(0.223)
Science Honors Placement	0.756	$(0.121)^{*}$	0.756	$(0.125)^{*}$
Math Test Score	1.040	(0.119)	1.044	(0.119)
Science Test Score	0.998	(0.070)	0.993	(0.072)
Interaction Effects				
Female X Science Grade			0.977	$(0.011)^{**}$
Constant	2.634	(1.925)	0.988	(0.986)
Observations	1513			

Note: OR—Odds Ratios; *SE*—Robust Standard Errors (eform); Sig: $^{***}p < 0.01$, $^{**}p < 0.05$, $^{*}p < 0.1$, two tailed test.

reveals that Hispanic females are slightly over two times as likely as males to be in the low STEM group rather than the neutral STEM group. Additionally, with an odds ratio less than one (OR = .812) we see that LEP students are less likely than non-LEP students to be in the low STEM group than the neutral STEM group. Stated conversely, this means that LEP students are more likely to be in the neutral group. Turning to our indicators of prior academic performance, we find a significant effect for middle school math grades. Specifically, the odds ratio less than one (OR = .992) means that Hispanic students with higher math grades are somewhat less likely to be in the low STEM category compared to the neutral category. Similarly, students who were in a science honors class in middle school are also less likely to be in the low STEM than the neutral STEM category (OR = .756). Thus there is some evidence that those students that have low expectations for entering any STEM field in college have lower performance in math and science than their peers in the neutral STEM category. Furthermore, in testing for gender interactions, we found a significant interaction between gender and science grades. The results of this model are shown in Model 2 of Table 5.1. The main effect of science grades is very close to one and not significant, and the interaction between female and science grades is significant with an odds ratio less than one (OR = .977). Thus, while science grades have no impact on the likelihood of being in low STEM for Hispanic boys (net of all the other indicators in the model), they negatively predict membership in the low STEM vs. the neutral STEM category for Hispanic girls.

Predicting Computer Science/Engineering vs. Neutral STEM

In Table 5.2, we present the results of a model predicting the likelihood of having a preference for a CS/E major vs. having neutral expectations across all STEM majors. As discussed before, females are less likely to be in CS/E vs. the STEM neutral category (OR = .450). Additionally, LEP students are almost two times more likely to have a preference for CS/E vs. the STEM neutral category.

The results reveal that higher previous math performance predicts a preference for CS/E. Specifically, students with higher math grades and those who were in math honors in middle school are significantly more likely to be in the CS/E rather than the STEM neutral category. In contrast, net of other variables in the model, those with higher science grades are less likely to be in the CS/E category (or conversely, more likely to be in the neutral category). Finally, we observed no significant interactions between gender and the academic indicators, revealing that the patterns for math and science grades and math course-taking are consistent for both Hispanic males and females.

TABLE 5.2 Multinomial Logistic Regression Results Predicting Computer Science/Engineering vs. Neutral STEM Among Hispanic Early High School Students

	OR	Model 1 (SE) Sig
Female	0.450	(0.066)***
LEP Status	1.797	(0.325)***
Middle School Academic Profile Math grade	1.041	(0.010)***
Science grade	0.974	(0.011)**
Math honors placement	1.612	(0.388)**
Science honors placement	0.880	(0.187)
Math test score	1.005	(0.137)
Science test score	1.163	(0.144)
Constant	0.110	(0.055)***
Observations	1137	

Note: OR—Odds Ratios; *SE*—Robust Standard Errors (eform); Sig: ***$p < 0.01$, **$p < 0.05$, *$p < 0.1$, two tailed test.

Predicting Physical Science Versus Neutral STEM

In Table 5.3 we present the results of a model predicting the likelihood of having a preference for a physical science major vs. having neutral STEM expectations across all fields. First, there is not a significant main effect for gender, as Hispanic females are as likely as Hispanic males to be in the physical science category compared to the neutral STEM category. Additionally, there is not a significant effect of LEP status. Of all of the academic indicators, only one is statistically significant. Having a higher score on the standardized science test administered by the district in middle school is associated with higher odds of being in the physical science vs. neutral STEM categories.

There are two significant interactions between gender and the academic indicators, specifically for both advanced math and science course-taking. Turning to models displaying the results of the interactions in Table 5.3, we see that the odds ratios for the interaction between gender and both the indicator for math honors and for science honors are less than one (OR = .622 and .672, respectively). Thus, in contrast to males, Hispanic females who were in either math or science honors classes in middle school are less likely to have a preference for physical science, or more likely to be in the neutral STEM group. For example, girls who took an advanced science class have a .3 probability of being in the physical science group rather than the neutral group, compared to a probability of .4 for girls who had not taken advanced science.

TABLE 5.3   Multinomial Logistic Regression Results Predicting Physical Science vs. Neutral STEM Among Hispanic Early High School Students

	OR	Model 1 (SE) Sig	OR	Model 2 (SE) Sig	OR	Model 3 (SE) Sig
Female	1.143	(0.134)	1.532	(0.237)***	1.488	(0.280)**
LEP Status	1.141	(0.125)	1.143	(0.130)	1.141	(0.128)
Middle School Academic Profile Math Grade	1.002	(0.006)	1.003	(0.005)	1.002	(0.006)
Science Grade	0.991	(0.008)	0.989	(0.009)	0.990	(0.008)
Math Honors Placement	1.077	(0.178)	1.353	(0.166)**	1.085	(0.179)
Science Honors Placement	0.795	(0.172)	0.802	(0.181)	0.965	(0.234)
Math Test Score	1.023	(0.133)	1.027	(0.125)	1.017	(0.129)
Science Test Score	1.259	(0.154)*	1.263	(0.157)*	1.260	(0.158)*
Interaction Effects						
Female X Math Honors Placement		0.622(0.171)*				
Female X Science Honors Placement					0.672(0.155)*	
Constant	0.778	(0.651)	0.744	(0.616)	0.701(0.584)	
Observations	1146		1146		1146	

Note: OR—Odds Ratios; *SE*—Robust Standard Errors (eform); Sig: ***$p < 0.01$, **$p < 0.05$, *$p < 0.1$, two-tailed test.

Predicting Physical Science vs. Computer Science/Engineering

Our final set of comparisons contrasts those students who exhibit a strong preference for a particular STEM field, either physical science on the one hand or CS/E on the other. As seen in Table 5.4, Hispanic females are almost two and a half times more likely to have a preference for physical science rather than CS/E. LEP students are significantly less likely to have a preference for physical science (*OR* = .655), or alternatively more likely to have a preference for CS/E.

The remainder of the model indicates contrasting effects of prior math and science grades. Math grades significantly predict a slightly lower likelihood of preferring physical science over CS/E (*OR* = .959), while high science grades predict a slightly higher likelihood of preferring physical science over CS/E (*OR* = 1.016). Lastly, there is a significant gender interaction with science test scores. Model 2 indicates that while the odds ratio for the main effect of science test score is more than one (although not statistically significant), the gender interaction is less than one and significant

TABLE 5.4 Multinomial Logistic Regression Results Predicting Physical Science vs. Computer Science/Engineering Among Hispanic Early High School Students

	OR	Model 1 (*SE*) Sig	OR	Model 2 (*SE*) Sig
Female	2.447	(0.476)***	2.735	(0.422)***
LEP Status	0.655	(0.131)**	0.655	(0.131)**
Middle School Academic Profile Math Grade	0.959	(0.011)***	0.959	(0.011)***
Science Grade	1.016	(0.007)**	1.016	(0.007)**
Math Honors Placement	0.724	(0.204)	0.739	(0.218)
Science Honors Placement	0.871	(0.263)	0.860	(0.269)
Math Test Score	0.998	(0.190)	0.975	(0.189)
Science Test Score	1.136	(0.212)	1.303	(0.238)
Interaction Effects				
Female X Science Test Score			0.710	(0.129)*
Constant	10.560	(7.276)***	9.930	(6.871)***
Observations	729		729	

Note: OR—Odds Ratios; *SE*—Robust Standard Errors (eform); Sig: ***$p < 0.01$, **$p < 0.05$, *$p < 0.1$, two-tailed test.

($OR = .710$). Thus while higher science test scores may shape the development of a preference for physical science vs. CS/E for Hispanic boys, this is not the case for girls.

CONCLUSIONS

STEM postsecondary and occupational fields have historically been male-dominated, and consequently, researchers and policymakers have long focused on understanding obstacles to females' participation. Given the instrumental role of early expectations for shaping later STEM pathways, recent research has turned to examine gender disparities in the early ambitions and interests expressed by adolescents and young adults (Legewie & Diprete, 2014b; Morgan, Gelbgser et al., 2013; Xie & Shauman, 2003). While there is a growing body of research on this topic, most studies focus on aggregate differences between males and females at the national level. Given the rapidly changing demographic composition of our nation's youth, there is a need for more research on minorities, particularly Hispanic youth who are often overlooked in the STEM literature. Therefore, a primary focus of this study is exploring the early STEM expectations of high school students in a predominantly Hispanic school district.

In order to examine both gender and racial/ethnic differences in STEM expectations, we utilized Latent Profile Analyses (LPA) to empirically explore students' reported intentions to major in each of five different STEM fields. Results revealed four distinct classes of students: those who had very low expectations of majoring in any STEM field, those who held neutral expectations for all STEM fields, those who had a strong preference for majoring in physical science, and those who had a strong preference for computer science or engineering. Female students of all racial/ethnic groups were most likely to be in the low STEM expectations category. In fact, almost half of young women in our sample fell into this group, revealing that they had virtually no expectation of majoring in any STEM field. Given research that finds that adolescents very rarely reconsider an educational or occupational option that they have previously ruled out, this is quite a sobering finding (Eccles, 2005).

Yet our analyses also revealed that compared to their White and Black peers, Hispanic youth of both genders were more likely to be in the group that expressed a preference for computer science and engineering. This is promising evidence of strong interest in these particular STEM fields among a certain portion of the minority adolescent population. We do not know to what extent schools and teachers are aware of this interest, or whether and how they work to cultivate it. Perhaps Hispanic youth in this generally economically disadvantaged district perceive computer science and engineering as fields where they can earn lucrative salaries and stable employment, as well as higher social status. This is clearly an avenue for more research.

The second part of our analysis focuses specifically on the Hispanic majority within the district and examines how prior academic performance in math and science during middle school predicts students' STEM expectations at the beginning of high school. While some research has suggested that minority youth's educational ambitions are not strongly tied to their academic performance (Morgan & Mehta, 2004), our results offer contrary evidence. Specifically, we find that students in the low STEM expectation group (those that do not expect to major in any STEM field) generally have lower levels of math and science performance than their peers in the neutral STEM group. Additionally, we find that math performance tends to predict a preference for computer science and engineering, while science performance more strongly predicts preference for a physical science major. This suggests that at least some youth view STEM fields distinctly at this age and are developing notions of the skills suited to each.

However, while lower performance tends to similarly predict low expectations for both male and female Hispanic students, among students in other STEM expectation categories, we find evidence that prior performance works differently for Hispanic girls compared to their male peers. For example, the results of gender interactions reveal that while taking advanced courses in math in middle school positively predicts boys having a preference for a future physical science major (vs. having neutral STEM expectations), this is not the case for girls. For Hispanic females, taking advanced math is associated with a higher probability of being in the neutral STEM category than the physical science category. A similar pattern is apparent for advanced science course-taking. The reasons for this are not known; perhaps girls are somehow discouraged by the normative environment or some aspects of the curriculum in advanced math and science classes. Yet whatever the cause, it is important to note that many young Hispanic women with relatively strong math and science credentials report neutral expectations towards pursuing STEM fields. We suggest that future research should investigate what it takes to encourage girls to move past viewing all STEM fields as a "maybe yes/maybe no" proposition to instead develop a preference for a particular STEM field.

In closing we note that our study, like any other, has limitations. Specifically, due to small sample sizes for White and Black youth, we are unable to reliably model gender differences within these other ethnic groups, and therefore unable to compare their patterns to those of Hispanic youth. Such comparisons that would enable us to more effectively capture the intersection of gender and race/ethnicity would be ideal. Yet given the lack of attention towards Hispanic adolescents in so much of the quantitative research on STEM inequality, we think that our particular focus is nevertheless a welcome and needed one. Finally, our study was limited to the experiences of students in one predominantly minority, generally economically disadvantaged, school district. Given the increasing economic and racial/ethnic segregation of American schools (Orfield & Lee, 2004), however, the district we studied likely has much in common with the schools attended by most minority youth in the country. Understanding the experiences and STEM ambitions of students in these contexts is critical for changing larger societal patterns of inequality.

NOTE

1. We tested for statistical significance between groups using *t*-tests, and additionally confirmed the results via logistic regression analyses with robust standard errors calculated to account for clustering of students within schools.

REFERENCES

Andersen, M. L. (2005). Thinking about women: A quarter century's view. *Gender & Society, 19*(4), 437–455.

Archer-Banks, D. A. M., & Behar-Horenstein, L. S. (2012). Ogbu revisited: Unpacking high-achieving African American girls' high school experiences. *Urban Education, 47*(1), 198–223.

Barton, A. C., Tan, E., & Rivet, A. (2008). Creating hybrid spaces for engaging school science among urban middle school girls. *American Education Research Journal, 45*(1), 68–103.

Blickenstaff, J. C. (2005). Women and science careers: Leaky pipeline or gender filter? *Gender and Education, 17*(4), 369–386.

Bobbitt-Zeher, D. (2007). The gender income gap and the role of education. *Sociology of Education, 80*(1), 1–22.

Browne, I., & Misra, J. (2003). The intersection of gender and race in the labor market. *Annual Review of Sociology, 29*(1), 487–513.

Constentino de Cohen, C., & Deterding, N. (2009). Widening the net: National estimates of gender disparities in engineering. *Journal of Engineering Education, 98*(3), 211–226.

Correll, S. J. (2001). Gender and the career choice process: The role of biased self-assessments. *American Journal of Sociology, 106*(6), 1691–1730.

DiPrete, T. A., & Buchmann, C. (2013). *The rise of women: The growing gender gap in education and what it means for American Schools.* New York, NY: Russell Sage Foundation.

Dondero, M., & Muller, C. (2012). School stratification in new and established Latino destinations. *Social Forces, 91*(2), 477–502.

Eccles, J. S. (2005). Studying gender and ethnic differences in participation in math, physical science, and information technology. *New Directions for Child and Adolescent Development, 110*(1), 7–14.

Eccles, J. S. (2009). Who am I and what am I going to do with my life? Personal and collective identities as motivators or action. *Educational Psychologist, 44,* 78–89.

England, P. (2010). The gender revolution: Uneven and stalled. *Gender & Society, 24*(2), 149–166.

Glass, J. L., Sassler, S., Levitte, Y., & Michelmore, K. M. (2013). What's so special about STEM? A comparison of women's retention in STEM and professional occupations. *Social Forces, 92*(2), 723–756.

Greenfield, T. A. (1997). Gender- and grade-level differences in science interest and participation. *Science Education, 81*(3), 259–276.

Griffith, A. L. (2010). Persistence of women and minorities in STEM field majors: Is it the school that matters? *Economics of Education Review, 29*(6), 911–922.

Hanson, S. L. (2006). African American women in science: Experiences from high school through the post-secondary years and beyond. In J. Bystydzienski & S. Bird (Eds.), *Removing barriers: Women in academic science, technology, engineering, and mathematics* (pp. 123–141). Bloomington: Indiana University Press.

Harklau, L. (2013). Why Izzie didn't go to college: Choosing work over college as Latina feminism. *Teachers College Record, 11*(1)5, 1–32.

Kane, E. W. (2000). Racial and ethnic variations in gender-related attitudes. *Annual Review of Sociology, 26*(1), 419–439.

Katz, S. D., Allbritton, D., Aronis, J., Wilson, C., & Soffa, M. L. (2006). Gender, achievement, and persistence in an undergraduate computer science program. *SIGMIS Database, 37*(4), 42–57.

Landivar, C. L. (2013). *Disparities in STEM employment by sex, race, and Hispanic origin.* American Community Survey Reports (ACS-24). Washington, DC: U.S. Census Bureau.

Legewie, J., & Diprete, T. A. (2014a). The high school environment and the gender gap in science and engineering. *Sociology of Education, 87*(4), 259–280.

Legewie, J., & Diprete, T. A. (2014b). Pathways to science and engineering bachelor's degrees for men and women. *Sociological Science, 1*(1), 41–48.

Maltese, A. V., & Tai, R. H. (2011). Pipeline persistence: Examining the association of educational experiences with earned degrees in STEM among US students. *Science Education, 95*(5), 877–907.

Mann, A., & DiPrete, T. A. (2013). Trends in gender segregation in the choice of science and engineering majors. *Social Science Research, 42*(2), 1519–1541.

Mickelson, R. A. (1990). The attitude-achievement paradox among Black adolescents. *Sociology of Education, 63*(1), 44–61.

Montoya, L. J. (1996). Latino gender differences in public opinion: Results from the Latino national political survey. *Hispanic Journal of Behavioral Sciences, 18*(2), 255–276.

Morgan, S. L., Gelbgser, D., & Weeden, K. A. (2013a). Feeding the pipeline: Gender, occupational plans, and college major selection. *Social Science Research, 42*(4), 98–105.

Morgan, S. L., Leenman, T. S., Todd, J. L., & Weeden, K. A. (2013b). Occupational plans, beliefs about educational requirements, and patterns of college entry. *Sociology of Education, 86*(3), 197–217.

Morgan, S. L., & Mehta, J. D. (2004). Beyond the laboratory: Evaluating the survey evidence for the disidentification explanation of black-white differences in achievement. *Sociology of Education, 77*(1), 82–101.

National Academy of Sciences. (2007). *Beyond bias and barriers: Fulfilling the potential of women in academic science and engineering.* Washington, DC: National Academics Press.

National Research Council. (2011). *Expanding underrepresented minority participation: America's science and technology talent at the crossroads.* Washington, DC: National Academies Press.

National Science Board. (2014). *Science and engineering indicators 2014.* Arlington, VA: National Science Foundation.

Orfield, G., & Lee, C. (2004). *Brown at 50: King's dream or Plessy's nightmare.* Cambridge, MA: The Civil Rights Project.

Ost, B. (2010). The role of peers and grades in determining major persistence in the sciences. *Economics of Education Review, 29*(6), 923–934.

Ovink, S. M. (2014). "They always call me an investment": Gendered familism and Latino/a college pathways. *Gender & Society, 28*(2), 265–288.

Pew Research Center. (2012). *Hispanic student enrollments reach new highs in 2011.* Washington, DC: Pew Hispanic Center. Retrieved from https://www.pewresearch.org/hispanic/2012/08/20/hispanic-student-enrollments-reach-new-highs-in-2011/

Riegle-Crumb, C., Farkas, G., & Muller, C. (2006). The role of gender and friendship in advanced course taking. *Sociology of Education, 79*(3), 206–228.

Riegle-Crumb, C., & King, B. (2010). Questioning a white male advantage in STEM: Examining disparities in college major. *Educational Researcher, 39*(9), 656–664.

Riegle-Crumb, C., King, B., Grodsky, E., & Muller, C. (2012). The more things change, the more they stay the same? Prior achievement fails to explain gender inequality in entry into STEM college majors over time. *American Educational Research Journal, 49*(4), 1048–1073.

Riegle-Crumb, C., Moore, C., & Ramos-Wada, A. (2011). Who wants to have a career in science or math? Exploring adolescents' future aspirations by gender and race/ethnicity. *Science Education, 95*(3), 458–476.

Sadler, P. M., Sonnert, G., Hazari, Z., & Tai, R. (2012). Stability and volatility of STEM career interest in high school: A gender study. *Science Education, 96*(2), 411–427.

Schneider, B., & Stevenson, D. (1999). *The Ambitious generation: America's teenagers, motivated but directionless.* New Haven, CT: Yale University Press.

Seymour, E., & Hewitt, N. M. (1997). *Talking about leaving: Why undergraduates leave the sciences.* Boulder, CO: Westview Press.

Sorge, C. (2007). What happens: Relationship of age and gender with science attitudes from elementary to middle school. *Science Educator, 16*(2), 33–37.

Tai, R. H., Lui, C. Q., Maltese, A. V., & Fan, X. (2006). Planning early for careers in science. *Science, 312*(5779), 1143–1144.

Turley, R. N. L. (2009). College proximity: Mapping access to opportunity. *Sociology of Education, 82*(2), 126–146.

Xie, Y., & Shauman, K. (2003). *Women in science: Career processes and outcomes.* Cambridge, MA: Harvard University Press.

Zarrett, N. R., & Malanchuk, O. (2005). Who's computing? Gender and race differences in young adults' decisions to pursue an information technology career. *New Directions for child and Adolescent Development, 110*(1), 65–84.

CHAPTER 6

BLACK WOMEN AND GIRLS, SCIENCE ACHIEVEMENT, AND EDUCATION POLICY

Black Feminist and Critical Race Feminist Perspectives

Theodorea Regina Berry
Reanna S. Roby

> The effectiveness of science teachers is often measured by the success of the students. In order to ensure student success in science, research about how students learn science and how teachers should be teaching science must be taken into account by policy makers. (Owens, 2009, p. 49)

Eleven years ago, Owens (2009) published work that encouraged readers to examine changes to educational policy that could improve student science achievement, specifically stating that "research about how students learn science and how teachers should be teaching science must be taken into account by policy makers" (p. 49). Owens discussed ways in which federal policies address education, how science achievement is measured, how students are taught science, and the ways in which students learn science. Owens concluded this research with the implications for science education and policy.

Girls and Women of Color In STEM, pages 91–104
Copyright © 2020 by Information Age Publishing
91

STATEMENT OF NEED

There are data and research that articulate the ways in which Black girls lag behind in science. Research conducted by Farinde and Lewis (2012) indicated that African American/Black girls "lag behind both white male and female students" (p. 427). In the National Assessment for Educational Progress (NAEP) 2011 national report card in science, the national average score in eighth grade NAEP science reported in terms of scaled scores was 159 and the average scores by race/ethnicity in eighth grade NAEP science are as follows: White, 163; Black, 129; Hispanic, 137; Asian/Pacific Islander, 159; American Indian/Alaskan Native, 141 (NCES, 2012). Male students have an average score of 154 while female students' average score is 149.

Espinosa (2011) recognized that there is a limited presence of women of color in STEM fields. Catsambis (1994, as cited in Farinde & Lewis, 2012) stated that "women of color were significantly absent in STEM fields" (p. 421). For the purpose of this study, women of color are identified as "African American, Asian American, Latina, Native American, and Pacific Islander" (Espinosa, 2011, p. 210). Equally important, is the limited data and research available on why Black women do not embrace science and other STEM fields as careers.

In the *Profile of Undergraduate Students: 2011–2012* (NCES, 2014) data reveal that 15.9% of all students enrolled in U.S. colleges and universities majored in science, technology, engineering, and mathematics (STEM) fields. While more Black women (62.8%) than Black men (37.2%) are enrolled in colleges and universities, NCES and Census data reveal a limited number of Black women pursuing STEM fields. In the NCES study, *Higher Education: Gaps in Access and Persistence Study* (Ross et al., 2012), data reveal Black women earned 20% of degrees conferred by degree-granting institutions in STEM fields. In comparison, Black men earned 22% of degrees conferred, White women earned 23% of degrees conferred, and White men earned 27% of degrees conferred by degree-granting institutions in STEM fields. Furthermore, current data (NCES, 2013) clearly indicate a limited pool of Black women as aspiring science educators.

Researchers, Maltese and Tai (2010) and Spencer and Walker (2011), indicated that interest in science education begins in the K–12 environment. Owens (2009) clearly acknowledged the variety of skills, dispositions, and learning styles students possess upon entering the science classroom. While Owens sufficiently addressed the nexus of educational policy and science education, Owens did not specifically address Black women and girls in the ways in which science is taught and how students learn science.

PURPOSE OF THE STUDY

The purpose of this theoretical research study was to address the ways in which Black feminist thought and critical race feminism (CRF) can be integrated into science teaching to make it more accessible to Black girls. To fulfill this purpose, one question served to guide this theoretical research study: In what ways can Black feminist thought and CRF address how science is taught and how students learn science that would, potentially, benefit Black women and girls?

REVIEW OF THE LITERATURE

Black women have a high initial interest in STEM but face unique barriers to completion of STEM degrees such as negative race-based stereotyping (O'Brien, Blodorn, Adams, Garcia, & Hammer, 2014). These barriers to degree completion can, in turn, lead to a limited number of Black women who become employed in STEM fields. It is important to engage girls and other marginalized groups in science as early as possible. In order to do so, we must address issues of the nature and culture of science in the classroom and in society (Brotman & Moore, 2008). Identifying factors that create differences in STEM participation may help to inform interventions aimed at increasing women's overall participation (O'Brien et al., 2014).

Taking into consideration the complexities of identities, Black girls face challenges that their White counterparts do not in STEM and society (National Women's Law Center & NAACP Legal Defense Fund, 2014; Pringle, Brkich, Adams, West-Olatunii, & Archer-Banks, 2012). Owens (2009) is an example of how research that addresses the ways in which students learn science, does not traditionally consider the intersectionality of Black identities. Thus, more research is needed to define the unique barriers that Black women face in STEM-related fields at multiple levels (O'Brien et al., 2014). Targeting the access of Black girls and women in STEM ultimately benefits everyone (NWLC, 2014).

Black Women and Girls in the Classroom

Collins (1990) posited, "All African American women share the common experience of being Black women in a society that denigrates women of African descent" (p. 22). The classroom is a microcosm of the society and, as such, the denigration of Black women and girls also occurs in these spaces. Sadker and Sadker (1986) pioneered work on girls in the classroom and included issues that specifically relate to Black girls in the classroom.

Organizations such as the American Association of University Women (AAUW) have well documented the disparity of treatment amongst boys and girls in the classroom by both male and female teachers (AAUW, 1992). The research from AAUW has indicated that despite the disparity of such treatment, African American girls persevere in the classroom setting. This is illustrated in this quote published by the AAUW:

> Black girls have less interaction with teachers than White girls or than boys of either race. Research indicates that teachers may unconsciously rebuff these Black girls, who eventually turn to peers for interaction, often becoming the class enforcer or go-between for other students. Black females also receive less reinforcement from teachers than do other students, although their academic performance is often better than boys. In fact, when Black girls do as well as White boys in school, teachers attribute their success to hard work but assume that the White boys are not working up to their full potential. (1992, pp. 122–123)

Other researchers Fordham (1993) and Evans-Winters (2005) have engaged in research that specifically address the ways in which Black girls interact with one another, interact with teachers, and engage in learning.

African American/Black girls who can, subsequently, become prospective teachers negotiate the realities of two worlds in classroom settings. Current African American/Black teachers possess the ideas, concepts, beliefs, and values commonly found both in their communities and in the majority society (Ladson-Billings, 1994). The negotiation of this merger typically occurs in the collegiate classroom. "Prospective teachers do not easily relinquish beliefs—about themselves or others" (Ladson-Billings, 1994, p. 143). What occurs in classrooms for teacher education and during preservice practical applications is merged with the K–12 experience and influences what educational professionals do in the K–12 classroom. For those African American/Black female prospective teachers who experience the centering of their voices through a critical lens (Berry, 2005, 2009, 2012), the negotiation of identity with experience, belief, and praxis is made explicit.

However, for the African American/Black female who often experiences degradation of self-worth and personal knowledge in the collegiate classroom (Delpit, 1995), the dilemma is not only great as a preservice teacher but also significant within her in-service teaching practice. "Most of the Black and Native teachers interviewed [by Delpit] believe accounts of their own experiences are not validated in teacher education programs or in their subsequent teaching lives" (Delpit, 1995, p. 108). The presence and/or absence of such validation may account, in some measure, for the presence or absence of Black female teachers in K–12 schools.

Black Women and Girls in Science Education

Farinde and Lewis (2012) asserted that the disparities in education limit the opportunities for African American girls to take upper-level science courses in high school. Such disparities can lead to the limited presence of these women as science educators and/or professionals within STEM fields. Solorzano (2004) and Whiting (2009) also indicated the absence of African American girls in high-level advanced placement courses.

Farinde and Lewis (2012) provided recommendations for teaching Black women and girls as it directly relates to math and science education. Specifically, the researchers advised that

> Educators must nurture African American female students' interests in math and science, initially encouraging these girls to pursue a non-traditional career path...Teachers should not allow African American females to passively engage in memorizing math/science concepts. Hands-on application through active cooperative learning groups should be the norm...Teachers should infuse culturally relevant teaching strategies into math/science instruction. This includes, but is not limited to, acknowledging the contributions of African American women within math and science will help validate young African American female students' presence in STEM areas in their mind. (p. 429)

Black Women and Girls in STEM Fields

Exclusion of women and minorities in science is evident by the lack of ethnic and gender diversity in STEM careers (Pringle et al., 2012). This trend can be attributed to the culture of science. Since 2001, women have accounted for over 50% of the degrees awarded in science and engineering, however, the number of all women represented in science and engineering professions is only 27% (Hill, Corbet, & St. Rose, 2010). Black women account for 10.4% of that total (National Science Foundation, 2013). Science can be improved by broadening the diversity of its practitioners across gender, ethnic, and racial lines (Clark Blickenstaff, 2005). Social and environmental factors act as barriers to women's full participation in STEM fields (Hill, Corbet, & St. Rose, 2010).

Gender bias is locked in place in fields like science by male dominance at all the levels of decision-making; women are barely visible at these levels, fixing the subconscious idea that science belongs to men (Science for all, 2013). As a result, many women are deterred from pursuing careers in science at the highest levels (NWLC, 2014). However, science and engineering departments that support the integration of female faculty with mentoring and effective work–life policies can expect to recruit and retain more women (Hill et al., 2010). Increasing the number of girls and women who enter and remain in science and engineering fields is critical for both equity and innovation (AAUW, 2010).

Positionality Statement

As women of color who engage in our work within the field of education through the lenses of our experiences, we honor and value the ways in which our race and gender provide unique perspectives to our work.

> Race beyond the discussion of African American men and gender beyond the topic of White women reveal an often neglected, yet unique perspective, which, from a noticeable member of a historically inferior race and sex, exposes subtle and at times blatant institutionalized barriers. (Farinde & Lewis, 2012, p. 422)

As women of color who engage in science and who teach women who are potential/future science educators (Berry, 2009, 2005), we fully understand the significance of the presence of Black women in STEM fields and as science educators. More importantly, we fully understand the ways in which our multiple and intersecting identities influence and inform what we know and how we know what we know.

THEORETICAL LENSES

There has been considerable work that addresses CRF in the context of education and teacher education (Berry, 2005, 2009, 2012). To date, there has not been theoretical nor empirical work that addresses CRF in the context of science education, science education policy, nor STEM/science teacher education. Such a perspective can provide insights on the ways in which Black women and girls perform in science, learn science, and teach science.

Black feminist thought has also gained significant voice within the field of education. However, there is a gap in the literature in how this framework can be integrated into the context of science education and science education policy (Mcpherson, 2012). Both of these theoretical constructs are included as the lenses with which we analyzed the need to increase science participation for Black women and girls. Both of these theories are described in depth as follows.

Critical Race Feminism

Critical race feminism, an outgrowth of critical race theory (CRT; Delgado & Stefancic, 2001), acknowledges and examines oppression at the intersections of race and gender. As an outgrowth of CRT, CRF espouses the tenets of CRT. Berry and Candis (2015) articulated the necessity of CRT as a result of social and legal events inextricably tied to race in the United States. CRT founders Derrick Bell and Alan Freeman developed this theory and its central tenets as a result of their work in critical legal studies. CRT entered the field of education through the scholarship of Gloria Ladson-Billings and William Tate (1995) as it primarily rests upon these foundational tenets/ elements: (a) essentialism and anti-essentialism/intersectionality, (b) the normalization of race and racism, (c) interest convergence, (d) dismantling color-blind notions of equality, (e) race as a social construction, and (f) using storytelling/counter-storytelling for voices of color.

Three key concepts of CRT, anti-essentialism/intersectionality, normalization of race and racism, and storytelling/counter-storytelling, play significant roles in the development and theorizing central to CRF. Berry and Stovall (2013) defined and conceptualized intersectionality and multidimensionality, accordingly:

> Intersectionality of identity occurs when individuals possess two or more social markers simultaneously (e.g., race, gender, ethnicity, class). Multi-dimensionality of identity occurs when individuals possess two or more individualities that function at the same time, informing one another in practice (e.g., teacher as parent, teacher as parent and community member, historian as traveler). In many cases, intersectionality and multi-dimensionality function together. (p. 590)

Legal scholar Adrien Katherine Wing (1997) centralized multidimensionality as a key concept of this theory and views CRF as a means of centering the voices of women of color in ways that scholarship regarding Black men and White women often leave silent. "CRF constitutes a race intervention in feminist discourse, in that it necessarily embraces feminism's emphasis on gender oppression within a system of patriarchy" (Wing, 2003, p. 7) while paying full attention to White supremacy within the feminist movement. In this way, CRF addresses the long-standing problem of racism and race bias within feminist issues and the feminist movement while acknowledging the double bind of race and gender.

Black Feminist Thought

Collins (1990) defined Black feminist thought as the ideas that clarify a standpoint of and for black women. As we consider the representation of Black women and girls in science, this standpoint is useful in addressing how women and girls become interested in science and what keeps them there. Three themes to consider within this standpoint are: Black women's self-definition and self-valuation, the interlocking nature of oppression, and the importance of Black women's culture. Taking into consideration that identity formation is essential to learning, (Brotman & Moore, 2005) and a part of the lives of Black girls and women, we utilize these themes to reconstruct ways in which science is learned and taught.

Learning and Teaching Science: Black Feminist and Critical Race Feminist Perspectives

Bell (1984) and Ladson-Billings (2012) asserted that Black people live their lives across multiple categories of being and that social, educational, and legal constructs should not essentialize our lived experiences. This is especially poignant as we use two theoretical frameworks to understand and conceptualize the ways in which Black women and girls engage with science and how such engagement can influence science education policy.

Owens (2009) identified three ways in which science is learned: (a) inquiry, (b) peer-to-peer interactions, and (c) incorporation of prior knowledge and connection to ideas. In regard to how science is taught, Owens (2009) stated:

> Creating an open, student-centered learning environment that encourages curiosity and exploration is more conducive to learning science than the traditional teacher-centered approach to instruction…accomplished science teachers use a variety of instructional approaches to guide learners toward knowledge about science…Relating science content to students' real life experiences can be very effective in motivating learning…Using guided inquiry as a method of instruction has been shown to be an effective teaching strategy…In scientific inquiry, students need to be given opportunities to engage in discourse with one another…verbal and written… (p. 52)

In the subsections that follow, Owens' (2009) notions of science learning and teaching are placed in the context of Black feminist thought and CRF.

Black Feminist Thought and How Science Is Taught

Feminist research that focuses on equity is critically important in establishing the significance of attending to gender issues in science education (Brickhouse, 2001). Thus, the integration of Black feminist thought seeks to do the same, while considering specific teaching ideals and including all students.

To retain young girls' interest in the sciences, there is a need for radical changes in the approaches of teaching science (Naugah & Watts, 2013). A Black feminist standpoint allows for this by considering the themes of Black feminist thought. Understanding that scientific knowledge is culturally situated and, therefore, reflects the gender and racial ideologies of societies (Brickhouse, 2001), it is important for teachers to be aware of ways in which science has marginalized various populations and the way it can be depicted in textbooks and science lessons. By teaching science in a way that does not allow voice, can be crippling—or oppressive—for students who do not see themselves as a scientist or capable of understanding science.

Black Feminist Thought and How Science Is Learned

Owens (2009) spoke of the way in which students learn science, by bringing in their skills and through a number of techniques. Science pedagogy can reinforce girls' negative attitudes about science by devaluing the contributions of female students and emphasizing rote learning (Clark Blickenstaff, 2005). The Black feminist tenets that support Black women's self-definition and self-valuation, as well as the importance of Black women's culture, is pertinent to this claim. Girls who are already interested in science might be able to develop correlations between their lived experiences as well as those presented in science classrooms. This, in turn, may be beneficial for girls who perform well within the sciences by elevating their self-valuation. However, understanding how one's performance plays a role in self-definition and self-valuation is important for both women and girls in the sciences.

Brickhouse, Lowery, and Schultz (2000) address some of these same ideas in a study of four Black girls interested in science. Through their study, they were able to address how science is something that is culturally mediated. This finding should push educators to be concerned about their students' identities inside and outside of the classroom and how they essentially play a role in the way students learn and how they—educators—teach science.

Critical Race Feminism and How Science Is Taught

Critical race feminism offers Black women who teach science a unique perspective in planning instruction. To address this matter, this subsection (as well as the subsequent subsection) will focus on four key characteristics of CRF: (a) anti-essentialism/intersectionality, (b) normalization of race and racism, (c) uniqueness of voice via storytelling/counter-storytelling, and (d) multidimensionality.

Using a variety of instructional strategies in the teaching of science validates CRF's notions of anti-essentialism. Such strategies acknowledge that Black female science educators can integrate the depth and breadth of their unique experiences into the science classroom. These experiences will, often, be ladened with cultural overtones connected to their identities as women of color. Intersectionality not only allows Black women as science educators to incorporate things we know based on our race and gender but also allows us to address multiple disciplines that connect with science education and science inquiry (i.e., history, geography, reading, writing).

Science teachers who work to relate science content to students' real life experiences should consider multi-dimensionality as a way of understanding these experiences. Identities and experiences do not operate in isolation; they inform one another and possess the potential to assist in the scaffolding of knowledge for students. If students learn a concept from a particular experience based on a role they have outside of the science classroom, they could learn a science concept based on that experience.

However, to access such experiences, science educators must also value narratives or stories that differ from what is considered normal. The concept of uniqueness of voice provides space for Black women and girls to have such experiences heard and validated in the science classroom.

Guided inquiry can allow all participants in the science learning classroom to work as teacher and student through the concept of anti-essentialism. "Guidance can be very direct . . . or very limited" (Owens, 2009, p. 52). However, an anti-essentialist viewpoint could promote a balance of power in the classroom and limit student stereotyping concerning who can be science "expert" based on race and/or gender.

Critical Race Feminism and How Science Is Learned

As noted earlier in this chapter, Black women and girls are learning science; however, the data indicates that (a) a limited number of girls are learning science at levels considered proficient and (b) a limited number of Black women are choosing to engage in science learning. Concepts and tenets from CRF should be considered for science learning.

Owens (2009) noted "students learn science by doing science" (p. 51). Inquiry for science learning speaks to CRF's notions of anti-essentialism and multidimensionality, specifically Wing's (1997) theory of multiplicative praxis. Inquiry as an anti-essentialist notion values a process of "critical thinking to come up with explanations that aid in the development of student understanding of science" (Owens, 2009, p. 51). Critical thinking in science inquiry may manifest itself differently in Black women and girls as it will take into account the varied experiences these students will have based on their intersectional identities of Black and female.

This is where validation of counter-storytelling is significant in both peer-to-peer interactions and the incorporation of prior knowledge in science learning for Black women and girls. Owens (2009) indicated "communication is a main component in the scientific process" (p. 51). Yet, both teachers and students in the science classroom must value the multiple and varying stories Black women and girls will provide in their explanation. Additionally, all "students come to the classroom with prior knowledge about how the world works" (Owens, 2009, p. 51). Black women and girls are likely to present a world that may be very different from their majoritarian peers. If, in fact, students can only learn science when prior knowledge is considered and integrated into the learning of new concepts, the experiences of Black women and girls must be fully included through their counter stories. The uniqueness of their voices could assist all students in accessing new concepts from a different vantage point.

CONCLUSION AND IMPLICATIONS

The perspectives and experiences of those science educators and science education policy makers can make a difference in the ways in which science is taught and learned for Black women and girls. "Faculty perspectives and research trajectories have long-lasting effects on the nature of scientific inquiry and on the learning experiences of students across the entire higher education landscape" (Espinosa, 2011, p. 211). Additionally, education policy, specifically science education policy, possesses the potential to outlive an administration's tenure.

The Digest for Education Statistics (NCES, 2012) indicated that reading and mathematics are priorities for academic performance in Grades K through 8. Yet, Owens (2009) noted science becomes a priority in high school. If the desire is to promote interest in science amongst Black girls, then science education policy should reflect the necessity to prioritize science learning before high school. This would give Black girls more opportunities to engage their unique voices and experiences in the context of science learning and make it more relevant to their lives.

Science education policy should seek to reform national and state curriculum and standards that, according to Owens (2009), focus on the quality of knowledge rather than the quantity of knowledge. If students can explore and engage (rather than memorize and learn), Black women and girls will have more opportunities to integrate their lived experiences into science teaching and learning. Should more depth be permitted in the scope and sequence of how science is taught and learned, Black women and girls' stories can be used to address multiple concepts.

Science education policy has focused on science achievement based on performance on standardized tests. The goal of such policy is to improve science achievement nationally, and to improve the United States, standing in science achievement internationally. Aligning science education policy to concepts and tenets of Black feminist thought and CRF possess the potential for all students to succeed. Validation/self-validation, voice, and experience possess the potential to increase the depth of the science curriculum. This could make the United States competitive with the top "10 highest achieving countries in science" (Owens, 2009, p. 53) at all grade levels.

Finally, science education policy promotes the use of research for effective science instruction and teaching. Much of the research cited in federal government policy does not address science teaching and learning for Black students and, specifically, Black women and girls. If "research about how students learn science should be used to develop teaching strategies that facilitate student learning" (Owens, 2009, p. 54), then policymakers must understand that the identities and experiences of Black women and girls must matter more if their numbers are to be increased in STEM fields.

REFERENCES

American Association of University Women. (1992). *How schools shortchange girls.* New York, NY: Marlowe & Company.

Berry, T. R. (2012). Understanding equity: A brown lesson in a teacher education program from a critical race feminist perspective. In S. Hughes & T. R. Berry (Eds.), *The evolving significance of race in education: Living, learning, and teaching.* New York, NY: Peter Lang.

Berry, T. R. (2009). Women of color in a bilingual/dialectical dilemma: Critical race feminism against a curriculum of oppression in teacher education. *International Journal of Qualitative Studies in Education, 22*(6), 745–753.

Berry, T. R. (2005). Black on Black education: Personally engaged pedagogy for/by African American pre-service teachers. *Urban Review, 37*(1), 31–48.

Bell, D. A. (1984). A hurdle too high: Class-based roadblocks to racial remediation. *Buffalo Law Review, 33,* 1–34.

Berry, T. R., & Candis, M. R. (2015). Cultural identity and education: A critical race perspective. *Educational Foundations, 27*(3/4), 43–64.

Berry, T. R., & Stovall, D. O. (2013). Trayvon Martin and the curriculum of tragedy: Critical race lesson for education. *Race, Ethnicity, and Education, 16*(4), 587–602.

Brickhouse, N. W. (2001). Embodying science: A feminist perspective on learning. *Journal of Research in Science Teaching, 38*(3), 282–295.

Brickhouse, N. W., Lowery, P., & Schultz, K. (2000). What kind of a girl does science? The construction of school science identities. *Journal of Research in Science Teaching, 37*(5), 441–458.

Brotman, J., & Moore, F. (2008). Girls and science: A review of four themes in the science education literature. *Journal of Research in Science Teaching, 45*(9), 971–1002.

Clark Blickenstaff, J. (2005). Women and science careers: Leaky pipeline or gender filter? *Gender and Education, 17*(4), 369–386.

Collins, P. H. (1990). *Black feminist thought.* New York, NY: Routledge.

Delgado, R., & Stefancic, J. (2001). *Critical race theory: An introduction.* New York, NY: New York University Press.

Delpit, L. (1995). *Other people's children: Cultural conflict in the classroom.* New York, NY: The New Press.

Espinosa, L. L. (2011). Pipelines and pathways: Women of color in undergraduate STEM majors and the college experiences that contribute to persistence. *Harvard Educational Review, 81*(2), 209–240.

Evans-Winters, V. E. (2005). *Teaching black girls: Resiliency in urban classrooms* (Vol. 279). New York, NY: Peter Lang.

Farinde, A. A., & Lewis, C. W. (2012). The underrepresentation of African American female students in STEM fields: Implications for classroom teachers. *U.S.–China Education Review B, 4*, 412–430.

Fordham, S. (1993). "Those loud Black girls": (Black) women, silence, and gender "passing" in the academy. *Anthropology & Education Quarterly, 24*(1), 3–32.

Hill, C., Corbett, C., & St Rose, A. (2010). *Why so few? Women in science, technology, engineering, and mathematics.* Washington, DC: American Association of University Women.

Ladson-Billings, G. (2012). Through a glass darkly: The persistence of race in education research and scholarship. *Educational Researcher, 41*(4), 115–120.

Ladson-Billings, G. (1994). *The dreamkeepers: Successful teachers of African American children.* San Francisco, CA: Josey-Bass.

Ladson-Billings, G., & Tate, W.F. (1995). Toward a critical race theory. *Teachers College Record, 97*(1), 47–68.

Maltese, A. V., & Tai, R. H. (2010). Eyeballs in the fridge: Sources of early interest in science. *International Journal of Science Education, 32*(5), 669–685.

Mcpherson, E. (2012). *Undergraduate African American women's narratives on persistence in science majors at a PWI* (Unpublished doctoral dissertation). University of Illinois at Urbana-Champaign, Urbana, IL. Retrieved from http://hdl .handle.net/2142/34524

National Center for Education Statistics. (2014). *Web tables: Profile of Undergraduate Students: 2011–12* (NCES 2015-167). Washington, DC: U.S. Department of Education Institute of Education Sciences. Retrieved from http://nces .ed.gov/pubs2015/2015167.pdf

National Center for Education Statistics. (2012). *The nation's report card: Science 2011* (NCES 2012-465). Washington, DC: U.S. Department of Education Institute for Education Sciences.

National Science Foundation. (2013). *Women, minorities, and persons with disabilities in science and engineering* (Special Report NSF 13-304). Arlington, VA: Author. Retrieved from http://www.nsf.gov/statistics/wmpd/

National Women's Law Center & NAACP Legal Defense Fund. (2014). *Unlocking opportunity for African American girls: A call to action for educational equity.* Washington, DC: Author.

Naugah, J., & Watts, M. (2013). Girls and science education in Mauritius: A study of science class practices and their effects on girls. *Research in Science & Technological Education, 31*(3), 252–268.

O'Brien, L. T., Blodorn, A., Adams, G., Garcia, D. M., & Hammer, E. (2014). Ethnic variation in gender-STEM stereotypes and STEM participation: An intersectional approach. *Cultural Diversity and Ethnic Minority Psychology,* *21*(2), 169–180. http://dx.doi.org/10.1037/a0037944

Owens, T. M. (2009). Improving science achievement through changes in education policy. *Science Educator, 18*(2), 49–55.

Pringle, R., Brkich, K., Adams, T., West-Olatunii, C., & Archer-Banks, D. (2012). Factors influencing elementary teachers' positioning of African American girls as science and mathematics learners. *School Science and Mathematics, 112*(4), 217–229.

Ross, T., Kena, G., Rathbun, A., KewalRamani, A., Zhang, J., Kristapovich, P., & Manning, E. (2012). *Higher education: Gaps in access and persistence study.* Statistical Analysis Report. NCES 2012-046. Washington, DC: National Center for Education Statistics.

Sadker, M., & Sadker, D. (1986). Sexism in the classroom: From grade school to graduate school. *The Phi Delta Kappan, 67*(7), 512–515.

Science for all. (2013). *Nature, 495*(7439), 5-5. doi:10.1038/495005a

Spencer, T. L., & Walker, T. M. (2011). Creating a love for science for elementary students through inquiry-based learning. *Journal of Virginia Science Education, 4*(2), 18–25.

Solorzano, D. (2004). A critical race analysis of Latina/o and African American advanced placement enrollment in public high schools. *High School Journal, 87*(3), 15.

Whiting, G.Y. (2009). Black students and advanced placement classes: Summary, concerns, and recommendations. *Gifted Child Today, 32*(1), 23.

Wing, A. K. (2003). Introduction. In A. K. Wing (Ed.), *Critical race feminism: A reader* (2nd ed.; pp. 1–19). New York, NY: New York University Press.

Wing, A. K. (1997). Brief reflections toward a multiplicative theory. In A.K. Wing (Ed.), *Critical race feminism: A reader,* (pp. 27–34). New York: New York University Press.

CHAPTER 7

AFRICAN AMERICAN FEMALE ACHIEVEMENT IN STEM

AP Courses Provide a Different Story?

Jemimah L. Young
Jamaal Young

Culturally and linguistically diverse (CLD) student populations such as women, African Americans, and Latinos constitute a substantial portion of the nation's K–12 population. However, these students pursue science, technology, engineering, and mathematics (STEM) degrees and professions at lower rates than White and Asian males. Specifically, CLD student populations represent 40% of the nation's K–12 enrollment but constitute only 18% of those receiving degrees in STEM fields (Hrabowski, 2012). African American females constitute a unique and growing population of K–12 learners, college educated women, and young professionals. The enrollment trends for African American females suggests that African American females represent approximately half the population of all African American students enrolled in Grades K–8 in the United States with 7.28% of the total 14.54% of African American students (U.S. Census Bureau, 2020). In Grades 9–12, however, slightly fewer African American females are enrolled

Girls and Women of Color In STEM, pages 105–116
Copyright © 2020 by Information Age Publishing
105

at 7.86% compared to 8.31% of African American males (U.S. Census Bureau, 2020).

This study uses empirical data to provide a counter-narrative to common conclusions drawn from studies of African American female achievement. Albeit the achievement gap is a well-documented phenomenon, the researchers in this study critically analyze African American female achievement across multiple content areas in search of areas of academic dominance instead of achievement disparities. Deficit thinking continues to plague African American research literature. However, researchers are calling for alternative perspectives and analysis of African American achievement (Robinson, Vega, Moore, Mayes, & Robinson, 2014). Although, these perspectives have largely come from the qualitative research paradigm, here the researchers utilize quantitative data analysis to illuminate African American female achievement—not the lack thereof. This study adjusts the focus from an emphasis on "gap gazing" to a focus on "success seeking." Through this paradigm shift, the researchers hope to appropriate space in current literature for the purposes of highlighting the academic successes, rather than failures of African American students.

The research process for this study was guided by two objectives. First, this study sought to critically analyze trends in access and participation in STEM Advanced Placement (AP) courses for African American female students. The goal of this analysis was to identify content areas in which participation in STEM AP courses was strongest, and provide conclusions and implications based on trends, to increase participation in other areas. Secondly, this study compared African American female achievement within each analogous STEM AP content discipline. The goal of this analysis was to identify the specific standardized examination within content strands where African American female students excelled. Researchers sought to compare performance in the mathematics content strand by comparing African American female scores on the AB Calculus, BC Calculus, and statistics examinations. This analysis removes the comparisons between African Americans and other ethnic groups, which subsequently fail to yield viable information to support African American female achievement because the results are convoluted.

THEORETICAL FRAMEWORK

Feminist epistemologies and race-based epistemologies tend to work in isolation and with narrow foci on White females and African American males which allow the needs of African American females to fall through the cracks (Evans-Winters, 2005). This research in feminist scholarship sometimes fails to include the voices of African American girls. The lack of intersections between the two epistemologies creates a significant need for more scholarship in education that focuses on the African American female subgroup. However, critical race feminism (CRF) in education may provide legal and academic stratagem for studying and eradicating race, class, and gender oppression in educational institutions (Evan-Winters & Esposito, 2010, p. 19).

This study used CRF critique as a complementary framework to critical race theory (CRT). The intersection between race and gender is an essential element in the analysis of African American female achievement because issues of race and gender are not mutually exclusive or simply additive. Wing (2000) asserts that identity is not additive; thus, African American women cannot be described as "White women plus color, nor as African American men plus gender" (p. 7). This assertion draws attention to the over simplification of racial and gender issues that has led to much of the underrepresentation of African American female achievement reported in the literature. Because of the complexity of the interactions and associations between race and gender, CRF scholarship necessitates a multidisciplinary approach to research and practice. At the root of CRF, is a strong affinity for social justice that resonates through its methodology that fosters political, social, and economic transformations necessary to benefit the populations of interest (Few, 2007). As earlier noted, the multiplicity and intersectionality of identities are essential to the application of CRT (Berry, 2009). Thus, researchers should pay particular attention to how multiplicity and intersectionality manifest throughout the research when applying the CRF framework. The experiences of female students of color must be examined holistically to capture the unique perspectives at the intersection of race and gender. Due to the intersection of race and gender, African American girls face both systemic and systematic forms of discrimination.

METHODS

This research study utilized a descriptive research design. Descriptive research elucidates natural and man-made phenomena—their form, actions, changes over time, and similarities with other phenomena (Gall, Gall, & Borg, 2007, p. 300). This design was chosen for several reasons. First, the goal of this study was to present data that supported theories to explain African American female achievement as an educational phenomenon. Accordingly, this study is exploratory not confirmatory by design. Thus, the goal was not to substantiate a particular theory or set of theories, but rather to explore African American female achievement across different AP exam content areas but not in comparison to other groups' achievement. This data should subsequently be used to develop theories that can later be substantiated or refuted.

Participants

The participants for this study were a representative sample of African American girls from public and private schools across the United States. Race and ethnicity were based on self-reported data collected by the College Board. The sample was comprised of $N = 97,745$ total students. Of this total number of students 20,919 were 9th- or 10th-grade students, 36,272 were 11th-grade students, 39043 were 12th-grade students, and 1,483 were pre-high school students.

Analysis

Data were extracted from the 2012 AP exam archived data sets provided by the College Board. African American female data were removed and then prepared for analysis in Microsoft Excel. The analysis consists primarily of descriptive statistics to further ascertain the nature of African American female achievement on AP examinations. Confidence intervals and pie charts were used to present the African American female achievement data pictorially.

Confidence intervals were selected because they provide point estimates population parameters, as well as a measure of the precision of these estimates that were used to compare across administrations (Cumming & Finch, 2001). The point estimates are sample statistics, two of the most commonly used of which are means and effect sizes (Zientek, Thompson, & Yetkiner, 2010). The sample statistics were referred to as point estimates because they approximate population parameters. The estimates are unique for each sample and should be compared to establish trends. This action is important because each sample or administration of the AP exam is unique. Moreover, this unique sample comes with various amounts of error. The confidence intervals allow the amount of error to be quantified from sample to sample for comparison. The level of precision in each point estimate controls the error associated with each point estimate. The width of the confidence interval represents the precision associated with each point estimate, specifically, the smaller the width of the confidence interval, the more precise the measurement and the wider the confidence interval, the less precise the measurement (Cumming & Finch, 2007).

Furthermore, the width of the confidence interval is directly related to the standard deviated and inversely related to sample size, two major components of measurement precision in statistics. Appropriately, if the variability (standard deviation) is small then the point estimate is more precise, and likewise, a larger sample size is more representative, which increases the precision of the point estimate.

A 95% confidence interval was chosen by convention, a 90% or any other level would be equally valid, but the 95% confidence interval is a stricter measure (Zientek, Thompson, & Yetkiner, 2010). An appropriate interpretation of these intervals is necessary. A 95% confidence interval does not indicate that a point estimate correctly represents the population parameter with 95% certainty, but rather that if an infinite number of confidence intervals are constructed one can be 95% certain that the population parameter is present. To access the differences in performance between African American females and males in mathematics and reading, mean difference confidence intervals were created. The mean difference confidence intervals were calculated using the following formulas:

Lower Limit $= M_1 - M_2 - (t_{CL})\ (Sm1 - m2)$
Upper Limit $= M_1 - M_2 + (t_{CL})\ (Sm1 - m2)$

M_1 represented the mean of the African American female scores and M_2 was the mean of the African American male scores. The t_{CL} represented the t critical for the 95% confidence intervals, found using Microsoft Excel macro, and $Sm1 - m2$ is the difference in African American females' and males' standard errors calculated from the AP exam data. The confidence intervals were calculated in Microsoft Excel using the confidence macro present in the available Excel macros. To perform these calculations one needs the mean, standard deviation, and population size, all of which were retrieved from the College Board's AP archived data website. Once this data were retrieved and the proper calculations made, the data were graphed in Microsoft Excel using the High–Low–Close stock graphing procedure (Zientek, Thompson, & Yetkiner, 2010).

The means scale score difference confidence intervals for each administration were plotted on the same graph for each STEM content strand. The AP examinations analyzed in this study were divided into mathematics and science content strands. The mathematics content strand was comprised of the following examinations: Calculus AB, Calculus BC, and statistics. While the science examination contained the following examinations: biology, chemistry, computer science, environmental science, Physics B, and Physics C. The mean differences between student performances on each examination was assessed by examining the amount of overlap present between the different confidence intervals (Cumming & Finch, 2007).

In this article, Cumming and Finch (2007) suggest that statistically significant differences can be assessed by means of visual inspection. According to Cumming and Finch, differences are notable if the mean difference confidence intervals do not intersect with the *x*-axis or zero. This was the process that was used to assess the difference in African American male and female achievement in mathematics and reading across administrations.

RESULTS

African American female AP exam participation was assessed in the STEM content strands mathematics and science. The distribution of mathematics AP exams completed by African American females can be seen in Figure 7.1. The data in Figure 7.1 suggest that the Calculus AB exam was completed with the most frequency by African American female students in 2012. The statistics exam was the second most frequent exam completed followed by the Calculus BC exam.

The science strand was comprised of substantially more AP exams. The data in Figure 7.2 suggest that African American female students completed the AP Biology exam with a frequency of 44%. This was almost twice the frequency of completion of the next two exams—chemistry and environmental science. Computer science, Physics B, and Physics C were the three least completed examinations in 2102.

The 95% mean score confidence intervals for the mathematics AP exams are presented in Figure 7.3. The data in Figure 7.3 presents a pictorial representation of the differences in mean scores on the three exams.

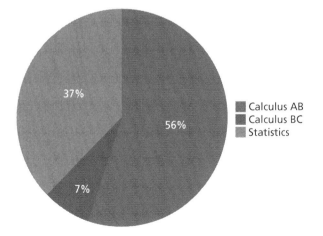

Figure 7.1 African American female student mathematics AP exam completion distribution.

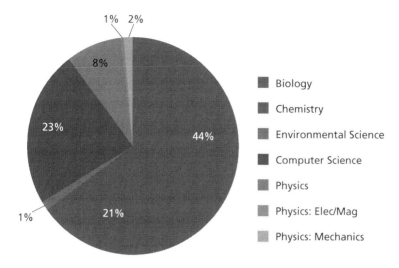

Figure 7.2 African American female student science AP exam completion distribution.

As previously mentioned confidence intervals can be used to examine the precision of measurements and the difference between point estimates. In Figure 7.3, the width of each confidence band depicts the precision of the measurement of each confidence interval. The narrower the confidence band the more accurate the measurement. Thus, the scores for the Calculus BC exam are the least precise of the score point estimate confidence intervals. However, the band is not substantially wide, but rather the Calculus

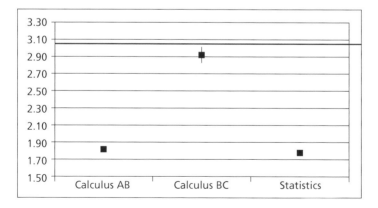

Figure 7.3 A 95% CI for African American female student mean scores on mathematics AP exams.

AB and statistics exam confidence bands are extremely narrow. The African American female scores on the Calculus BC exam are statistically significantly higher than the Calculus AB and statistics exam. AP exams are scored on a scale of 1–5, where 1 is the lowest score and 5 is the highest. Most public colleges and universities will accept a score of 3 on an AP exam for credit in the equivalent college level course. African American female mean scores for the Calculus BC exam were right below the mean score of 3. Unfortunately, the mean scores for the Calculus AB and the statistics examination were substantially lower than a score of 3, which is needed to receive college credit by examination in most public institutions.

The 95% confidence intervals for the Science AP examinations are presented in Figure 7.4. Substantial precision was presented in all exam score measurements except for the Physics C examination. Furthermore, the African American student performance was statistically significantly higher for the Physics C examination, as shown in the lack of overlap between the Physics C confidence bands in the other examination confidence bands. All AP examinations are scored on the same scale, thus a score of 3 or above is necessary to receive credit by exam on any of the science AP exams. Similarly to the results for the mathematics examinations, only the Physics C exam was relatively close to three criteria for credit by examination.

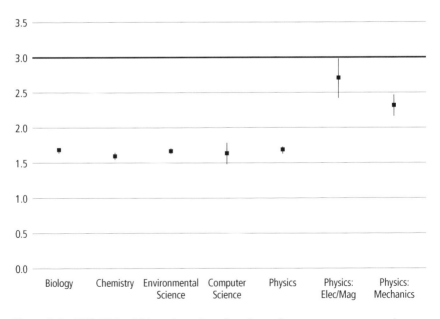

Figure 7.4 95% CI for African American female student mean scores on science AP exams.

CONCLUSIONS

The results of this study suggest that African American girls attempt substantially more Calculus AB examinations, but do not perform at the minimum level required to receive college credit by examination. While, African American girls attempted the Calculus BC exam with the least frequency their performance was statistically, significantly higher on this examination. One explanation for this phenomena is that the Calculus BC test is an examination of the content in Calculus 1 and Calculus 2, thus this exam is recommended for only the top mathematics students in the nation. Since participation in the Calculus BC exam is offered in fewer schools and fewer African American female students have access to this exam, the African American students that completed the exam may not be representative of the population as a whole. Furthermore, given the exams rarity, it is typically only accessible in affluent school districts with substantial resources.

A similar trend was present in the results of the science AP examinations. The Physics C exam was one of the least attempted exams by the African American students in this study, yet it was the exam with the highest mean score for the science examination. The results also suggest that African American female students may lack access to many of the science AP exams directly related to STEM professions. For instance, the computer science and both physics examinations were the least attempted science exams in this study. However, these exams are amongst the least common AP examinations administered each year. Another possible explanation is that many African American female students may not feel as competent in the science examinations that require substantial applied mathematics. Further investigation however is necessary to substantiate these conclusions.

The results of this study have significant implications to the trajectory and successful matriculation of African American females in STEM higher education. A study of College Board data revealed that only 33% of the expected frequency of underrepresented African Americans and Hispanics participated in AP courses (Burton, Whitman, Yepes-Baraya, Cline, & Kim, 2002). While numerous barriers affect African American student enrollment in STEM-related AP courses, several factors are common: (a) lack of awareness, (b) resistance from school personnel, and (c) feelings of isolation (Yonezawa, Wells, & Serna, 2002). This examination postulates that access, participation, and achievement in STEM AP courses are a means to propel African American female students to pursue STEM-related careers.

This research provides a foundation to guide further critical inquiry of African American female achievement. Specifically, these results provide implications for further research. According to a study conducted by Silverstein (2006), race and gender data were reported in less than 10% of the multicultural body of research indexed in Silverstein (2006) from 1990 to 2004. Thus, 90% of the research reported in PsycINFO across this period did not take into account the intersectionality of race and gender. Intersectionality makes plain that gender, race, class, and sexuality simultaneously affect the perceptions, experiences, and opportunities for everyone living in a society stratified along these dimensions (Cole, 2009, p. 177).

Thus, to fully understand the achievement of African American females, research must begin to consciously report racial and gender data for all experiments in the social and behavioral sciences. Aside from disaggregated achievement, researchers may begin to utilize CRT and CRF as theoretical as well as methodological frameworks to guide future investigations. These investigations may focus on: (a) recognizing the intercentricity of race and racism with other forms of subordination, (b) challenging the dominant ideology, (c) a commitment to social justice, (d) placing experiential knowledge at the center of the investigation, and (e) applying a transdisciplinary perspective (Solórzano & Yosso, 2002).

African American females successfully complete higher education and earn advanced degrees at much higher rates than African American males, but as the results of this study indicate, African American females scored lower on all educational tests presented compared to Asian American and White females. Thus, despite underachievement across all content areas, African American females have an academic resilience that allows them to overcome many of the detrimental environmental and social factors particular to their racial and gender group. According to Morales (2010), academic resilience can be fostered and maintained through mentoring relationships and specialized educational out of school experiences.

Classroom practices must utilize this resilience to propel African American females ahead earlier in their academic careers. Based on graduation rates and degree attainment, it is evident that African American females have the intellect to achieve at a high level in all academic content areas; however, this potential seems to remain untapped until postsecondary education. Specialized instructional programs must be developed to cultivate this resilience and improve the academic performance of African American female students in K–12 educational settings. Particular emphasis must be placed on the adolescent academic grade spansbecause this is where African American female performance is the least consistent and most troubling regarding the inter-gender racial achievement gap. Ladson-Billings (2006) identified four areas in education where CRT was most applicable. Thus, CRT must be applied to the development and evaluation of educational programs and practices in (a) curriculum, (b) instruction, (c) assessment, and (d) school funding as these are key areas where transformation can occur.

The academic and professional achievements of African American females warrants attention, but more attention given the substantial academic resilience exhibited by African American females. The construction of race and gender identity within the African American community presents many questions concerning the academic performance of African American females in relation to their male counterparts. How does the apparent "gender role duality" influence or hinder the academic performance of African American females? Does exhibiting masculine and feminine qualities create higher self-esteem in African American females or just an increase in pressure to perform? Does non-gender role conformity create undue tension in academic settings between teachers and African American females or does the apparent assertive nature of African American females place them in high esteem with classroom teachers? These questions are beyond the scope of this study. However, the results of this study set the groundwork to begin further investigation into the influence of African American females' constructions of race and gender on academic achievement.

This study examined the academic performance of African American females across multiple content domains. The results indicate that despite underachievement across all areas compared to their female counterparts the performance of African American females can be improved drastically based on strong growth trends and postsecondary achievement data. Suggestions for better research and educational practices are proposed, and implications for future work were presented. The application of these suggestions should help to begin to inform better practice through a more intersectional view of African American student achievement.

REFERENCES

Berry, T. R. (2009). Women of color in a bilingual/dialectal dilemma: Critical race feminism against a curriculum of oppression in teacher education. *International Journal of Qualitative Studies in Education, 22*(6), 745–753.

Burton, N., Whitman, N., Yepes-Baraya, M., Cline, F., & Kim, R. (2002). *Minority student success: The role of teachers in Advanced Placement program (AP) courses* (College Board Research Rep. No. 2002-8, ETS RR-02-17). New York, NY: College Entrance Examination Board.

Cole, E. R. (2009). Intersectionality and research in psychology. *American Psychologist, 64*(3), 170–180.

Cumming, G., & Finch, S. (2001). A primer on the understanding, use, and calculation of confidence intervals that are based on central and non-central distributions. *Educational and Psychological Measurement, 61*(4), 532–574.

Cumming, G., & Finch, S. (2007). Inference by eye: Confidence intervals and how to read pictures of data. *American Psychologist, 60*(2), 170–180.

Evans-Winters, V. (2005). *Teaching Black girls: Resiliency in urban schools*. New York, NY: Peter Lang.

Evans-Winter, V., & Esposito, J. (2010). Other people's daughters: Critical race feminism and black girls' education. *Educational Foundations, 24*(1), 11–14.

Few, A. L. (2007). Integrating Black consciousness and critical race feminism into family studies research. *Journal of Family Issues, 28*(4), 452–473.

Gall, M. D., Gall, J. P., & Borg, W. R. (2007). Collecting research data with questionnaires and interviews. In *Educational research: An introduction* (pp. 227–261). Boston, MA: Pearson.

Hrabowski, F. A., III. (2012). Broadening participation in the American STEM workforce. *BioScience, 62*(4), 325–326.

Ladson-Billings, G. (2006). From the achievement gap to the education debt: Understanding achievement in U.S. schools. *Educational Researcher, 35*(7), 3–12.

Morales, E. E. (2010). Linking strengths: Identifying and exploring protective factor clusters in academically resilient low-socioeconomic urban students of color. *Roeper Review, 32*(3), 164–175.

Robinson, D. V., Vega, D., Moore, J. L., Mayes, R. D., & Robinson, J. R. (2014). Chutes and ladders: Young African American males navigating potholes to achieve academic success. In J. L. Moore & C. W. Lewis (Eds.), *African American male students in preK–12 schools: Informing research, policy, and practice* (Vol. 2; pp. 107–124). Bingley, England: Emerald.

Silverstein. L. B. (2006). Integrating feminism and multiculturalism: Scientific fact or science fiction? *Professional Psychology: Research and Practice, 37*(1), 21–28.

Solórzano, D. G., & Yosso, T. J. (2002). Critical race theory methodology: Counter- storytelling as an analytical framework for education research. *Qualitative Inquiry, 8*(1), 23–44.

U.S. Census Bureau (2020, September). *School enrollment in the United States: October 2012-detailed tables*. Retrieved from https://www.census.gov/data/tables/2012/demo/school-enrollment/2012-cps.html

Wing, A. K. (Ed.). (2000). *Global critical race feminism: An international reader*. New York, NY: New York University Press.

Yonezawa, S., Wells, A. S., & Serna, I. (2002). Choosing tracks: "Freedom of choice" in detracking schools. *American Educational Research Journal, 39*(1), 37–67.

Zientek, L. R., Thompson, B., & Yetkiner, Z. E. (2010). Characterizing the mathematics anxiety literature using confidence intervals as a literature review mechanism. The *Journal of Educational Research, 103*(6), 424–438.

CHAPTER 8

KENYAN SECONDARY SCHOOL STUDENTS' PERCEPTIONS OF THEIR SCIENCE CLASSROOM

Influence of Gender, School Type, and Instructional Context

Lee Shumow
Teresa A. Wasonga

Development and management of Kenya's abundant natural resources and outstanding agricultural conditions for and by the Kenyan people require a workforce with considerable scientific skills and knowledge. The Kenyan government has identified science, technology, and innovation as "critical to the socio-economic transformation of the country" (Republic of Kenya, 2007, p. 19) intending to use schools to enhance quality, equity, and access to science and technology. However, like many other countries in the world, Kenya has struggled with attaining needed levels of scientific literacy among their citizens (Keraro, Wachanga, & Orora, 2006; Republic

Girls and Women of Color In STEM, pages 117–133
Copyright © 2020 by Information Age Publishing

of Kenya, 2012). One possible reason for that struggle is secondary school students' lack of self-determination in pursuing science education. In this mixed method study, the authors examine students' motivation to learn science in Kenyan secondary schools and test whether students' motivation varies by gender, school type, and classroom processes and practices in classrooms serving mainstream (not wealthy or elite) students. This study is designed to fill a need for more studies that specifically examine motivation to learn mathematics and science in the African secondary school system.

In Kenya, there is an 8–4–4 education system, including 8 years of primary work, 4 years of secondary schooling, and 4 years at the university level. The majority of primary and secondary schools are public although private schools serve a significant number of children. Public schools are highly selective, based on a tier system (national, county, and district). The country uses a national curriculum that exposes all students in public and government registered private schools to the same subjects, most of which are compulsory. At the secondary level, compulsory subjects include languages (Kiswahili and English), mathematics, physical sciences (physics, chemistry, and biology), and social sciences (history and civics, geography, and religion). All of these subjects are learned every year in a hierarchical order from the basic essentials to applied knowledge. All secondary school teachers are graduates of accredited universities and certified by the Teachers Service Commission (TSC), a constitutionally mandated commission charged with the management of teacher functions.

THEORETICAL PERSPECTIVE

Self-Determination Theory

Our description and comparison of motivational processes is framed by a well-known motivational theory, self-determination theory (Deci & Ryan, 1991). Self-determination theory posits that individuals have a basic need to feel autonomous, competent, and related within contexts like classrooms cross-culturally and that these factors are crucial in sustaining students' interest and commitment to learning (Chirkov, 2009; Deci & Ryan, 1991, 2002). To the extent that a social context like a classroom allows for the fulfillment of those innate tendencies, students experience greater motivation and persistence. We focus our investigation on students' subjective experience of those needs and their related sense of task relevance within classrooms.

Some evidence suggests that SDT is applicable to Kenyan education. It has been widely used, for example, in designing HIV prevention and other health programs. At least one study suggests that some principles of

SDT apply to Kenyan secondary school science (Changeiywo, Wambugu, & Wachanga, 2011), but that speculation has not been tested.

According to SDT, students who play a part in determining the environment by having some choice and control in daily activities are more likely to persist in those activities and pursue personal goals associated with the subject. Similarly, students who pursue an activity for intrinsic reasons, like interest, relevance, and attaining personal goals, will be more persistent and successful in that activity than those motivated by extrinsic reasons (Ames, 1992). Perceptions of competence, which refer to a belief in one's ability to succeed in a given task, make students more likely to attempt and keep trying the task, an idea supported by some evidence in U.S. studies (Grolnick, Gurland, Jacob, & Decourcey, 2002). Students' sense of relatedness with others within a learning context fosters a sense of belonging, which is considered an important motivator by SDT (Deci & Ryan, 2002). This study uses students' sense of competitiveness and cooperativeness as indicators of relatedness.

LITERATURE REVIEW

Science Education and Gender in Kenya

Motivation to learn is an essential precursor of engagement, skill, success, and career choice. In Kenya, performance in science on the national examinations has been poor, especially among girls (Republic of Kenya, 2004; Republic of Kenya, 2005). Historically, females have had less access to secondary education. Those females who attended secondary school received less adequate preparation for higher education and careers dependent on science knowledge than males did. This has led to fewer females than males majoring in science-oriented fields in Kenyan institutions of higher education (Agesa & Agesa, 2003; Logan & Beoku-Betts, 1996). As a result, fewer women have transitioned into jobs requiring scientific skills, which tend to provide greater stability and relatively good salaries. Recently, females comprised 44% of the students attending technical, industrial, vocational, and entrepreneurship training (TIVET) schools in Kenya, but only about 5% of those females enrolled in science-oriented courses at TIVET schools (Republic of Kenya, 2012). Gender disparity in science is even more acute in higher education and workplaces that focus on science related skills (Ministry of Education, 2008).

Given the gap in science achievement and career pursuit between male and female students, the first question investigated in the current study is whether male and female secondary school students in Kenya differ in motivational processes highlighted by SDT during science class. Kenyan female students may feel that they have less control and competence than males and feel less sense of relevance and relatedness in class than males because girls have had few role models in science and the inequities described here may have influenced the self-determination beliefs of female students in science negatively. On the other hand, girls may equal or exceed boys in these areas of self-determination because they perceive their educational opportunity to be of great value.

Recent research on students' motivation during science classes in G-8 countries and Australia has demonstrated that females experience high school science classes very differently from males, with females reporting less control and competence in science (DeBacker & Nelson, 2000; Freeman, 2004; Nosek et al., 2009; Preston, 2004). Studies on gender, motivation, and science or mathematics achievement are beginning to emerge in Kenya. A few studies have documented gender differences in motivation to learn mathematics and science with females reporting lower success and motivation in secondary school mathematics than males, a situation that was compounded for females in coeducational schools (Githua & Mwangi, 2003). Among students attending single-sex schools, Muchera, Dixon, Hartley, and Hardin (2010) recently found higher scores on self-concept among males than females even though females performed better in mathematics. Shihusa and Keraro (2009) found that male students scored significantly higher on both motivation and performance in biology class. However, another recent study found no gender differences in motivation to learn physics among students attending several coeducational schools in one region of Eastern Kenya (Changeiywo, Wambugu, & Wachanga, 2011). These studies suggested that school type might be an important motivational factor.

School Type and Gender in Kenyan Secondary Schools

Secondary schools in Kenya are traditionally single-sex boarding but coeducational and day secondary schools are emerging and growing in popularity. The relative merits of single-sex and coeducational schools have been hotly debated in Kenya (Bosire, Mondoh, & Barmao, 2008). A number of Kenyans assume, based on cultural beliefs, that single-sex schools have a positive effect especially on girls in terms of academic performance.

Indeed, single-sex classrooms or schools have been proposed as one solution for the disparity between males and females in math and science observed in Kenya (Bosire, Mondoh, & Barmao, 2008), the Unite States (Sax, Arms, Woodruff, Riggers, & Eagan, 2009), Europe (Kessels & Hannover, 2008; Sullivan, Joshi, & Leonard, 2010), and Korea (Park & Behrman, 2010). Proponents of single-sex schools argue that such schools offer the best opportunity to redress inequities and point to evidence that females who attend single-sex schools are more motivated and engaged in their education than females who attend otherwise similar schools, especially in scientific and technical subjects (Lee & Lockheed, 1990; Sax et al., 2009). Opponents argue that single-sex schools undermine educational opportunity and compound bias. Some argue that both males and females will benefit in single-sex schools as a result of greater focus on academics and less exposure to adolescent subcultures (Mensch, Clark, Lloyd, & Erulkar, 1999). To test these speculations, we first compare students attending all male, all female, and coeducational schools. We then separately compare males and females who are attending single-sex schools with those attending coeducational schools.

One study in Kenya (Bosire, Mondoh, & Barmao, 2008) found that females performed considerably better in single-sex mathematics classrooms than in mixed classrooms. Several studies conducted on teaching methods in Kenya suggest that motivation in science might differ by school type for males and females, an inference that we test in this study. For example, an intervention study in chemistry found that males in single-sex schools benefitted more from a quasi-experiment in cooperative learning than males attending coeducational schools (Wachanga & Mwangi, 2004). Another intervention study found that both males and females in two coeducational schools benefited in terms of increased motivation to learn biology after participating in a cooperative learning intervention (Keraro, Wachanga, & Orora, 2006).

Classroom Instructional Context

Some scholars have suggested that contextual factors like instruction explain persistent gender gaps and demotivation in science (Else-Quest, Hyde, & Linn, 2010). The banking method, in which learning is characterized by memorization and compliance with authority, is common in Kenyan schools where it mirrors cultural and political practices. Just as children and ordinary people are expected to submit to their parents and leaders respectively, students and teachers submit unequivocally to teachers and school leaders respectively. The situation may be more complex for female students who may also be expected, culturally to submit to the authority of male students. Scholars in science education have embraced instruction which focuses on thinking, making content relevant, conversation, and active learning (Duschl, 2008; Krajcik & Sutherland, 2010). We observed in each of the classrooms in which we sampled students' reports of their self-determination recording the mode of instruction, the extent to which teachers promoted critical thinking, relevance of the material, and responsiveness to students. We also rated teacher support for independence and attempts to engage students in the class. We investigated whether these aspects of instruction differed by school type and whether they were related to student reports of self-determination.

METHOD AND DATA SOURCE

Context: Structure of Secondary Schools in Kenya

Most Kenyan secondary schools are single-sex and residential; some are coeducational schools and some are day schools (the high cost of boarding having led to growth in the number of day schools). Another phenomenon in Kenyan secondary schools is stratification into national, county, and district schools. National schools are the most prestigious and well-funded admitting students with the highest scores on the national Kenya Certificate of Primary Education (KCPE). Many of them attended high quality private primary schools well resourced with facilities, equipment, and teachers (Sawamura & Sifuna, 2008). Thus, while the intention of national schools was to bring together bright students from all over the country irrespective of socioeconomic background, they tend to serve the rich students. County and district schools educate the majority of Kenyan students, although county schools have more stringent admission score requirements. Government subsidy is higher for national schools. Consequently, facilities and equipment in county and district schools are insufficient, the schools are overcrowded, and they lack enough teachers.

Participants

Students ($N = 377$: $n = 152$ males, 225 females) from nine science classrooms in six secondary schools in western Kenya comprised the sample for this study. Three participating schools were single-sex (1 male; 2 female) and three were coeducational schools. Three schools were boarding and three were day schools. Three were provincial and three were district schools. Five of the schools were public/government and one of the coeducational schools was owned by a semi-government corporation. Nearly every student in each class agreed to participate in the study. Because, admissions depend on the national examination score, each of the five public schools has similar ranges of students in academic ability and socioeconomic status; class sizes ranged from 50–57. The semi-government school, where class size was about 40, serves students from self-selected middle and upper middle income Kenyan families.

Procedure

All classrooms were visited in the same week early in the Kenyan school year. Two researchers observed each of the classrooms for one class period. At the end of the lesson, students completed a questionnaire.

Measures

Student reports were obtained through a modification of the experience sampling method (ESM) similar to that used by others (Schwinle & Turner, 2006) which has been used to document variations by gender and classroom activity in secondary school science classes (Shumow & Schmidt, 2012). Experience sampling method has extensive validity and reliability (Hektner, Schmidt, & Csikszentmihalyi, 2007). Following the science lesson, students used Likert scales (0 = *not at all*, 1 = *a little*, 2 = *somewhat*, 3 = *very much*) to report on their subjective experience that day as reflected in Table 8.1 under the results section.

Classroom Observations

Time Sample Observations

Classrooms were observed in cycles of 1 minute observe, 15 second record, which meant that 80% of each class period was observed systematically while 20% of the time was spent recording aspects of instruction. For example, we recorded whether particular instructional modes had been used. Choices included: lecture, lecture recitation, discussion, seat work (individual or small group), student presentation, film or video, lab, testing, classroom organization (passing out materials), or not science focused. It was also noted whether the teacher made bids for the students to think critically or drew attention to the relevance of the material. Finally, it was recorded if the teacher or the students had initiated teachers' verbalizations.

Global Ratings of Classroom Teachers

At the end of each class period, observers completed global ratings of several elements of the teachers' interactions with the students using a scale of *rarely*, *somewhat*, or *often*. Items rated the extent to which teachers: (a) supported independence, (b) engaged student participation, (c) promoted critical thinking, and (d) disciplined students. Any classroom disruptions were also noted.

Most (66%) of the ratings were completed by two observers. Percent agreement of 84% indicated reliability of the ratings. Disagreements were decided by the code developer.

RESULTS

Self-Determination Reports by Students

Gender Overall

In Table 8.1, we share the results from comparing student reports of self-determination by gender. Compared to males, female students reported experiencing less control in their science classes. Females reported marginally less success than males during class, although there were no differences in perceived skill. Females also felt more competitive during science class than males but males and females did not differ in their reported feelings of cooperation. No gender differences were found in terms of experiencing science class as relevant.

Coeducational Versus Single-Sex Schools

Results of analyses by school type are shown in Table 8.2. In general, students in coeducational schools reported perceiving themselves as having greater control, competence, success, and sense of cooperativeness than students in single-sex schools. Students in female only schools reported higher competitiveness than students in the other school types. However,

TABLE 8.1 Students' Perceptions and Motivation in Science Classrooms by Gender

Theoretical Construct of Self Determination	Student Rating of Their:	Male	Female	Significance
Autonomy	Control	2.52(.75)	2.25(1.0)	2.92**
Relevance	Interest	2.76(.71)	2.75(.68)	NS
	Future Goal Relevance	2.86(.50)	2.85(.53)	NS
	Importance Self	2.94(.24)	2.94(.35)	NS
Competence	Skill	2.30(.79)	2.26(.80)	NS
	Success	2.63(.63)	2.50(80)	1.68^
Relatedness	Cooperation	2.81(.52)	2.75(.64)	NS
	Competition	2.31(.94)	2.51(.84)	−2.2*

Note: Analyses adjusted for any unequal variances
NS = Not significant
$p < .1$, $^*p < .05$, $^{**}p < .01$, $^{***}p < .001$

TABLE 8.2   Students' Perceptions and Motivation in Science Classrooms by School Type

Theoretical Construct of Self Determination	Measure	Single Sex School		Coed	Significance
		Male	Female		
Autonomy	Control	2.46(.78)	2.16(1.1)	2.54(.79)	F = 7.01**
	Interest	2.71(.72)	2.74(.71)	2.79(.67)	NS
	Relevance	2.92(.33)	2.90(.40)	2.77(.65)	F = 3.14*
	Importance	2.98(.14)	2.93(.37)	2.92(.29)	NS
Competence	Skill	2.08(.81)	2.22(.82)	2.42(.74)	F = 4.59*
	Success	2.35(.79)	2.43(.83)	2.77(.54)	F = 11.19***
Relatedness	Cooperation	2.77(.51)	2.70(.68)	2.85(.49)	F = 2.66^
	Competition	2.00(1.0)	2.53(.80)	2.47(.89)	F = 7.45**

Note: NS = Not significant
$p < .1$, $^*p < .05$, $^{**}p < .01$, $^{***}p < .001$.

students in coeducational schools scored significantly lower on future relevance than students attending single-sex schools.

Gender by School Type

Table 8.3 reflects findings comparing male students in the single-sex school with male students in coed schools and female students in single-sex schools with female students in coed schools. Males attending coed schools reported greater skill, success, and competition than males attending the single-sex school. Females in coeducational schools reported significantly higher control, success, and cooperation; females in single-sex schools reported significantly higher scores in future relevance.

Classroom Instructional Context

Classroom instruction was characterized by the banking method (Friere, 1993). Lecture, lecture-recitation, and teacher directed seat work or laboratory activities comprised the vast majority of instruction. Teacher student interaction was overwhelmingly teacher, not student, initiated. Only one teacher engaged students in discussion and that was briefly. Time was used exclusively for instruction in the Kenyan classrooms. In no case was more than one minute used on classroom organization; no time was used on discipline as students were compliant.

There were no differences in methods or instructional interactions between teachers in single-sex or coeducational schools. There was some variation among teachers in the extent to which they supported student

TABLE 8.3 Students' Perceptions and Motivation in Science Classrooms by Gender and School Type

Self Determination Theoretical Construct	Measure	Males			Females		
		SS	Coed	Significance	SS	Coed	Significance
Autonomy	Control	2.46(0.78)	2.56(0.74)	NS	2.16(1.08)	2.53(0.90)	F = 4.93*
	Interest	2.71(0.72)	2.79(0.71)	NS	2.74(0.71)	2.79(0.60)	NS
	Future Relevance	2.92(0.33)	2.82(0.56)	NS	2.90(0.40)	2.67(0.79)	F = 7.68**
	Importance to Self	2.98(0.14)	2.91(0.28)	NS	2.93(0.37)	2.94(0.31)	NS
Competence	Skill	2.08(0.81)	2.42(0.75)	F = 6.64*	2.22(0.82)	2.40(0.72)	NS
	Success	2.35(0.79)	2.78(0.46)	F = 18.23***	2.43(0.83)	2.73(0.66)	F = 5.64*
Relatedness	Cooperation	2.77(0.51)	2.82(0.52)	NS	2.70(0.68)	2.91(0.45)	F = 4.16*
	Competition	2.00(1.00)	2.47(0.87)	F = 8.70**	2.53(0.80)	2.47(0.95)	NS

Note: NS = Not significant
$p<.1$, $^*p<.05$, $^{**}p<.01$, $^{***}p<.001$.

TABLE 8.4	**Summary of Observations**					
Teacher	School Type	Support Independence	Engage Participation	Dominant Methods	Critical Thinking	Relevance
1	SS F	Some	Often	Lecture-Recitation	Some	Minimal
2	SS M	Rare	Rare	Lecture	Rare	Minimal
3	SS F	Some	Often	Lecture-Recitation	Often	None
4	SS F	Some	Some	Lecture	Some	Considerable
5	SS F	Some	Rare	Lab, Lecture	Rare	None
6	Coed	Rare	Rare F > M	Lecture	Rare	Considerable
7	Coed	Some	Some M = F	Lecture-Recitation	Some	None
8	Coed	Often	Often M = F	Lab, Lecture-Recitation	Rare	None
9	Coed	Rare	Often M > F	Lab, Lecture-Recitation	Some	Minimal

independence on classroom tasks, asked for student participation (recitation), fostered critical thinking, and connected content to aspects of "real life" (relevance). In Table 8.4, we summarize our observations.

We correlated our ratings and time sample estimates of instruction with the average class rating students provided for various self-determination measures. Spearman's rho was used to test for significant differences. Consistent with the theory, the amount of time teachers used lecture was associated negatively with student ratings of autonomy, interest, skill, success, and relatedness (both cooperation and competition). Also consistent with theory, teacher support for independence was related positively to students' reports that they felt skilled during class. In general, fostering thinking, making content relevant, and student initiation were not associated with students' subjective experience in ways predicted by SDT. More time fostering thinking during class was associated positively with student reported interest but negatively with students' reported autonomy and skill. Teacher initiated making content relevant was associated negatively with student reported autonomy, interest, and skill. Finally, more student initiated teacher responses was associated negatively with students reported autonomy, skill, and success.

DISCUSSION

Overall, female Kenyan secondary school students reported a lower sense of control, marginally less success, and more competitiveness than male students. No gender differences were found in terms of students' perception of their skill, interest, relevance, and cooperation in science class. Thus, some gender differences similar to those of students in other nations were found but those differences were fewer and weaker among Kenyan students. These results were unexpected given the fact that Kenyan female students have few role models in science and a history of unequal opportunity.

There are several possible explanations for these findings. For one, cultural factors, elaborated on below, may explain female students' lower sense of control compared to male students as well as their need to compete to succeed. However, it is important to note that the mean female autonomy (control) ratings fell between *somewhat* and *very much*, which are dramatically higher than those reported by U.S. female secondary school students. Recent actionable Kenyan policy directives to enhance the status of girls might be having a positive impact on these female secondary school students' sense of self-determination. Several specific strategies addressing different forms of biases against girls have been implemented in schools to address cultural and other barriers that hinder many girls from fully participating in education, as well as extra support in terms of science equipment and related materials to girls' schools (Ministry of Education, 2008, p. 38).

Another possible explanation is that the girls feel extraordinarily fortunate to be attending school. They may feel skillful because they have attained the scores to be admitted and competitive because they "won" the intense school admission competition. Their interest and sense of relevance may also stem from a sense of good fortune and hope for the future related to the opportunity to attend secondary school.

Yet another possible explanation for female students' lower sense of control and success is that, in this study, all but one teacher were males. Although research is inconclusive on the impact of teachers' gender on female students (Mensch & Lloyd, 1998), traditional values pertaining to male authority in Kenya may lead female students to feel less sense of self-determination than if more of their teachers were female. Because only one teacher was female (and she taught in a single-sex school), we are not able to test for associations. A future study could examine that question in depth.

The second issue investigated pertained to school type. Overall, students' sense of autonomy, competence, relatedness, and future relevance differed between students attending male single-sex, female single-sex, and coeducational schools. The results were not consistent with the argument that single-sex schools benefit both males and females in science. In fact, male students attending coeducational schools had higher perceptions of competence than the male students attending the single-sex school and did not differ on the other motivational process variables. Female students attending coeducational school reported more autonomy, success, and marginally more cooperativeness than female students attending single-sex schools.

Females in single-sex schools reported more competitiveness and more sense of future relevance than females attending coeducational schools but did not differ on reported interest or importance of the material to them.

It is particularly interesting that there were some benefits in terms of self-determination associated with attending coeducational schools. This was despite the fact that many students who attend coeducational public schools are those whose parents cannot afford public boarding schools. Further, the single-sex schools required higher scores on the Kenya Certificate of Primary Education (KCPE) than the coeducational schools. The relatively high scores of coeducational school students on self-determination constructs like control, success, and cooperation may be indicative of resiliency. Their lower sense of future relevance in comparison to their more advantaged peers attending single-sex schools may suggest a sense of uncertainty about the future despite their current success.

On the other hand, male and female students in coeducational schools may feel successful, and females in those schools may feel more autonomous and cooperative than students in single-sex schools precisely because they recognize the coeducational nature of the adult world. They increasingly see women working in businesses, offices, schools, and medical facilities in their communities. In addition, they are exposed to men and women working together every day. This might lead them to feel that they are functioning in a more "adult setting" than single-sex secondary school students, which could influence their sense of self-determination positively.

Classroom instruction was observed and described because it was expected to influence students' self-determination. The observations revealed that the banking method of teaching was pervasive in all of the schools. Science was not taught in ways that promoted application, citizenship, or critical thinking. Teachers' ratings of their classes indicated that they thought a good science lesson was one in which students listened, took notes, and responded to rote recall questions. The teacher initiated the vast majority of their verbalizations to students; students responded as directed. Experiments were demonstrated by the teacher and observed by students. When the students did experiments, these were prescribed and controlled with little room for discovery. Conversations with science teachers revealed the beliefs that science is "cut and dry" comprising a prescribed set of content knowledge, the teacher's role is to tell the students what the facts are, and the students' role is to master what is taught.

Teachers' use of the lecture and lecture-recitation methods during class took a toll in terms of the students' self-determination as lower ratings were associated with greater amounts of time that teachers used those methods. Students reported being more interested when teachers engaged them by fostering thinking and felt more competent when teachers supported their independence. However, despite this partial support for SDT, in contrast to studies conducted in the United States, some expected relationships between self-determination and instructional context were not found. For example, given the predominance of the banking method and passive discourse in the classes, the means of student reports showed that they believed they were learning (successful) and students were both observed to be and reported being engaged. All class time was spent on task and not even one incident was observed in which a student disrupted class, or a teacher had to discipline a student. In the United States, many students report being bored and disengaged during lessons characterized by the banking method (Hektner, Schmidt, & Csikszentmihalyi, 2007).

Another unexpected finding was that students reported having less control and competence when teachers attempted to foster their thinking or when teachers responded to students. Why did these secondary students in Kenya respond like they did? One possibility is that students interpreted student initiation of teacher responses as meaning they, the students, were confused and lacking, not that their perspective was welcomed or that they were welcome to begin an instructional conversation. Similarly, students could interpret challenging thought questions as threatening to their competence. They are used to rapid fire recitation of facts in science and may feel unskilled and uneasy when questions are complex and difficult.

Another possible explanation for these unexpected associations between instructional context and students' self-determination is that Kenyan students are brought up within a cultural system that does not support questioning of authority. Acceptance of passive discourse is a reflection of cultural norms rooted in traditional values and assumptions that emphasize the unequal status of men and women, boys and girls, and teachers and students (Mensch & Lloyd, 1998). Traditionally, the notion that knowledge exclusively resides in elders is considered absolute and morally true (Bloch, 1993, as cited in Mensch & Lloyd, 1998). In school, teachers take the role of elders and the knowledge they give is accepted unconditionally. These norms manifest in classrooms. Students refrain from asking questions, initiating conversation, or talking unless they are asked.

Our findings indicate that teachers and students may both acquiesce to traditional values in the classroom. Nevertheless, for students to engage with science in a way that facilitates their self-determination and engages them in learning about issues facing themselves and their societies, science education cannot depend on the banking method of instruction only. Self-determination theory researchers in education have identified approaches that facilitate self-determination (Ryan & Deci, 2009). Those approaches dovetail well with inquiry and constructivist approaches to science. Students who are inculcated into an authoritarian system of education within a hierarchical traditional culture are likely to require encouragement to discuss or talk about difficult and complex issues in science as an essential part of learning. Educators will need to try and test ideas for transitioning teachers and students. In Kenya, it might be useful to begin by developing several interdisciplinary units which integrate science with civics classes where students consider and debate social issues which require some scientific knowledge to solve.

In this study we found that SDT provides a lens through which to evaluate the experience of mainstream Kenyan secondary school students in their science classrooms. Students with a greater sense of agency, competence, relatedness, and relevance in science class will be advantaged in developing and using scientific literacy to meet their own needs. We conclude that these students' ability to make decisions about critical societal issues will be enhanced as well.

REFERENCES

Agesa, J., & Agesa, R. (2002). Gender differences in public and private university enrollment in Kenya: What do they mask? *The Review of Black Political Economy, 30*(1), 29–55.

Ames, C. (1992). Classrooms: Goals, structures, and student motivation. *Journal of educational psychology, 84*(3), 261.

Bosire, J., Mondoh, H., & Barmao, A. (2008). Effect of streaming by gender on student achievement in mathematics in secondary schools in Kenya. *South African Journal of Education, 28*(4), 595–607.

Changeiywo, J., Wambugu, P. , & Wachanga, S. (2011). Investigations of students' motivation towards learning secondary school physics through mastery learning. *International Journal of Science and Mathematics Education, 9*(6), 1333–1350.

Chirkov, V. (2009). A cross-cultural analysis of autonomy in education: A self-determination theory perspective. *Theory and Research in Education, 7*(2), 253–262.

DeBacker, T. K., & Nelson, R. M. (2000). Motivation to learn science: Differences related to gender, class type, and ability. *Journal of Educational Research, 93*(4), 245–254.

Deci, E., & Ryan, R. (1991). A motivational approach to self: Integration in personality. In R. Dienstbier (Ed.), *Nebraska symposium on motivation, 1990: Perspectives on motivation* (Vol. 38; pp. 237–288). Lincoln: University Nebraska Press.

Deci, E., & Ryan, R. M. (2002). An overview of self-determination theory: An organismic-dialectical perspective. In E. Deci & R. M. Ryan (Eds.), *Handbook of self-determination research* (pp. 3–36). Rochester, NY: University of Rochester Press.

Duschl, R. (2008). Science education in three-part harmony: Balancing conceptual, epistemic and social learning goals. *Review of Research in Education. 32*(1), 268–291.

Else-Quest, N., Hyde, J. S., & Linn, M. (2010). Cross-national patterns of gender differences in mathematics: A meta-analysis. *Psychological Bulletin, 136*(1), 103–127.

Freeman, C. E. (2004). *Trends in educational equity of girls and women* (NCES2005-016). Washington, DC: National Center for Educational Statistics.

Friere, P. (1993). *Pedagogy of the oppressed.* New York, NY: Continuum.

Githua, B., & Mwangi, J. (2003). Students' mathematics self-concept and motivation to learn mathematics: Relationship and gender differences among Kenya's secondary-school students in Nairobi and Rift Valley provinces, *International Journal of Educational Development, 23*(5), 487–499. Retrieved from http://www.sciencedirect.com/science/article/pii/S0738059303000257

Grolnick, W. S., Gurland, S. T., Jacob, K. F., & Decourcey, W. (2002). The development of self-determination in middle childhood and adolescence. In A. Wigfield & J. S. Eccles (Eds.), *Development of achievement motivation* (pp. 147–171). Cambridge, MA: Academic Press. Retrieved from https://www.researchgate.net/profile/Wendy_Grolnick/publication/232580776_Chapter_6._The_Development_of_SelfDetermination_in_Middle_Childhood_and_Adolescence/links/0c960521d2896aa2a2000000.pdf

Hektner, J., Schmidt, J., & Csikszentmihalyi, M. (2007). *Experience sampling method: Measuring the quality of everyday life.* Thousand Oaks, CA: SAGE.

Keraro, F., Wachanga, S., & Orora, W. (2007). Effects of cooperative concept mapping teaching approach on secondary school students motivation in Gucha District, Kenya. *International Journal of Science and Mathematics Education, 5*(1), 111–124.

Kessels, U., & Hannover, B. (2008). When being a girl matters less: Accessibility of gender-related self-knowledge in single-sex and coeducational classes and its impact on students' physics-related self-concept of ability. *British Journal of Educational Psychology, 78*(Pt 2), 273–289.

Krajcik, J. S., & Sutherland, L. M. (2010). Supporting students in developing literacy in science. *Science, 328*(5977), 456–459.

Lee, E. V., & Lockheed, M. E. (1990). The effects of single sex schooling on achievement and attitudes in Nigeria. *Comparative Education Review, 34*(20), 209–231.

Logan, B. I., & Beoku-Betts, J. (1996). Women and education in Africa. *Journal of Asian and African Studies, 31*(3/4), 217–239.

Mensch, S. M., Clark, W. H., Lloyd, C. B., & Erulkar, A. S. (1999). *Premarital sex and school dropout in Kenya: Can schools make a difference?* New York, NY: Population Council.

Mensch, B. S., & Lloyd, C. B. (1998). Gender differences in the schooling experiences of adolescents in low-income countries: The case of Kenya. *Studies in Family Planning 29*(2), 167–184.

Ministry of Education. (2008, November). *The development of education: National report of Kenya.* Report presented at the International Conference on Education, Geneva, Switzerland. Retrieved from http://www.ibe.unesco.org/en/ibedocs/national-reports

Muchera, W., Dixon, F., Hartley, K., & Hardin, T. (2010). Perceptions of self-concept and actual academic performance in math and English among high school students in Kenya. *Education Research, 1*(8). 263–275.

Nosek, B., Smyth, F., Sriram, N., Lindner, N., Devos, T., Ayala, A., . . . Greenwald, A. (2009). National differences in gender–science stereotypes predict national sex differences in science and math achievement. *Proceedings of the National Academy of Sciences in the USA, 106*(26), 10593–10597. Retrieved from http://www.pnas.org/content/106/26/10593.full

Park, H., & Behrman, J. (2010). *Causal effects of single-sex schools on college attendance: Random assignment in korean high schools* (PSC Working Paper Series). Retrieved from http://works.bepress.com/hyunjoon_park/8

Preston, A. E. (2004). *Leaving science: Occupational exit from scientific careers.* New York, NY: SAGE.

Republic of Kenya. (2007). *Kenya vision 2030: A globally competitive and prosperous Kenya.* Nairobi: Government of Kenya.

Republic of Kenya. (2005). *Kenya education sector support program 2005–2010: Delivering quality equitable education and training to all Kenyans.* Nairobi, Kenya: Ministry of Education, Science and Technology. Retrieved from https://planipolis .iiep.unesco.org/sites/planipolis/files/ressources/kenya_kessp_final_2005 .pdf

Republic of Kenya. (2004). *Sessional paper No. 1 of 2004 on meeting the challenges of education, training and research in Kenya in the 21st century: A policy framework for education, training and research.* Nairobi, Kenya: Ministry of Education, Science and Technology. Retrieved from http://www.knqa.go.ke/wp-content/ uploads/2018/10/sessional-paper-sept.-2005-final.pdf

Republic of Kenya. (2012). *Towards a globally competitive quality education for sustainable development: Report of the task force.* Nairobi, Kenya: Ministry of Education. Retrieved from https://vision2030.go.ke/publication/towards-a-globally -competitive-quality-education-for-sustainable-development/

Ryan, R. M., & Deci, E. L. (2009). Promoting self-determined school engagement: Motivation, learning, and well-being. In K. R. Wentzel & A. Wigfield (Eds.), *Handbook on motivation at school* (pp. 171–196). New York, NY: Routledge.

Sawamura, N., & Sifuna, D. N. (2008). Universalizing primary education in Kenya: Is it beneficial and sustainable. *Journal of International Cooperation in Education, 11*(3), 103–118.

Sax, L. J., Arms, E., Woodruff, M., Riggers, T., & Eagan, K. (2009). *Women graduates of single sex and coeducational high schools: Differences in their characteristics and the transition to college.* Los Angeles, CA: Sudikoff Family Institute for Education & New Media, UCLA Graduate School of Education & Information Studies. Retrieved from http://heri.ucla.edu/PDFs/Sax_FINAL%20REPORT_ Sing_1F02B4.pdf

Shumow, L., & Schimdt, J. A. (2012, March). *Change in science self-efficacy of male and female adolescents: Role of gender and classroom context.* Poster presented at the biennial meeting of the Society for Research in Adolescence. Vancouver B.C.

Schwinle, A., & Turner, J. C. (2006). Striking the right balance: Students' motivational experiences and affect in upper elementary mathematics classes. *Journal of Educational Research, 99*(5), 271–293.

Shihusa, H., & Keraro, F. N. (2009). Using advanced organizers to enhance students' motivation in learning biology. *Eurasia Journal of Mathematics, Science and Technology Education, 5*(4), 413–420.

Sullivan, A., Joshi, H., & Leonard, D. (2010). Single-sex schooling and academic attainment at school and through the lifecourse. *American Educational Research Journal, 47*(1), 6–36.

Wachanga, S., & Mwangi, J. (2004). Effects of the cooperative class experiment teaching method on secondary school students' chemistry achievement in Kenya's Nakuru District. *International Education Journal, 5*(1), 26–36.

CHAPTER 9

AFRICAN AMERICAN MIDDLE SCHOOL GIRLS IN A COMMUNITY-BASED INFORMAL PROGRAM

Mining Rare Gems to Pursue STEM

Natalie S. King
Rose M. Pringle
Mayra L. Cordero
Natalie Ridgewell

Nationally, there is overwhelming concern about preparing the next generation of scientifically-literate American citizens to actively engage in science, technology, engineering, and mathematics (STEM) fields. The economy of the United States and preparedness to compete in the 21st century global market depends greatly on the expertise of all citizens in STEM (Bass, Contant, & Carin, 2008; National Academy of Sciences, 2007). To maintain the national security and global competitiveness, it is imperative that *all* students, including those from underrepresented populations in

Girls and Women of Color In STEM, pages 135–155
Copyright © 2020 by Information Age Publishing

America develop the necessary knowledge and skills to become functional citizens and promote their participation in STEM careers, thus ensuring the pipeline of related expertise. Knowledgeable citizens are better able to make informed and intentional decisions about public policy issues, which can influence choices made on a personal, state, and national level. It is for these reasons that all students should have access to high quality science education. The Framework for K–12 Science Education (National Research Council [NRC], 2013) was designed to help realize a vision for science and engineering education and recommends that students actively engage in inquiry-based science and engineering practices related to disciplinary core ideas (NRC, 2012). Educators agree that systematically engaging in such practices across K–12 would be effective in positioning students as STEM learners and in their developing a greater appreciation for the importance of the disciplines in their individual lives as citizens. However, the number of students who are motivated to pursue careers in STEM is currently low, especially amongst girls and underrepresented populations (Hanson, 2009; Hill, Corbett, & St. Rose, 2010). This situation has raised concerns among a range of stakeholders, and a number of educational and social reforms have tried to meet this need.

Some critical factors that have impacted whether or not girls pursue STEM professions are culturally prescribed gender roles, interests, and beliefs about their preparedness or ability to succeed. As such, many girls and women report that they are not interested in science and engineering. In a 2009 poll of youth ages 8–17 by the American Society for Quality, only 5% of girls said that they were interested in an engineering career, compared to 24% of boys. Another recent poll reported that 74% of college-bound boys between the ages of 13 to 17 stated that computer science or computing would be a good college major for them compared to only 32% of their female peers (WGBH Education Foundation & Association for Computing Machinery, 2009). From early adolescence, girls often express being less interested in math or science careers than boys (Lapan, Adams, Turner, & Hinkelman, 2000; Turner et al., 2008). Even girls and women who excel in mathematics often do not pursue STEM fields, and in studies of high math achievers, it was reported that women are more likely to secure degrees in the life sciences, social sciences, and humanities, than in math, engineering, physical science, or computer science (Lubinski & Benbow, 2006). Although girls are participating in high school science and math courses at the same rate as boys and are earning slightly higher grades in these classes, the number of females in STEM still remains low (NCES, 2010). Additionally, students from historically disadvantaged groups such as African American and Hispanic students, both females and males, are less likely to have access to advanced math and science courses in high school, which negatively affects their ability to enter and successfully complete STEM majors in college

(King & Pringle, 2019; May & Chubin, 2003). Attracting and retaining these groups of students will maximize creativity, diversity, and innovation in the STEM fields.

Many reform efforts in science and math education that seek to promote effective instruction still fail to meet the needs of underrepresented populations, especially African American girls (Pringle, Brkich, Adams, West-Olatunji, & Archer-Banks, 2012). Research suggests that the interdependent relationship between gender and race results in multiple burdens including marginalization and other social disadvantages (Patterson, Cameron, & Lalonde, 1996). Because of their race and gender, African American girls have to navigate the "double bind" if they pursue careers in the STEM fields. The term "double bind" refutes the myth that women of color are less interested in pursuing the STEM trajectory and provides insight into the inequities that they face as it relates to their underutilization and underrepresentation in STEM fields (Ong, Wright, Espinosa, & Orfield, 2011).

Current studies on gender differences in science indicate a closing of the achievement gap (Hill, Corbett, & St. Rose, 2010). However, disaggregation of the data in general, reveals that while girls are doing better overall, African American girls are consistently scoring below basic proficiency levels in science when compared to their White counterparts (NCES, 2010). Furthermore, research indicates that although African American girls are interested in science, they experience racism and sexism in the science domain and hence remain underrepresented in science programs and careers. The effects from these "isms" often discourage African American girls from pursuing careers in science. Therefore, those who remain highly motivated to continue studying science must swim against the tide (Hanson, 2009). While young African American women express more interest in STEM fields than do young White women (Hanson, 2009; Fouad & Walker, 2005), only a limited number of African American women pursue STEM careers, suggesting that other barriers are important for this community.

In addition to gender and race, achievement and interest are also shaped by the environment (Hill, Corbett, & St. Rose, 2010) but too often in middle schools, science curricula do not give substantial attention to the "cultural capital" of the learners. We appropriate the term cultural capital as economic position, class, race, occupation, and gender roles that are usually privileged and help people navigate their way through society (Bourdieu, 1993; Hinchey, 2010; Lareau & Calarco, 2012; Sensoy & DiAngelo, 2012; Yosso, 2005).

Research points to curricula that do not attend to the culture of learners as a major factor contributing to the underrepresentation of African American girls in STEM. While there has been substantial research and theorizing relative to the importance of attending to the cultural experiences of learners, these ideas are weakly realized in the enactment of the formal curriculum in the middle grades. In our informal learning STEM program described in this chapter, we seek to provide African American middle school girls with interactive and reform-based STEM learning experiences with an emphasis on science and their cultural resources. In the process, we investigate the impact of the program on their perception of themselves as learners and their receptiveness to STEM learning activities.

THE NEED FOR INFORMAL STEM PROGRAMS FOR AFRICAN AMERICAN MIDDLE SCHOOL GIRLS

Overall, middle school science education in the United States is in crisis. According to the 2010 National Assessment of Education Progress (NAEP) results, only 32% of eighth grade students performed at or above the "proficient" level in science (NCES, 2010). Unfortunately, if students have negative learning experiences in middle school, they become disengaged in STEM as they transition to high school and into college (Gallagher, 1994; Tai, Liu, Maltese, & Fan, 2006). Currently, the science instruction in middle school is still dominated by lecture, textbooks, and worksheets, which do not align with contemporary views of effective science instruction (Darby, 2005; Logan & Skamp, 2008; Marshall, Horton, Igo, & Switzer, 2009; Speering & Rennie, 1996). Additionally, this method of teaching does not support our current understanding of how learning occurs, as research suggests that students who have participated in inquiry-based science experience higher science achievement (Martin, Mullis, Foy, & Stanco, 2012). This more hands-on approach to science instruction embraces students as active participants in the learning process as recommended by current K–12 science education reform-based documents (Duschl, Schweingruber, & Shouse, 2007; National Research Council, 2012) and gives credence to the funds of knowledge or the "historically accumulated and culturally developed bodies of knowledge and skills essential for household or individual functioning and well-being" (Moll, Amanti, Neff, & Gonzalez, 1992, p. 133) that they bring to the learning environment.

Moreover, Hill, Corbett, and St. Rose (2010) discuss the importance of the learning environment and culture on cultivating the abilities and interests of underrepresented populations in STEM. They contend that in order to overcome the stereotypes that pervade our culture and encourage more participation in STEM, special attention must be given to the classroom and work environments. No longer are schools considered to be the almighty equalizer, but instead they are now implicitly and explicitly contributing to a great divide among children (Welner & Carter, 2013, p. 3). Due to their race and gender, African American girls often have difficulty navigating not only in schools, but more specifically, careers in the STEM fields. The barriers to pursuing this trajectory are compounded if these girls experience poverty in their home life. This intersection of race, gender, and low socioeconomic status creates a dire need for additional learning opportunities. Researchers suggest that informal learning environments, which utilize culturally relevant curriculum, can provide the appropriate space and place for these girls to reach their maximum potential (Anderson & Ellenbogen, 2012; Aubusson, Griffin, & Kearney, 2012; Slaton & Barton, 2012; Tal, 2012). Rennie (2007) defines informal science education as learning science outside of the formal school environment. Such experiences include museums, aquariums, zoos, media, home, and community-based programs. There is a general consensus that STEM enrichment programs positively impact women of color and provide safe and conducive spaces to validate their identities as scientists, mathematicians, and even engineers (Ong, 2005; Ong, Wright, Espinosa, & Orfield, 2011).

THE IMPACT OF POVERTY

Typically, fewer tax dollars are spent on the education of students living in areas of poverty when compared to students living in more affluent communities (Darling-Hammond, 2013). Because of the lack of funds and resources available to school districts in low-income areas, the facilities are more often dilapidated, the technology is out-of-date, and/or the buildings are unaccommodating in size and scope to fit the needs of students (Darling-Hammond, 2013; Gamoran, 2008; Ladson-Billings, 2013). In addition, poorly resourced schools often offer fewer or less challenging curriculum to their students, while wealthier school districts often provide advanced programs such as the Gifted and Talented, International Baccalaureate (IB), Honors Programs, and/or Advanced Placement (AP). All children need access to these resources, and at an early age, because delaying children's exposure to high-quality educational resources can cause long-term negative effects such as increased high school dropout rates, lower academic achievement, and higher rates of truancy and misconduct (Barnett & Lamy, 2013). The discrepancies in the access to, and level of, high-quality educational resources and exposure to STEM impede the opportunities for all students to reach their maximum potential and pursue this trajectory. Consistent with Rennie, Feher, Dierking, and Falk (2003) and Slaton and Barton (2012), we contend that informal STEM education, facilitated through a community-based program has the potential to support the academic development of African American learners especially middle school girls with the potential to impact their perceptions about their participation in STEM careers.

I AM STEM AS A S̲TEM ENRICHMENT PROGRAM EMBRACING CULTURE

I AM STEM, an informal learning program, was developed to serve K–12 students from low socioeconomic status with the intent to improve their interests, identity, and engagement in STEM education. This iteration of the program lasted for 5 weeks during the summer and most of the participants were from underrepresented populations. In this chapter, the researchers specifically focus on the experiences of the middle school girls enrolled in the S̲TEM Program. I AM STEM provided high-quality, hands-on experiences in technology, math, and engineering embedded within an inquiry-based science curriculum. We underlined the "S" in "STEM" because science was used as the vehicle to promote STEM by integrating technology, math, and engineering in scientific core concepts and practices. Our program could also be considered a S̲TEAM program because students utilized visual and performing *a*rts to demonstrate their understandings of *s*cientific, *t*echnological, *e*ngineering, and *m*athematical concepts. The enacted curriculum was developed and implemented in partnerships with a local university and volunteers from hospitals, businesses, and organizations related to STEM.

I AM STEM camp incorporated the culture of African American girls in the curriculum and created a safe and inclusive learning environment that embraced and valued their lives. Connections were made to the girls' lived experiences in ways that allowed abstract concepts to become more concrete and to form a foundation for learning the new knowledge and skills. Specific activities such as developing a cookbook for their peers and creating a solar oven encouraged their critical and creative thinking and afforded much flexibility in the ways that they shared their ideas and participated in various group activities to achieve set tasks. In other activities, efforts were made to harness and nourish the unique talents of each girl in ways that supported the development of learning communities within the informal setting. In addition, all instructors communicated high expectations of the girls while adhering to standards of high academic excellence.

Many of America's most struggling and marginalized students have not fully participated in the public education system. Scholars such as Ware (2006); Ladson-Billings (2009); Ross, Bondy, Gallingane, and Hambacher (2008); Siddle Walker (1996); Siddle Walker (2011); Hayes and Juárez (2012); Carter (2013); Ladson-Billings (2013); and Carter and Welner (2013); among many others, have long stated the characteristics and benefits of utilizing pedagogies that embrace and include the cultures of all students. We need culture-specific teaching to encourage the engagement of African American girls in science because culture is central to learning and shapes how we think and communicate with others. I AM STEM embraces culturally responsive teaching (CRT) in the curriculum to acknowledge, celebrate, and value culturally diverse students so that all participants have equitable access to education. CRT taps into the higher learning potentials of ethnically diverse students while cultivating their psychosocial and academic abilities (Gay, 2002, 2010). This approach to teaching allows teachers to teach to and through the strengths of diverse students by validating their cultural knowledge and experiences so that learning becomes relevant. CRT is multidimensional and includes the content, learning context, student–teacher relationship, classroom management, instructional techniques, and performance assessments (Gay, 2010). This form of teaching is empowering, liberating, and makes success a nonnegotiable and attainable goal. Teachers and students have the opportunity to tap into a range of diverse cultural knowledge, experiences, and perspectives to make authentic knowledge about different groups of people. CRT reshapes the curriculum so that it is student-centered and teachers transcend their own cultural biases to facilitate the learning and participation of all students. Furthermore, culturally relevant pedagogy (CRP) has similar tenets but its foundation is rooted in African American culture embracing a social justice stance. Ladson-Billings (1995) asserts that "culturally relevant pedagogy is designed to problematize teaching and encourage teachers to ask about the nature of the student–teacher relationship, the curriculum, schooling, and society" (p. 21). Additionally, CRP "explores teachers' identity, beliefs, attitudes, dispositions, and practice as a core correlation to student achievement and success" (Houchen, 2013, p. 97). Both of these practices serve to support diverse student learners and marginalized students in unique ways and are comprised of the following: building meaningful relationships with students; recognizing students' assets, rather than their deficits; knowing about students' cultures and backgrounds; creating meaningful relationships with parents, guardians, and the community; and helping students reach their "highest potential" (Carter, 2013; Carter & Welner, 2013; Delpit, 2006; Hayes & Juárez, 2012; Ladson-Billings, 2013; Siddle Walker, 2011; Ware, 2006).

I AM STEM used cultural referents to impart knowledge and skills and empower students emotionally, intellectually, and socially. We employed culturally CRT and CRP to support the learning needs of all students, but especially the African American middle school girls in the STEM content areas. The girls were encouraged to share their experiences in classroom discussions, activities, and projects. In I AM STEM camp, the African American middle school girls were engaged in STEM learning experiences that sought to provide them with hands-on experiences and introduced them to careers in STEM. They engaged in a range of high-quality activities that included learning experiences selected from the formal school mathematics and science curriculum and complemented with related activities provided by STEM personnel, interactions with scientists and engineers, and partnerships with a local university's College of Education and College of Engineering. Women often persist in STEM if they have role models and mentors, feel a sense of belonging, and can foster relationships with other women in the STEM field (Goodman Research Group, 2002; Seymour & Hewitt, 1997). As such, the culture and context of I AM STEM fostered a learning environment that was conducive for the African American middle school girls in several ways, and the volunteers and mentors in I AM STEM were all individuals of color in the STEM fields. In our study of I AM STEM, we explored the African American girls' experiences with STEM to determine the extent to which the informal learning experiences sparked their interests in STEM and encouraged them to potentially pursue careers in the STEM fields. Specifically, we asked the following questions: (a) "How do African American middle school girls experience an informal summer program that focuses on STEM and cultural relevance?" and (b) "What is the impact of a summer informal STEM program on African American middle school girls' perceptions of themselves as learners?" Investigating how they experienced the activities and documenting their perspectives on STEM have the potential to point educators in directions that can contribute to our approaches in fostering the development of the girls as STEM learners.

DATA COLLECTION AND ANALYSIS

The study was conducted during the summer of 2014, and the researchers used an interpretive design with multiple data sources that were consistent with established methods of qualitative research (Bogdan & Biklen, 1992; Glaser & Strauss, 1967; Miles & Huberman, 1994; Strauss, 1987). The research participants included African American middle school girls and their STEM instructors. The following data sources were used to respond to the research questions and also to evaluate the effectiveness of the program: informal observations with anecdotal field notes, focus group interviews, formal interviews with the science and technology instructors, and samples of students' work. The researchers observed students' interactions with selected volunteers who were session providers and mathematics, science, and technology instructors, as well as researchers' field notes and personal reflections, samples of students' work, and video and audio recordings of selected students' activities. Additional data were collected from the instructors and parents and used for formative feedback during the enactment of the project. That is, much value was placed on the voices of the parents and other caregivers as important participants as we sought to "mine the gems." The parents also offered rich descriptions of the effectiveness of the program activities and shared their perspectives on the impacts on their daughters and on the quality of the learning and social activities.

Engaging in Hatch's (2002) inductive data analysis, the research team identified themes, patterns, and relationships among the data sources and across domains as we unearthed connections between the themes. The following themes emerged: Becoming aware of STEM career options allowed the girls the opportunities to dream of possibilities and to project themselves into that image; culturally aware STEM teachers are able to embrace their roles as mentors and role models beyond being just mediators of content knowledge; and the informal STEM learning environment can provide African American middle school girls with a sense of belonging, exposure and interest in STEM careers, as they develop confidence in their ability to achieve in STEM.

UNEARTHING THE DREAMS: AFRICAN AMERICAN GIRLS' VISIONS FROM AWARENESS TO POSSIBILITIES CONNECTING TO THEIR CULTURES

The literature provides much evidence on the importance of accessing and harnessing students' funds of knowledge as an important element in effective teaching of students who are outside of mainstream culture (Barton & Tan, 2010; Moll, Amanti, Neff, & Gonzalez, 1992). Such funds of knowledge, according to educators, counter deficit perspectives and use their lived experiences as a knowledge base instead of a barrier (González, Moll, & Amanti, 2005). I AM STEM camp provided the facilitators and girls with a "hybrid space" (Barton & Tan, 2009; Barton, Tan, & Rivet, 2008) to merge their social worlds and science learning in an informal setting. In the formal school curriculum, teaching and learning are usually dictated by national and state mandates with teachers' practices directed to the high-stakes assessment used to determine their effectiveness. Even though I AM STEM had similar goals of increasing students' achievement levels, it operated outside the constraints of formal school curriculum; the activities in I AM STEM deliberately used the African American cultural experiences as the base for learning. Lessons selected for use in the program specifically included examples that tapped into the experiences of the girls.

For example, in the unit of study on light, the science teacher, Ms. Mays, designed a lesson that used ultraviolet (UV) light sensitive beads to teach the core concept of absorption of non-visible light. Before beginning the lesson, the instructor surfaced the girls' prior knowledge on their experiences with beads. The girls discussed how they wore beads in their hair when they were younger and shared stories of their mom, or "aunties," or cousins braiding their hair in different styles and putting beads on the ends. Once students were engaged and showed familiarity with the beads through their culture, the instructor taught a lesson about ultraviolet light

and the girls wrote their observations about the beads in their science journals inside and outside of the classroom, noting how the beads changed colors when they went outside in the sun. In addition, Ms. Mays allowed them
to rub sunscreen on the UV beads. She used this opportunity to ask about
their experiences with sunscreen. Many of them did not use sunscreen because as one student, Lana, remarked, "sunscreen is for White people."
However, a few of them were familiar with sunscreen and used it regularly.
Dena's reason for applying sunscreen was "because *I* don't wanna get any
blacker [*sic*]." Whatever the case, Ms. Mays used this activity to debunk the
myth that African Americans do not need sunscreen because they do get
sunburned. The girls were highly engaged in this lesson and openly shared
stories of their experiences in relation to the science lesson. They asked
questions and greeted this lesson with many laughs and a sense of self.

EMBRACING THEIR CARING NATURE AND FACILITATING DISCUSSIONS ABOUT THE FUTURE

During many of the science lessons, the African American girls repeatedly
talked about their future and goals. They understood their socioeconomic
status (SES) and the need to make choices in careers that will allow them
to be champions of their community. Many expressed their interest in careers related to health and social services and communicated a will to take
care of others. For example, Janice, in identifying a litany of possibilities
was clear that all of her selections would serve to help those in her community. She said she wanted to be a "doctor, or nurse, teacher, firefighter,
police, army man, and soccer player." When asked why so many careers,
she responded, "All of these things help people out and even in the sport."
Janice was clear in describing the inspiration of her choices: "In one of the
activities, with the doctors in the white coat, we had to look after a friend
who was in an accident and had a large wound. I had to get up and move
quickly to help... to get a piece of cloth and hold around the leg and other
body parts so that my friend will get well. That is what doctors and teachers
do... they get up and keep moving and help" (Personal communication,
July 31, 2014).

The math curriculum was also enriched with opportunities for the girls
to incorporate their culture and lived experiences. Instructors in integrating math into other subject areas, allowed the girls to share their aspirations
and dreams. For example, as part of the math lessons, our teachers talked
about the importance of ownership. Many of the girls at the camp lived in
apartments that their parent(s) rented. This sparked a conversation about
the difference between paying rent and a mortgage. The guest lecturer explained: "When you rent, you only have the right to live in that place for a

specified amount of time and there are no tangible benefits. Mortgage payments give you an ability to remain in that residence, build equity, and claim the interest payments on your taxes." Not only did this create awareness and spark many questions and conversations, the girls started talking about the mansions that they could see themselves living in and wanted better for themselves. They were then asked to design their dream home or business and draw it to scale. Once the girls drew their blueprints, they worked together in groups to build one home or business using cardboard. Not only was financial literacy incorporated into the math lessons, but also architecture, creativity, and engineering. The activities provided a safe space for the girls to share their experiences with money, their aspirations, and how they will achieve their goals. Dana stated, "When I was younger around 10 and growing up, I had a lot of money. I saved up my money to buy shoes. Half of the time I had to earn the money then, or on the other hand I was given money. I earned money by doing stuff that was asked and making people proud. Who gave me money was my mom, other family members, my neighbor, and adult friends of the family" (Personal communication, August 1, 2014). Experiences such as this in an informal setting have the potential to positively impact the formal setting where math is typically presented in a decontextualized manner and "non-dominant" students are often disconnected (Moll & Ruiz, 2002; Tan & Barton, 2012; Tate, 1994). Not only were students measuring and learning to draw to scale, but they were also motivated, worked together, had thoughtful and rich conversations related to the lessons, and offered words of encouragement to each other.

CULTURALLY AWARE STEM TEACHERS EMBRACED THEIR ROLES AS MENTORS BEYOND MEDIATORS OF CONTENT KNOWLEDGE

Making a Difference: The Role of Culturally Aware Teachers

From their teaching credentials, it was clear that the facilitators who enacted the formal STEM curriculum during I AM STEM had the ability to develop the students academically especially in their areas of expertise. Take the case of Nikki, she was grateful for the interactions she had with the instructors and noted,

> I think it increased my knowledge a little bit 'cause some stuff that I learned I didn't even know about. And then some of the stuff I didn't get, Mr. Rodney, Ms. Kandy, and everybody else who was there helped us. Like some of the math problems were really hard but Mr. Rodney went over it with us individually and that helped me [*sic*]. (Focus group interview, August 1, 2014)

The instructors took the time to address their needs, answer their questions, and stimulate their interests. Although the curriculum was rigorous and challenging, the teachers truly cared and presented the material in relevant and engaging ways.

Ms. Mays, a middle school science teacher volunteered her time in I AM STEM because she wanted to make a difference in the science learning of the girls. In one of her early interviews with project leaders, she said,

> I use many different strategies to support the learning of all my students. My interest in supporting the learning of African American girls began last year when I noticed that some of these girls worked really hard in class, however, they did not perform well on the standardized tests... participating in I AM STEM camp will give me an opportunity to get to know them in a different environment. (Personal communication, March 15, 2014)

Ms. Mays was quick to note her marginal successes with African American girls during the regular school year after this rich interaction with African American girls in I AM STEM camp during the summer. In fact, she recently conducted a teacher inquiry project as a capstone project in a graduate program that focused on pedagogical practices that sought to increase engagement and science achievement among the 6th grade students in her science classes who were from underserved populations. Furthermore, she consistently expressed a willingness to nurture and support the development of her cultural competence to better meet the needs of all her learners in the middle school in our local school district.

Cultivating Working/Learning Relationships With African American Girls

In a written reflection, Ms. Mays noted that developing strong respectful relationships with the African American girls takes time. The girls were more open and trusting of each other at first, than they were with the instructors. During one lesson, the girls discussed their career goals and if they will need science to achieve those goals. Below is an excerpt of the conversation:

> **Kelsi:** I want to be an endocrinologist, a diabetes doctor.
> **Janna:** Cool. Diabetes is in your blood and blood is connected to science.
> **Michelle:** What makes you wanna become a diabetes doctor?
> **Kelsi:** Because I have diabetes.
> **Janna:** My great grandma has diabetes because she ate a lot of sugar. Too many sweets and stuff.

Instructor: Is that the reason why you have diabetes?
      Kelsi: No.
Instructor: Why do you have diabetes?
   Michelle: Were you born with it?
      Kelsi: No I wasn't born with it. I got it when I was three. I have Type 1 diabetes.
   Michelle: Is that good or bad?
      Kelsi: It's better than Type 2.
      Janna: What's the difference between Type 1 and Type 2?
      Kelsi: Type 2 has to do with what you eat and Type 1 you have to take insulin.
   Michelle: Is that like when you have a port sitting right there? (points to stomach)
      Kelsi: No, I'm gonna get that when I turn 13 though. I hope.
      Janna: A port?
      Kelsi: Yeah it's a port that the insulin goes in your body so you don't have to keep taking the needle out. It stays [*sic*].

This conversation shifted from a discussion about Kelsi's career goals to her lived experience with diabetes. Many of the girls attend different schools and only know each other through I AM STEM camp. However, they quickly fostered strong relationships and friendships through conversations like the one above. Ms. Mays was not an active participant in many of their discussions and simply listened; however, the girls developed a strong and respectful relationship with her by the end of the program. Although the girls' conversations may not have been directly aligned to the learning goals for the day, this informal setting was a safe space for the girls to share and connect their own personal and cultural experiences within a science lesson. According to Cox-Petersen, Melber, and Patchen (2012), developing strong relationships in the classroom is a necessary element in increasing students' access to science. Teachers must create safe learning spaces where students feel valued and are given opportunities to ask questions and take initiative of their own learning. In one of Ms. Mays' reflections, she expressed: "It is difficult to build this type of relationship in such a short period of time. However, when Kelsi was given an opportunity to explain her experiences with diabetes, I noticed a change . . . Kelsi began to participate more in the class" (Teacher journal entry, July 20, 2014). Kelsi used her experiences as a foundation for discussion. Her peers learned what an endocrinologist was, why she wanted to become one, and the difference between Type 1 and Type 2 diabetes. Although the information was not fully accurate, this conversation resulted in Kelsi choosing the endocrine system for further investigation for the human body systems project.

The instructors also gained an awareness of their roles as mediators of more than just discipline-specific knowledge. They communicated high expectations and used student backgrounds and culture in enriching the curricular activities. The teachers encouraged creativity which was well-received by many of the girls as they compared formal school to I AM STEM:

> We get to do activities like you get to like make what you're learning. What you're learning about is like right there in front of your face. We just like go to our books in class [referring to school] and just read... Instead of you just tryna make something out of using stuff. She'll [Ms. Mays] bring different stuff that you didn't even know that you could make it out of. Like I didn't know that you could make atoms with gummy bears to show it [*sic*]. (Aaliyah, Focus group interview, August 1, 2014)

I AM STEM AS AN INFORMAL LEARNING SPACE WAS EFFECTIVE IN ENGAGING THE GIRLS AND PROVIDING OPPORTUNITIES FOR CREATIVITY AND SUCCESS WITHIN STEM

Freedom of Expression: Situating Myself in STEM With Acceptance

An important element in contemporary beliefs about how children learn is providing students with opportunities to surface their prior knowledge. The seamless integration of all the disciplines in STEM allowed the girls to connect their lived experiences and to express their learning in ways that were comfortable. In the technology class, the participants created stop motion videos about the scientific concepts that they learned about in the camp. For example, one group of students created a video about the molecules that make up air and another group explained how people see. Our data analysis revealed that the girls were aware and excited about the opportunities that valued their experiences. For example Nicki, a very articulate girl noted, "I liked doing the video thing. Stop motion. That was fun. I did the elements, atoms, gold, and the halogens. Ms. Mays gave us a book and I studied it a little bit. When we came back to do the iPads, I had a little more information. So it was fascinating" (Focus group interview, August 1, 2014). Her description of the experience was supported by the technology instructor: "They were able to decide what kind of video they wanted and quite a few of them wrote poems and songs and raps. Some of them were dancing in their video. So, I think by being responsive to their interests. I mean that's a culturally responsive practice [*sic*]" (Personal communication, July 25, 2014). Throughout the STEM curriculum and activities, the girls had freedom of expression where they could display their knowledge of STEM in ways that made sense to them and connected to their interests and values. Alan Sitomer (2008), a high school teacher and author used hip-hop as a "tool to revolutionize academic success for disengaged teens while building a bridge to the classic curriculum of the language arts class" (p. 20). Our goal as teachers and project developers should be to create curricula that validates students' personal interests and is accessible, engaging, and relevant.

Similarly, in the engineering component of the program, participants were challenged to build a dome and a chair out of newspaper incorporating mathematical and scientific concepts. With each activity, a task was given with the expectation that the students could share ideas and work together to solve problems. The instructors simply provided guidance and content that could facilitate the process. The girls could see the relevance of the learning activities and the applicability to their everyday experiences, connecting the girls to the larger socioeconomic and political context. Engaging them in a culturally relevant STEM curriculum in an informal setting forced them to think beyond the classroom walls. This program cultivated a sense of belonging and a space where the girls became more informed citizens. A written statement from a parent whose daughter came home and attempted to teach her one of the science lessons also evidenced this: "Even though she was not clear explaining the whole lesson, I was impressed that she was so interested in talking to me about what she learned in the class." Furthermore, her daughter expressed in an interview, "All people can do and practice basic science; everybody can be a scientist" (Personal communication, August 15, 2014). Not only did she feel confident enough to teach her mother, but she was interested and passionate enough about the lessons that she continued to talk about it when she went home. Aaliyah took her freedom to express her understanding of the STEM concepts beyond the summer program.

I'm Ready for This: There's Room at the Top for Me

Even though the curriculum was rigorous, the girls appreciated the experience and the perceived benefits that their participation in I AM STEM would have when they went back to school. The girls openly expressed their feelings of preparedness for school and were excited about the success they were going to experience. Shayla wrote in her science journal: "The whole month I feel like I am very prepared for this year and I feel very ahead." During a focus group interview, Tiffany stated, "The math tests and reading tests and all these tests—It's getting us prepared for what's coming when we start back school. We will already have a little bit of knowledge about what we're gonna learn. I am excited about being ahead . . . I would like to come here every year because it increases my knowledge for the next grade level so that I can be ahead of the class [*sic*]" (August 1, 2014). There was a new sense of confidence and great anticipation to bring the knowledge that they have gained to the formal science classroom. These findings suggest that utilizing a culturally relevant curriculum in an informal learning environment can not only promote and sustain African American middle school girls' interest in STEM, but also provide a model that could be modified in a formal K–12 classroom.

IMPLICATIONS FOR PRACTICE

This study revealed implications for engaging underrepresented populations in STEM in informal settings and how this knowledge can inform pedagogy and student learning in formal contexts. Although an enacted curriculum may be inquiry-based, there is a strong need to include culturally relevant pedagogy (Ladson-Billings, 1995) to facilitate academic and personal growth in African American girls. Teachers have to see the limitations of the curriculum and understand that for African American girls to effectively learn science, they must find ways to incorporate culturally relevant practices in their middle school science classrooms. There is a great need to engage all learners in effective science to develop skills, attitudes and values necessary to function as scientifically literate citizenry—make decisions that will positively impact their lives based on understanding and sound reasoning, for employment in the sciences and in technology, and to enhance America's competitiveness and position in the global marketplace.

The researchers have developed 6 strategies that have the potential to increase the level of participation of African American girls pursuing the STEM trajectory in the formal setting so that the process of mining these rare gems can extend beyond the informal learning environment:

1. *Encourage critical and creative thinking:* Allow flexibility in the way ideas are constructed and communicated. Support various methods for diverse learners to communicate what they have learned so that they are able to think outside of the box. This initiative will help to create an inclusive environment that encourages a genuine interest in science.
2. *Leverage students' cultural strengths:* Take the time to evaluate the students' existing knowledge and use it as a foundation for future knowledge construction. Connect to the lived experiences and interests of underrepresented populations to allow abstract concepts to become more concrete. Teachers need to ensure that activities and lessons are contextualized and culturally relevant. This action

will promote both academic and social achievement and reduce the missed opportunities diverse students experience in the science classroom.

3. *Self-fulfilling prophecy is real:* Have high expectations for all students in your science and math classrooms. Do not lower your standards and be sure to embrace their interests and energy. Employ multi-dimensional forms of assessments so that you can get an accurate picture of their abilities and needs.

4. *Establish learning communities:* Learning communities provide a safe space where students can collaborate and "do" science and math. Feel at ease to learn along with your students. Become a mentor and facilitator of the classroom allowing space for diverse populations to discover the knowledge for themselves.

5. *Implement instructional conversations:* Have clear learning goals for these conversations so that students are purposefully engaged in dialogue. This goal will give all students an opportunity to exchange ideas and make connections with the science knowledge and their real life experiences. Critical conversations can also foster a collaborative learning environment.

6. *Science should be fun and engaging all year long:* Do not reserve the experiments and hands-on activities until after high-stakes tests. Instead, use these engaging activities to create meaningful learning opportunities throughout the year. All students, including underrepresented populations, enjoy being a part of science and math and "doing" so that they are not bored. Include and nourish their unique talents, cultures, and contributions in hands-on activities year round.

REFERENCES

Anderson, D., & Ellenbogen, K. M. (2012). Learning science in informal contexts–Epistemological perspectives and paradigms. In B. Fraser, K. Tobin, & C. McRobbie (Eds.), *Second international handbook of science education* (pp. 1179–1187). Dordrecht, Netherlands: Springer.

Aubusson, P., Griffin, J., & Kearney, M. (2012). Learning beyond the classroom: Implications for school science. In B. Fraser, K. Tobin, & C. McRobbie (Eds.), *Second international handbook of science education* (pp. 1123–1134). Dordrecht, Netherlands: Springer.

Barnett, W. S., & Lamy, C. E. (2013). Achievement gaps start early: Preschool can help. In P. L. Carter & K. G. Welner (Eds.), *Closing the opportunity gap: What America must do to give every child an even chance* (pp. 11–22). New York, NY: Oxford University Press.

Barton, A. C., & Tan, E. (2009). Funds of knowledge and discourses and hybrid space. *Journal of Research in Science Teaching, 46*(1), 50–73.

Barton, A. C., & Tan, E. (2010). We be burnin'! Agency, identity, and science learning. *The Journal of the Learning Sciences, 19*(2), 187–229.

Barton, A. C., Tan, E., & Rivet, A. (2008). Creating hybrid spaces for engaging school science among Urban middle school girls. *American Educational Research Journal, 45*(1), 68–103.

Bass, J. E., Contant, T. L., & Carin, A. A. (2008). *Methods for teaching science as inquiry.* Boston, MA: Pearson.

Bogdan, R., & Biklen, S. K. (1992). *Qualitative research for education.* Boston, MA: Allyn & Bacon.

Bourdieu, P. (1993). *The field of social production.* New York, NY: Columbia University Press.

Carter, P. L. (2013). Student and school cultures and the opportunity gap: Paying attention and to academic engagement and achievement. In P. L. Carter & K. G. Welner (Eds.), *Closing the opportunity gap: What America must do to give every child an even chance* (pp. 143–155). New York, NY: Oxford University Press.

Carter, P. L., & Welner, K. G. (2013). Achievement gaps arise from opportunity gaps. In P. L. Carter & K. G. Welner. (Eds.), *Closing the opportunity gap: What America must do to give every child an even chance* (pp. 1–10). New York, NY: Oxford University Press.

Cox-Petersen, A., Melber, L. M., & Patchen, T. (2012). *Teaching science to culturally and linguistically diverse elementary students.* Boston, MA: Pearson.

Darby, L. (2005). Science students' perceptions of engaging pedagogy. *Research in Science Education, 35*(4), 425–445.

Darling-Hammond, L. (2013). Inequality and school resources: What it will take to close the opportunity gap. In P. L. Carter & K. G. Welner (Eds.), *Closing the opportunity gap: What America must do to give every child an even chance* (pp. 77–97). New York, NY: Oxford University Press.

Delpit, L. (2006). *Other people's children: Cultural conflict in the classroom.* New York, NY: The New Press.

Duschl, R. A., Schweingruber, H. A., & Shouse, A. W. (2007). *Taking science to school: Learning and teaching science in grades K–8.* Washington, DC: National Research Council.

Fouad, N. A., & Walker, C. M. (2005). Cultural influences on responses to items on the Strong Interest Inventory. *Journal of Vocational Behavior, 66*(1), 104–123.

Gallagher, S. A. (1994). Middle school classroom predictors of science persistence. *Journal of Research in Science Teaching, 31*(7), 721–734.

Gamoran, A. (2008). Persisting social class inequality in US education. In L. Weiss (Ed.), *The way class works* (pp. 169–179). New York, NY: Routledge.

Gay, G. (2010). *Culturally responsive teaching: Theory, research, and practice.* New York, NY: Teachers College Press.

Gay, G. (2002). Preparing for culturally responsive teaching. *Journal of Teacher Education, 53*(2), 106–116.

Glaser, B. G., & Strauss, A. L. (1967). *The discovery of grounded theory: strategies for qualitative research.* Chicago, IL: Aldine.

González, N., Moll, L. C., & Amanti, C. (2005). *Funds of knowledge: theorizing practice in households, communities, and classrooms.* Mahwah, NJ: Erlbaum.

Goodman, I. F. (2002). *Final report of the women's experiences in college engineering (WECE) project.* Cambridge, MA: Goodman Research Group.

Hanson, S. L. (2009). *Swimming against the tide African American girls and science education.* Philadelphia, PA: Temple University Press.

Hatch, J. A. (2002). *Doing qualitative research in education settings.* Albany: State University of New York Press.

Hayes, C., & Juarez, B. (2012). There is no culturally responsive teaching spoken here: A critical race perspective. *Democracy and Education, 20*(1), 1–14.

Hill, C., Corbett, C., & St. Rose, A. (2010). *Why so few? Women in science, technology, engineering, and mathematics.* Washington, DC: AAUW.

Hinchey, P. H. (2010). *Finding freedom in the classroom: A practical introduction to critical theory* (revised ed.). New York, NY: Peter Lang.

Houchen, D. (2013). "Stakes is high" culturally relevant practitioner inquiry with African American students struggling to pass secondary reading exit exams. *Urban Education, 48*(1), 92–115.

King, N. S., & Pringle, R. M. (2019). Black girls speak STEM: Counterstories of informal and formal learning experiences. *Journal of Research in Science Teaching, 56*(5), 539–569.

Ladson-Billings, G. (1995). Toward a theory of culturally relevant pedagogy. *American Educational Research Journal, 32*(3), 465–491.

Ladson-Billings, G. (2009). *The dreamkeepers: Successful teachers of African American children.* San Francisco, CA: Wiley.

Ladson-Billings, G. (2013). Lack of achievement or loss of opportunity? In P. L. Carter & K. G. Welner (Eds.), *Closing the opportunity gap: What America must do to give every child an even chance* (pp. 11–22). New York, NY: Oxford University Press.

Lapan, R. T., Adams, A., Turner, S., & Hinkelman, J. M. (2000). Seventh graders' vocational interest and efficacy expectation patterns. *Journal of Career Development, 26*(3), 215–229.

Lareau, A., & Calarco, J. M. (2012). Class, cultural capital, and institutions: The case of families and schools. In S. T. Fiske & H. R Markus (Eds.), *Facing social class: How societal rank influences interaction* (pp. 61–86). New York, NY: Russell Sage Foundation.

Logan, M., & Skamp, K. (2008). Engaging students in science across the primary secondary interface: Listening to the students' voice. *Research in Science Education, 38*(4), 501–527.

Lubinski, D., & Benbow, C. P. (2006). Study of mathematically precocious youth after 35 years: Uncovering antecedents for the development of math-science expertise. *Perspectives on Psychological Science, 1*(4), 316–345.

Marshall, J. C., Horton, R., Igo, B. L., & Switzer, D. M. (2009). K–12 science and mathematics teachers' beliefs about and use of inquiry in the classroom. *International Journal of Science and Mathematics Education, 7*(3), 575–596.

Martin, M. O., Mullis, I. V. S., Foy, P., & Stanco, G. M. (2012). *TIMSS & PIRLS international study center.* Chestnut Hill, MA: Boston College.

May, G. S., & Chubin, D. E. (2003). A retrospective on undergraduate engineering success for underrepresented minority students. *Journal of Engineering Education, 92*(1), 27–39.

Miles, M. B., & Huberman, A. M. (1994). *Qualitative data analysis: An expanded source book*. Thousand Oaks, CA: SAGE.

Moll, L. C., Amanti, C., Neff, D., & Gonzalez, N. (1992). Funds of knowledge for teaching: Using a qualitative approach to connect homes and classrooms. *Theory into Practice, 31*(1), 132–141.

Moll, L., & Ruiz. (2002). The schooling of Latino children. In M. M. Suárez-Orozco & M. M. Páez (Eds.), *Latinos: Remaking America* (pp. 362–374). Berkeley: University of California Press.

National Academy of Sciences. (2007). *Rising above the gathering storm: Energizing and employing America for a brighter economic future*. Retrieved from https://www.nap.edu/catalog/11463/rising-above-the-gathering-storm-energizing-and-employing-america-for

National Center for Education Statistics. (2010). *An introduction to NAEP National Assessment of Educational Progress*. Washington, DC: Institute of Education Sciences.

National Research Council. (2013). *Next generation science standards: For states, by states*. Washington, DC: National Academic Press.

National Research Council. (2012). *A framework for K–12 science education: Practices, crosscutting concepts, and core ideas*. Washington, DC: The National Academies Press.

Ong, M. (2005). Body projects of young women of color in physics: Intersections of gender, race, and science. *Social Problems, 52*(4), 593–617.

Ong, M., Wright, C., Espinosa, L. L., & Orfield, G. (2011). Inside the double bind: A synthesis of empirical research on undergraduate and graduate women of color in science, technology, engineering, and mathematics. *Harvard Educational Review, 81*(2), 172–209.

Patterson, L. A., Cameron, J. E., & Lalonde, R. N. (1996). The intersection of race and gender: Examining the politics of identity in women's studies. *Canadian Journal of Behavioural Science/Revue canadienne des Sciences du comportement, 28*(3), 229–239.

Pringle, R. M., Brkich, K. M., Adams, T., West-Olatunji, C., & Archer-Banks, D. A. M. (*2012*). Factors influencing elementary teachers' positioning of African American girls as science and mathematics learners. *School Science & Mathematics, 112*(4), 217–229.

Rennie, L. J. (2007). Learning science outside of school. In S. K. Abell & N. G. Lederman (Eds.), *Handbook of research on science education* (pp. 125–167). Malwah, NJ: Erlbaum.

Rennie, L. J., Feher, E., Dierking, L. D., & Falk, J. H. (2003). Toward an agenda for advancing research on science learning in out-of-school settings. *Journal of Research in Science Teaching, 40*(2), 112–120.

Ross, D. D., Bondy, E., Gallingane, C., & Hambacher, E. (2008). Promoting academic engagement through insistence: Being a warm demander. *Childhood Education, 84*(3), 142–146.

Sensoy, Ö., & DiAngelo, R. (2012). *Is everyone really equal? An introduction to key concepts in social justice education*. New York, NY: Teachers College Press.

Seymour, E., & Hewitt, N. M. (1997). Talking about leaving: Why undergraduates leave the sciences. *Contemporary Sociology, 26*(5), 644.

Siddle Walker, V. (1996). *Their highest potential: An African American school community in the segregated South.* Chapel Hill: University of North Carolina Press.

Siddle Walker, V. (2011, October). *23rd Annual Benjamin E. Mays Lecture: Second-class education.* Speech presented at the 23rd Annual Benjamin E. Mays Lecture at Georgia State University, Atlanta, GA. Retrieved from: http://www.youtube.com/watch?v=rMVTQ0iFUMs

Sitomer, A. (2008). *Teaching teens & reaping results*: Stories, strategies, tools & tips from a three-time Teacher of the Year Award winner.* New York, NY: Scholastic.

Slaton, A., & Barton, A. C. (2012). Respect and Science Learning. In B. Fraser, K. Tobin, & C. McRobbie (Eds.), *Second international handbook of science education* (pp. 513–525). Dordrecht, Netherlands: Springer.

Speering, W., & Rennie, L. (1996). Students' perceptions about science: The impact of transition from primary to secondary school. *Research in Science Education, 26*(3), 283–298.

Strauss, A. L. (1987). *Qualitative analysis for social scientists.* Cambridge, England: Cambridge University Press.

Tai, R., Liu, C., Maltese, A., & Fan, X. (2006). Planning early for careers in science. *Science, 312*(5777), 1143–1144.

Tal, T. (2012). Out-of-school: learning experiences, teaching and students' learning. In B. Fraser, K. Tobin, & C. McRobbie (Eds.), *Second international handbook of science education* (pp. 1109–1122). Dordrecht, Netherlands: Springer.

Tan, E., & Barton, A. (2012). *Empowering science and mathematics education in urban schools.* Chicago, IL: The University of Chicago Press.

Tate, W. (1994). Mathematics standards and urban education: Is this the road to recovery? *Educational Forum, 58*(4), 380–390.

Turner, S. L., Conkel, J. L., Starkey, M., Landgraf, R., Lapan, R. T., Siewert, J. J.,... Huang, J. (2008). Gender differences in Holland vocational personality types: Implications for school counselors. *Professional School Counseling, 11*(5), 317–326.

Ware, F. (2006). Warm demander pedagogy: Culturally responsive teaching that supports a culture of achievement for African American students. *Urban Education, 41*(4), 427–456.

Welner, K. G., & Carter, P. L. (2013). Achievement gaps arise from opportunity gaps. In P. L. Carter & K. G. Welner (Eds.), *Closing the opportunity gap: What America must do to give every child an even chance* (pp. 1–10). New York, NY: Oxford University Press.

WGBH Education Foundation & Association for Computing Machinery. (2009). New image for computing: Report on market research. Retrieved from https://www.nsf.gov/awardsearch/showAward?AWD_ID=0753686

Yosso, T. J. (2005). Whose culture has capital? A critical race theory discussion of community cultural wealth. *Race, Ethnicity and Education, 8*(1), 69–92.

CHAPTER 10

LATINA PARENTAL INVOLVEMENT

Contributions to Persistence in STEM Fields

Katie Brkich
Alejandro J. Gallard Martinez
Alma D. Stevenson
Gillian Bayne
Wesley Pitts
Beth Wassell
Lorena Claeys
Belinda Bustos Flores

Increasing the representation of minorities in science, technology, engineering, and mathematics (STEM) fields has long been noted as an important goal by those concerned with equitable educational outcomes (e.g., Hagedorn & Purnamasari, 2012), especially because they contribute to strengthening interest and competence in secondary and college science course content (Achieve Inc., 2013), diversify the STEM workforce, and

Girls and Women of Color In STEM, pages 157–181
Copyright © 2020 by Information Age Publishing

improve the overall economic well-being of the nation. The issue of addressing the shortage of minorities (including women) in STEM fields has not escaped politicians' notice, with the U.S. Congress seeking to direct additional tax dollars into addressing the shortages through several pieces of legislation over the past 3 years: HR 4483 (Broadening Participation in STEM Education Act, 2012), HR 4833 Women and Minorities in STEM Booster Act of 2014, HR 5031 (STEM Education Act of 2014), HR 1020 (STEM Education Act of 2015), for example (Congress.Gov, 2015). At the time of this publication, only the STEM Education Act of 2015 had been made into law. Relating particularly to the STEM educational outcomes, Cole and Espinoza (2008) noted that of the science and engineering degrees awarded in 2005, Latin@s[1] earned only 7.3% of these—and of that portion, only 37% were earned by women. Additionally, of the 33% female recipients of STEM doctoral degrees awarded in 2006, only 2.5% of them were awarded to Latinas (College Board, 2010). Increasing the number of STEM degrees earned by Latinas is an important equity concern, and as minority student representation in STEM fields alone contributes to improved minority student performance (Hagedorn, Chi, Cepeda, & McLain, 2007), studying the features prompting Latinas to be resilient and persist is a valuable endeavor.

In considering the reasons for which some Latin@ students are resilient and persist in STEM fields, the role of parental support is of tremendous importance. Latin@ students may face a host of obstacles entirely different than those of White Americans in the pursuit of their education—such as immigration status, socioeconomic status, and language barriers (Baquedano-López, Alexander, & Hernandez, 2013; Jasis & Ordoñez-Jasis, 2012). Understanding the types of support Latin@ parents offer their children and how their children acknowledge this support may prompt a revisiting of White-normalized understandings of what constitutes "good parenting" in education. Understanding how Latin@ students characterize beneficial parental support may ultimately lead to challenging deficit views of parental involvement and eliminating dangerously self-fulfilling prophecies such as stereotype, or social identity threat (Steele, Spencer, & Aronson, 2002).

LITERATURE REVIEW

Parent involvement (PI) matters. This is a basic tenet of schooling in the United States. Hoover-Dempsey and associates (2005) found that an abundance of research positively links PI and school "success," including higher student grades, test scores, and participation in advanced courses, as well as lower retention and drop-out rates. PI has also been linked to important motivational, cognitive, social, and behavioral attributes like sense of personal competence and efficacy for learning, perceptions of personal control over school outcomes, self-regulation of knowledge and skills, adaptive school behavior, engagement with school and schoolwork, and beliefs about the importance of education (Hoover-Dempsey et al., 2005). These more personal processes and attributes that support student achievement were further shown to be susceptible to direct parent and teacher influence.

A Continuum of Parent Involvement/Engagement

Parental engagement with children's learning is not the same as PI with children's schools—nor should it be judged on that basis, even though it frequently is. There exists an important continuum from PI in and with schools to parent engagement with children's learning (Goodall & Montgomery, 2014). This is important, as parents of socioeconomically disadvantaged or ethnic and racial minority backgrounds may find engagement with schools difficult, but still are involved actively in their children's learning and education (Turney & Kao, 2009). However, the level of participation expected of some parents may not be the level at which they feel comfortable participating.

On one end of the continuum are instances where parents are involved in activities initiated and run by the school. One example is the "Meet the Teacher Night," at which parents move from teacher to teacher with little time for conversation beyond introductions. These nights are set up to provide a one-way flow of information from teacher to parent with minimal opportunity for dialogue. Other examples include parents being invited into the classroom to speak, read, or "help the teacher," each of which may result in parents taking off from work or getting a babysitter. Unfortunately, the planning of some of these activities often reflects a lack of consideration for diverse families' situations which may serve as obstacles to participation in school activities. Further, there often exists a disconnect between the lived experiences of White, middle-class teachers and their students of socioeconomically disadvantaged or ethnic and racial minority backgrounds, which can also lead to teachers making erroneously prejudicial assumptions about their parents (Horvat, Weininger, & Lareau, 2003; Rudney, 2005).

The next level of the continuum is parental involvement with schooling, defined by an interchange of information between parents and the school, but where the focus is schooling or the processes that surround learning. Parent–teacher conferences are an example of this level of the continuum, as parents and teachers share control of the flow of information. Parents helping with homework also fits here, as parents can choose how they help, but "the nature, direction, and content of the learning is set by the school" (Goodall & Montgomery, 2014, pp. 404–405). The largest barriers to involvement by parents of socioeconomically disadvantaged or ethnic and racial minority backgrounds appear to be their own negative experiences with schooling, as well as their academic and linguistic abilities with the content.

The final level of the continuum is parental engagement with children's learning. This allows for the most parental agency. At this level, parents' actions may be influenced by the school, but the choice of action rests with the parent. Parents' involvement is characterized by their own perceptions of their role as parents. Examples include providing supplemental learning opportunities for their children—such as after-school lessons, membership in sports, social, or religious organizations, or visits to informal learning locations like museums. Even further, this level exemplifies the role parents have played since their children's birth in teaching them to walk, talk, or interact with others (Goodall & Montgomery, 2014). The ways parents engage with their children's learning will vary significantly based on socioeconomic factors and cultural norms. For this reason, at all levels of this continuum, it is important to remember that the contexts of race, class, and family life have significant influence on the schools', teachers', and researchers' perspectives on parental involvement.

This continuum, as it moves from PI in schools to parent engagement with learning, represents a shift in emphasis and relational agency. For the purposes of this work, we recognize that the terms "parental involvement," "parental participation," "school–family partnerships," and "parental engagement" are often used to mean a variety of traditional and nontraditional approaches schools and teachers take toward the role of parents in their children's schooling. Unfortunately, the various interpretations of these terms by school personnel are often consistent with their own particular social location, institutional agendas, or visions of schooling, which often leads to situations in which White, middle-class teachers and administrators wonder at a perceived lack of parental involvement by certain groups (Jasis & Ordoñez-Jasis, 2012).

Our aim is to contribute to a growing body of critical sociocultural views of parent–school relationships that expands traditional notions of parental involvement and frames ethnic minority parents as productive and engaged participants in their children's schooling and education. We believe the broader understanding of parental engagement will create environments where all parents' support, no matter who observes it or where it takes place, is appreciated as "good" parenting. Therefore, we adopt Kim's (2009) definition of parental engagement as "parents' engagement in their children's lives to influence the children's overall actions" (p. 89) and any actions taken by parents towards that goal is included in evaluating parental engagement.

"Good" Parents

Vincent (1996) showed that teachers have a paternalistically limited view of what makes a "good" parent and that when parents are not "good," they need to be taught or trained. Crozier (1998) noted that teachers/schools have their own strategies for imposing their own "ideal type" of parent into the PI discussion. He further explains:

> Parental involvement in the normative sense is, in fact, underpinned by the specification of the "good" parent: constructed on the principles of universalism in the sense that they must be shared by everyone regardless...Although in another sense, the "good" parent also remains unspecified, there is an implication that the "good" parent can be equated with being white and middle class. (p. 333)

United States policy has often regulated the relationships between parents and schools through a normalizing perspective informed by middle-class values, which fails to consider more complex family arrangements and their economic situations, leading to negative views of parents of color (Baquedano-López et al., 2013).

Existing research indicates that traditional models of parental involvement—such as helping children with homework, attending parent–teacher conferences, and participating in organizations such as parent–teacher associations—only advance unequal distributions of cultural capital and resources favoring the privileged (Jasis & Ordoñez-Jasis, 2012). Traditionally valued parental involvement structures have thus been criticized as inadequate in involving families of color (Auerbach, 2009). Chief among the concerns is that for parents of nondominant students, they advance an undertone of remedy and deficit, which has led to use of "anti-deficit rhetoric" (or a discourse of "strengths") in more recent PI discussions and models (Baquedano-López et al., 2013). And while a rhetoric of strengths may present an expanded view of the family's role in education and schooling, Auerbach (1995) warns that while such a shift may come out of a neo-deficit ideology. Such "strength-based" models continue to exist in a deficit framework, in which parents whom school personnel view as uninvolved are seen as failing in their parental responsibilities, with no attention paid to the social injustices affecting them.

Recognizing the implications of the previous paragraph should justify prompting teachers and school personnel to examine not only the ways in which PI is evaluated, but also the role that their personal biases and assumptions play into those evaluations. As Crozier (2001) explains, "The rules of the game within the context of school are based upon [predominantly White and middle class] teachers'...definitions of involvement, partnership, cooperation, trust, and deference" (p. 334). Parents of socioeconomic disadvantage or from ethnic and racial minority backgrounds may not be knowledgeable of these rules, or if aware are heavily discouraged from playing the game in which their contributions are not seen as "good" (de Carvalho, 2000; Harris & Goodall, 2008).

Emerging research additionally shows that forms of parental engagement with learning which happens outside of school and in everyday life may be even more important than traditional models (Baquedano-López et al., 2013). This shows the significance of informing both parents of color and school personnel that it is engagement with learning—not involvement in schooling—which stands most to benefit the child. This work consequently seeks to show the ways in which Latina students acknowledged their Latin@ parents' engagement with their learning as being critical to their successes in pursuing STEM fields.

Latin@ Cultures and Parental Engagement

When discussing "culture," we use Sewell's (1999) conceptulizations of culture as both a "theoretically defined category or aspect of social life" and "a concrete and bounded world of beliefs and practices" (p. 39). We therefore operationalize *culture* to mean "a sphere of practical activity shot through by willful action, power relations, struggle, contradiction, and change" (p. 44). In researching Latin@ culture, we are attempting to examine the lived experiences of a rich and diverse multitude of realities from various backgrounds and locations. We use the term Latin@ to represent a vast segment of the population that identifies as having Latin American origin or ancestry, and view Latin@ as a category that is made of, in very general terms, a shared bond of culture, language, and history, as well as inequality and oppression (Ortiz & Ordoñez-Jasis, 2005). However, in an attempt to intentionally avoid over-generalizing all Latin@s, we focus on specific Latin@ individuals and families.

METHODS

Research Frameworks

Several research frameworks were used in examining the data for this study. Organized into the categories philosophical, analytical, and methodological frameworks, these frameworks included Vygotsky's (1978) framework for social constructivism, socioculturalism (Lemke, 2001); Sewell's (1999) conceptualizations of sociocultural theory. Yin's (2009) case study methodology was used as the methodological framework.

Philosophical Framework

As culture is not something defined statically (Sewell, 1999), examining the parental involvement of the study participants from a singular definitional lens would be inappropriate. Furthermore, given that culture is something which is contextually determined and socially mediated, applying a singular definitional lens of Latin@ culture to the study participants' experiences of parental involvement in their education as STEM learners—even when attempting to do so within a framework of cultural responsiveness (e.g., Ladson-Billings, 1995, 2007)—would stand the risk of colonizing the study participants' experiences strictly for the researchers' ends (see esp., Smith, 1999). For these reasons, this chapter adopts a Vygotskyan (1978) framework of social constructivism regarding both how it conceptualizes the notion of culture itself and how it applies in analyzing participating Latin@s' educational experiences with parental involvement. Vygotsky's (1978) framework for social constructivism holds that knowledge—and in the case of this research study, culture—is substantively real but is created cogeneratively and is shared amongst those participating in the knowing.

Analytical Framework

In addition to Vygotsky's (1978) philosophical framework of social constructivism, we have also adopted the analytical framework of socioculturalism (Lemke, 2001) in constructing an understanding of participating Latinas' experiences of parental involvement in their education as STEM learners. Sociocultural theory is one which "proposes that such cooperative human activity [as education] is only possible because we all grow up and live within larger-scale social organizations or institutions: family, school, church, community center" (Lemke, 2001, p. 296). This notion runs alongside Sewell's (1999) conceptualizations of culture as something theoretical, something transitory specifically devoted to semiotics and meaning-making, as well as loosely integrated, often contradictory, and always contested "distinct worlds of meaning" (p. 52).

Methodological Framework

Because typifying and generalizing Latin@ cultures as applied to participating Latinas' experiences of parental involvement in their education as STEM learners could be seen as running counter to Sewell's (1999) conceptualizations of sociocultural theory by failing to acknowledge the distinctiveness of each of the participants' experiences, we employed Yin's (2009) case study methodology. Case study methodology was the most appropriate approach to use because it holds at its core the acknowledgement of between-case differences as being central to their uniqueness and importance. Furthermore, the purpose of case study methodology is not to create population-wide theoretical generalizations. Though Yin (2009) encourages the use of cross-case analysis methods leading to the generation of a tentative typology of cases—which our research does—this tentative typology is not intended as a means of generalization, but rather to help understand between-case similarities and differences.

Study Participants

Existing research has demonstrated that gendering-othering in STEM fields occurs as early as elementary school, impacting whether girls—specifically girls of color—self-select out of STEM fields (Clewell & Campbell, 2002; Franz et al., 2010; Pringle, Brkich, Adams, West-Olatunji, & Archer-Banks, 2012; West-Olatunji et al., 2008; Wilkins, Gaskin, Kuluhiwa, & Sodersten, 2008). Engaging Latinas who had persisted through toward the end of their high school years or into their university studies would provide the most useful and relevant data regarding Latina resilience and persistence in STEM fields. Additionally, because such Latinas would have years of experience being resilient in the face of gender-based or culture-based discrimination, they could provide the richest of insights into their experiences with parental involvement and how this parental involvement contributed to their persistence as STEM learners. To this end, we recruited three Latinas—two at the end of their high school years and one pursuing a master's degree at a regionally accredited doctoral/research university in the southeastern United States. To protect their confidentiality, we assigned each pseudonyms—Dalia, Karmen, and Laurita.

Dalia

At the time of collection, Dalia—hailing originally from Elena, Mexico—was an aspiring and ambitious high school student who had set her sights on a career as a veterinarian. An honors student across all of her science classes, Dalia reported at the outset of the study that the non-Latin@ age-peers and adults in her life were surprised when she announced her career ambitions, as "they don't expect that from us Hispanics."

Karmen

A woman self-identifying as Puerto Rican and African American, Karmen was a graduate student pursuing a master's degree in physics education at a regionally accredited doctoral/research university in the southeastern United States. Though she reported occasionally "having a hard time with [her] master's stuff," she noted she would always take these struggles as opportunities to be successful.

Laurita

Born in Ixil, Mexico, Laurita was a high school senior who stood to be the first in her family not only to graduate high school but also to attend college. Though she faced considerable cultural discrimination regarding her parents' occupations—her father was a landscaper and her mother a housekeeper, leading age-peers to ask: "Are you going into lawn care?" or "Are you going to be a housekeeper?" Laurita noted her successes in AP Calculus and AP Physics would be that much more rewarding.

Data Collection

Over the course of one semester, the research team interviewed each participant three times for 1 hour using semi-structured interviews. Following Rubin's and Rubin's (2012) model of responsive interviewing, each interview partly informed the questions researchers posed in subsequent interviews. The interviews focused on five major strands of inquiry: (a) on what it means to be a girl, (b) on what it means to be Latin@, (c) on their educational and career aspirations, (d) on the obstacles they faced to their educational success, and (e) on the roles their parents played in their education. Collectively, approximately nine hours of digitally recorded audio transcribed onto approximately 170 pages constituted the research study's analyzed data corpus.

Data Analysis

Consistent with our methodological framework, we employed Yin's (2009) four stages of case study analysis. First, we attended to all the pertinent evidence at hand—and *only* the evidence which was pertinent to the role Latin@ parental involvement contributed to Latina resilience and persistence in STEM fields. Second, we considered possible rival interpretations to the data. Third, we restricted our analysis only to those elements we felt were most central to our case study, minimizing effectively the study's vulnerability to the possibility that "the main issue was being avoided because of possible negative findings" (p. 161)—a step consistent with our theoretical proposition. Finally, as former classroom teachers who have taught Latin@ students, we employed our own prior experience in refining our findings.

In addition to the above four stages of analysis, which we applied to each case—bound at the level of the individual Latina participant—we progressed through Yin's (2009) cross-case analysis method. The aim in using this method was the consideration of whether our three cases "reflect[ed] subgroups or categories of general cases—raising the possibility of a typology of cases that can be highly insightful" (p. 160). This cross-case analysis was both useful and appropriate in highlighting the differences between our participating Latinas' experiences of parental involvement in their education and in considering the impacts of culture on Latin@ parental involvement.

RESULTS

Dalia's, Karmen's, and Laurita's educational experiences showcase substantial challenges to the assertion that parents from families of color—particularly immigrant and migrant Latin@ families—are either uninvolved in or do not care about their children's education. Contrarily, while these girls' mothers and fathers did not all participate in ways characterized typically by White middle-class female teachers as "parental involvement" (e.g., attending parent–teacher conferences, participating in PTOs, or supporting school fundraisers), they all demonstrated substantial engagement with, interest in, and support of their daughters' academic pursuits. The ways in which Dalia's, Karmen's, and Laurita's parents' participated in their girls' education demonstrate how lived experience, circumstance, and values all contribute to a culturally informed system of support.

A Culture of High Expectations

One major fashion in which parents supported their daughters' education was through high academic expectations. Given existing bodies of research substantiating the link between high expectations and high levels of achievement, this represents an important source of support for their success. Dalia's parents, for example, made their expectations for overall success clear, even though Dalia described herself as lazy:

> My parents have always, I'm pretty sure their dream is for one of us, my sisters and me to be the valedictorian, they've always said they'd be really proud of us if we were the number one student. I mean, I would like for it but I'm pretty lazy, it's a lot of work.

Karmen's mother demonstrated similar expectations for success, but also connected these expectations to the responsibility of doing one's best work. On this, Karmen noted that "the only time it [her lack of success] was my fault was if I did not try my hardest. If I tried my hardest, it wasn't my fault anymore." Likewise, Laurita's parents established a culture of expectations in which a "'B' is okay, not great" as Laurita stated, adding, "We've been pushed to exceed the normal" in comparison to others.

Outperforming the Majority

The support of high expectations for their daughters was also specific for certain culturally driven purposes. First, all three girls stressed the importance of outperforming their White or English-speaking peers simply to keep pace, particularly as it relates to educational and work opportunities. Karmen addressed this point succinctly, along with the role her mother played in raising her awareness:

> My mother taught me regardless, you have to be better than everyone else because if you're equal to, (name) from Virginia used to say in reference to Black people and White people, say you're equal to the White person that is sitting next to you in the room. They might get the job over you because they are White, you need to make sure that does not happen by excelling [sic] them and being the absolute best of the best.

Laurita's resilience in the face of discrimination equally prompts a desire to outperform her age-peers—something which she attributes directly to her father. Regarding how she occasionally feels positioned, she stated that she doesn't like it "when people put me in a certain mindset" and that she takes pleasure in breaking them of their prejudices. By demonstrating to those who Other that they can not only keep pace but even outperform them, these Latinas demonstrated that success as a result of high expectations can in fact be an act of cultural defiance—all attributable to their parents.

Outperforming Their Parents and Brothers

The second major venue by which two parents—Dalia's and Laurita's—pushed high expectations for academic success comes by connection specifically to their gender. Both spoke on the importance of succeeding academically as a means of enjoying well-paying careers—but rather than this being a sufficient goal, it was phrased in contrast to doing better than their parents and not having to endure the hard physical labor to which many Latino men are relegated. Dalia spoke on how her father—a painter by trade—comes home tired all the time from work and how her mother pushes her to go to college so that her children can "succeed more than their parents." Likewise, Laurita noted that her father stressed consistently the importance of succeeding in school, such as if she "didn't do well [she'd] be stuck fitting into the stereotypical position of a Latino workplace." To drive this issue home, both Dalia's and Laurita's parents provided their daughters experiences working the kinds of jobs they do—Dalia helping her mom with housecleaning and Laurita working alongside her father on a landscaping site at age ten or alongside her mother in a finishing factory—as a means of a cautionary tale.

As a corollary to this, Laurita's parents pushed her to succeed in school so that they wouldn't have to endure a life of physically laborious work—but their gender, in comparison to those of Latino men generally or their brothers specifically, served as a particular push. Speaking on Latin@s generally, she noted that parents typically view their daughters to be frailer than their sons as noted in the following statement:

> Most parents see oh the boys they can do construction work, they can do hard laborious work, but it's the girls they're more worried about. I guess because they see us as more fragile or something, so it's the parents are putting more pressure on their girls so they achieve something greater.

In comparison to her brothers, Laurita noted that her parents pushed her a lot harder than they did her brothers—something she generalized to the Latin@ culture as a whole:

> Parents' focus right now for my generation is on girls. Get them an education, a job that's safe. You know that we won't struggle with. And I think most of it has to do with the moms. Because most of the moms now work in laborious, hard work and they don't want that for their daughters.

While all parents want their children to be successful, the extent to which Latinas are pushed to excel more than their male counterparts—on the grounds of avoiding backbreaking labor—appears entirely culturally grounded.

Supporting the Supportive Family

The final major venue by which the participating Latinas expressed the importance of succeeding academically was to be able to support the families which supported them in their formative years. While Dalia, Karmen, and Laurita never noted that their parents pushed them to be successful so that their daughters could care for them in their later years, nevertheless the girls spoke on the importance of being able to care for their families. Dalia, who had as a goal becoming an anesthesiologist, noted that "if I try hard, I'll be able to have a better life than my parents did and I know that one time when I get older I'll be able to pay them back for everything they helped with." Karmen noted that this desire to help family is "a cultural standard," and that it is important for girls "to set aside your own issues and be able to put up everything you have to help someone else that is there and needs your help. "

Laurita, while she did not speak on the importance of supporting her parents in their waning years, spoke on the importance of taking an active supporting role in the present. Though she noted her parents did much to push her substantially more than her younger brothers (aged 7 and 11), she took it upon herself to take care of them—much in the same way that her parents push her through high expectations. She frequently babysits them, "feed[s] them and make[s] sure they do their homework right." Likewise, as her parents pushed her to be successful—grounded in their concern that she would not have to work backbreaking hours in a labor-intensive job—so too she paid it forward with her brothers:

> Because I don't feel like just because they're boys they should get laid back. They have to work just as hard. If [the parents] are pushing the girls hard, they'll have to compete against the girls and so I push them hard too, because you need education regardless if you're a boy or a girl.

As her parents had high academic expectations for her, so too she held these for her brothers—because she wanted them to avoid the laborious work she was working to avoid as well.

Emotional Support

In addition to creating a culture of high academic expectations for their daughters, the parents of this study's participants ensured that they also provided for their daughters' emotional needs. Dalia, Karmen, and Laurita spoke of the roles their parents played as emotional nurturers, essential to academic success. Knowing that they can always count on their parents to care for them—without fail—provides them with a bulwark of emotional security. Dalia noted that her mom "is always going to be there for me" and is her "cover," while her father is her "protector." Karmen's mother likewise provided her such "cover" when her teacher unjustly accused her of cheating and again provided such "cover" in the form of relaxed parental discipline so as not to stifle or crush her daughter's spirited determination to succeed. Laurita's parents were described similarly; her mother provided the "cover" of unwavering emotional support, her father unwavering physical support and protection.

Supportive Shoulders and Listening Ears

One particular way in which the parents of two participants—Dalia and Laurita—were discussed as providing their daughters emotional support was to provide a safe and caring environment in which they could vent their frustrations. In Dalia's case, this manifested as advice on resolving problems she could not resolve on her own:

Like if I tell him [her father], "I'm having problems with something in school," like say, "I think the teacher's not doing something or not giving me enough time on a test." Like last year, he would be like, "Well, you probably need to go talk to him and say, 'Can you give me more time?'" And on the other hand, my mom would say, "Well, you need to work faster. You need to work up to his speed. If he wants you to work faster, you need to work faster, 'cause my teachers, they told me to work fast." That's how she would bring her story in when my dad would say, "Oh, you need to talk to your teacher."

While one could misinterpret this interaction as being one in which Dalia's parents were unwilling to provide support, in fact they were providing her with a safe space to vent her frustrations and advice on how to proceed while ensuring she retained the agency to solve her problems on her own. In this way, Dalia's parents were providing her with the means to resolve them without interfering, maximizing her resilience and problem-solving skills.

Laurita's parents also provided a very similar safe space, acting both as sources of advice as well as a release valve. She refers to her parents as her "main supporters," that they are "always there" for her and that she "can count on them" to provide a safe space:

Like when I have a bad day at school, I can tell my mom and she won't judge me and stuff, and she'll be like, "I understand." And she thinks she has an input, she'll tell me about it and not let me just rant to her. . . . [And her dad] he's like the comfort, he'll just hug me and he'll just sit there. And sometimes he'll give me his advice but just most of the time we just sit there and relax.

Stating that she "likes to complain a lot" and that—depending on Laurita's mood—her parents either will let her vent or will provide advice as needed, the relationship between Laurita and her parents is one such that she has unwavering emotional support with the knowledge that if she wanted additional layers of support, she had access to them. Additional support came only when solicited, denoting her parents' trust in her abilities either to solve her own issues or to seek out help without it being forced upon her.

Delaying Dating

Another way in which the participating Latinas' parents supported them emotionally was to create an environment in which dating—while not inherently frowned upon—was something they should delay until they completed their schoolwork. In terms of parenting this appears to be a norm across many Latin@ families; Laurita spoke of delaying dating as being a "very strong rule" which applied not only to her but to her Latina age-peers as a means of promoting academic success.

Acknowledging that such discouragements from dating might seem overly restrictive—Dalia spoke of overhearing many of her non-Latina age-peers wistfully wish, "Oh, I wish I had a boyfriend"—both Dalia's and Laurita's parents' admonitions for their daughters to delay dating serves as another form of emotional support. This is evident in the approach they take regarding the topic of dating all together. Rather than taking a stance of either "not now, not ever" or "not now, but later," these girls' parents have taken the stance of "not now, but later with our continued love, support, and encouragement." Laurita recounts her parents' position:

> Well, see, they phrase it funny, 'cause they're like, "Oh, whenever you get a boyfriend, we'd like to know. After you finish school, you know." So they imply that they will be okay with you getting a boyfriend, but after school.

Ultimately the emotional support which comes from this encouragement for Laurita to delay dating is one in which her parents do not exclusively forbid her from dating at her current age, but trust that she will make the choices which are in her own best interest. The trust seems to apply in Dalia's case—that she will wait until college or when she feels that it is "the appropriate time"—a position she has internalized.

Immunity to Insults

A final way in which participants' parents provided them with emotional support was to develop their resilience in the face of insults—and not to care what others think of them. Acknowledging the extensiveness of prejudice facing them, Dalia identified her ethnicity as a target, stating "I guess people go by stereotypes and people believe because you're Latino you can't be something." Karmen contrarily identified her gender as a target, particularly relating to her ability to succeed in STEM fields, noting that

> sometimes in school they talk about, "Oh, girls tend not to do well in this" or "They do better with this, and they do better in that." And for some people that gets ingrained in their head and if they struggle a little bit, they think that's what the problem is: "I'm a girl, I'm not going to be able to do this math as well as a boy."

Finally, on top of the targets of ethnicity and gender, Laurita noted that status as an immigrant—especially one for whom English was not a first language—stood as an issue her detractors exploited in their attacks:

> It was just like the typical I guess "What Mexicans do." Like, my dad's in lawn care—"Just like every other Mexican. Are you going to go into lawn care?" And we do housekeeping, me and my mom, so they're like, "Oh, are you going to grow up to be a housekeeper?"

Thus at nearly every turn, these strong young women were positioned as those who would not be able to succeed.

If one were operating from a deficits perspective, one might be tempted to note that the study participants—non-White, female, and from ELL/migrant families—had three strikes against them barring them from success. However, from a sociocultural perspective, these strong young women's families—and their parents in particular—provided them with the emotional support and training necessary to use these insults to fuel their successes as an act of defiance. Rather than breaking down and demonstrating weakness, Karmen spoke on the lesson her mother taught her: "I never let anything personal [such as her ethnicity or gender] affect me in school and that's for the simple fact that my mom taught me not to take my personal life out into the street."

Laurita similarly noted that her father in particular taught her that life wasn't fair. No matter what, one had to endure—*Lo que no mata, engorda*—and that teaching her to brush off insensitive remarks or to inure herself to them was the best way to endure and become successful. Dalia concurred, noting that from a very young age she faced insults based on her gender, ethnicity, and even height—and that the best way to counter these insults effectively was to rise above them: "I just ignore everyone else now, I just blow them off or say a smart comment to them." In this way, their parents built in them emotional resilience by teaching them—as Dalia's did—that they attend school "to learn, not to worry about what other people think about you."

School-Related Support

In contrast to typical White middle-class English-speaking notions of parental involvement—attending parent–teacher conferences, participating in PTOs, or supporting school fundraisers—this study's participants' parents nevertheless remained steadfastly engaged in promoting their daughters' education in a direct fashion. The reasons perhaps the typical White middle-class English-speaking classroom teacher overlooks their engagement may be grounded in cultural, ethnic, or racial differences to which these teachers may not be attuned or may be prejudicially predisposed to overlook. However, these parents provide a clear amount of school-related support for their Latina daughters.

Financial Investment

Though participants have previously spoken on the importance their parents placed on their education, the Latinas interviewed spoke substantively on the direct financial investments their parents made in their education. As Dalia's, Karmen's, and Laurita's parents worked long hours in arduous manual labor occupations, the girls were very aware of a dollar's value and its connection to work. Laurita spoke on how the relationship between her father's physically demanding work and the dinner table was always clear: "The food you're eating comes from your dad's work." As such, the girls' parents made sure that when it came to their schooling, they did not want for anything. Dalia noted the contrast between herself and her more financially secure peers:

> They never point out their financial issues to us because they don't want us to worry, but I guess when I compare the ways my friends live to how I live, I mean I know we're not missing anything 'cause we have everything, but they have more.

While her peers had more of everything she had, it is important to note that Dalia felt all of her needs were met, and that her parents bore the additional expense of her extracurricular activities.

Laurita similarly discussed the financial investments her parents made to ensure she was successful. Recounting an incident in which internet access went out at her home, she told of how her parents incurred substantial expense to ensure she could succeed:

> If I ever need anything it doesn't matter how hard the situation is, they're going to make it work. Our internet went off the last 2 months and I needed it for my virtual school class so they bought me a laptop so I could use the Wi-Fi at like the library and stuff.

Though Laurita's parents' solution was an expensive one, it was one which nevertheless allowed her mobility and freedom to work wherever she felt most comfortable—be it at a friend's place, a coffeehouse, or the library. Aside from this extreme event, Laurita acknowledged her parents would provide transportation wherever she needed to be regarding school or other activities and pick her up when done.

Study Sentinels

Another way in which participants' parents provided direct school-related support was to ensure that their daughters always completed their homework. This element of support comes in the form of immediately holding their daughters accountable to their academic responsibilities. For Dalia, someone who self-identified as having "a bad habit of not doing [her] homework," this direct parental supervision—"they always checked that I did my homework"—likely contributed substantially to her academic success. Laurita noted equally that her parents made sure she completed her homework, going so far as to keep a direct tab on what the teacher had assigned:

> [My mother] likes to get informed about what needs to get done. She'll be like "I heard…," 'cause my brothers like to lie to her and be like, "I don't have to do this," but if she goes, she'll be like, "Oh, your teacher says you have homework this day, this day, this day," and so they can't get away with it.

These girls' parents, by ensuring they monitored the completion of their daughters' homework, provided the direct school-related support teachers typically expect of parents.

While typical White middle-class English-speaking teachers may expect parents to help their children *directly* on their homework—with answers and such—this is not always how things work in Latin@ families. Acknowledging the possible existence of a language barrier or of differing levels of education—"It's not that they don't want to help their kid with their homework…my parents didn't have a high level of education"—participants ultimately benefited from the supervision their parents provided and from the trust their parents placed in them to complete their assignments on time. In Dalia's case, this trust resulted in her developing individual perseverance with regards to academic problems, relying on her parents only in a safety net capacity: "First, I analyze the problem and see if I can solve the problem myself. I'm going to solve it myself, and if I can't I'll go to my parents." In Laurita's case, she herself is entrusted by her parents to help her brothers with their homework and ensure it gets done in addition to her own homework assignments.

Attendance of Functions

One final way in which participants' parents provided direct school-related support was to attend parent–teacher organization meetings and to conference with their daughters' teachers on an individual basis. Their attendance of these functions is framed through a Latin@ lens, with hegemonic positioning shaping substantially the ways in which these interactions take place. This issue is particularly clear regarding the way in which Latin@ parents based their decisions on whether to attend meetings or not on the ways in which they were able to present themselves. Laurita, speaking of her mother, presents the situation thusly:

> My mom will never, ever go to a school meeting right from her job. She will go home, rush, shower, and change into something before she [goes]. They feel uncomfortable compared to the White population, how they're dressed.

While acknowledging that her parents do not feel ashamed of their jobs, Laurita nevertheless speaks to the awareness her parents have in terms of being socially stigmatized and positioned by those in positions of power. As Latin@ parents are keenly aware of these feelings of being positioned, they may face challenges as to whether to attend these school functions:

My mom taught us to be really clean and neat and that we need to be present-able because people will judge you on the way you dress. Even if you really don't care about how you dress, you need to present yourself properly. So that's how my mom, 'cause my mom is one of those people who will not go anywhere like school wise, and if she has to, she doesn't like to stay very long.

While participants' parents provided them with bulwarks of emotional support—teaching them to slough off insults—they nevertheless acknowl-edged the importance of always putting their best face forward. This may occasionally have precluded them from attending some functions—not be-cause they did not support their daughters' education, but rather because they did not want their daughters to risk additional potential stigmatization.

Parent–teacher meetings were also shaped by features of Latin@ culture or family life discussed previously here. Dalia noted that her parents would never avoid going to such meetings, as they had high expectations of her academically and were quick to show how proud of her they were. Fur-thermore, linguistic differences served as no obstacle to Dalia's mother in attending parent–teacher conferences: "My mom's like, 'I don't care if I can't speak it, I can understand it, so you guys can't stop me from going to parent–teacher conferences.'" In Laurita's case, both parents worked as a team to go to school functions, ensuring all events were covered. Because of the high value participants' parents placed on their daughters' education, they made sure to be present at school functions—not to make themselves be seen, but rather to ensure they had all the information necessary to best help their children.

DISCUSSION AND IMPLICATIONS

In this chapter, we postulate a typology of parental supports involving the promotion of a culture of high expectations and the provision of both emo-tional and school-based supports. A graphic representation of this typol-ogy can be seen in Figure 10.1. Drawing on the experiences of three Lati-nas—Dalia, Karmen, and Laurita—who demonstrated substantial success in STEM fields, our work explores the ways in which their perceptions of their parents' involvement in their education helped to promote their per-sistence in STEM fields. Understanding how Latin@ parents involve them-selves with, engage in, and support their children's education is an impor-tant step in challenging discriminatory and hegemonic narratives of what constitutes proper parental involvement in education—narratives which may serve as obstacles to Latina students' achievements within STEM fields. As Diana's, Karmen's, and Laurita's experiences indicate, Latin@ parents take a considerable interest in seeing their daughters succeed by providing them a combination of high academic expectations, emotional supports,

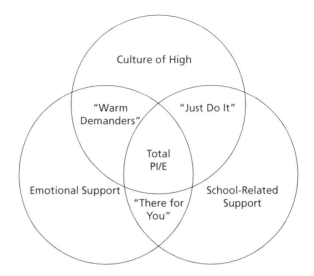

Figure 10.1 Typology of parental involvement/engagement.

and school-related supports that in many cases is not visible because of the filters created by a hegemony on proper parental involvement as illustrated in Table 10.1.

As existing research has shown that students who have parents engaged and involved in their education tend to have greater performance outcomes (e.g., Hoover-Dempsey et al., 2005), purposefully acknowledging the valued contributions Latin@ parents make in these areas within a sociocultural

TABLE 10.1 Participants' Discussions on Latin@ Parental Involvement			
Types of Support	**Dalia**	**Karmen**	**Laurita**
A Culture of High Expectations	X	X	X
Outperforming the majority	X	X	X
Outperforming their parents and brothers	X		X
Supporting the supportive family	X	X	X
Emotional Supports	X	X	X
Supporting Shoulders and Listening Ears	X		X
Delaying dating	X	X	X
Immunity to insults	X	X	X
School-Related Supports	X		X
Financial investment	X		X
Study sentinels	X		X
Attendance of functions	X		X

framework is crucial. However, Crozier (2001) noted that this is often not done for families falling outside dominant sociocultural groups:

> Given the apparent importance attributed to parents in the education of their children, one would expect the need to harness the support of the parents of these underachieving children in a concerted manner. However, the adoption of a "one size fits all" approach to parental involvement prevails. (p. 330)

Likewise, Baquedano-López and associates (2013) argued that traditional considerations of parental involvement typically "foster individualistic and school-centric approaches" which "do not engage the intersections of race, class, and immigration, which are relevant to the experiences of many parents from nondominant backgrounds" (p. 149). Rather than adopting singular "one size fits all" notions of what constitutes parental involvement, employing Latin@ parents' habitus and social capital as a lens (Bourdieu, 1977) may serve to break down barriers rather than erecting further obstacles in Latin@ students' paths.

As Vincent (1996) indicated, teachers have a rather narrow view of what constitutes "good parenting" and tend to advocate racist and paternalistic measures as remedies to perceived deficiencies. Without prompting reconsiderations through a sociocultural lens and accounting for the social capital Latin@ parents bring with them in their parent–child educational supports, Latin@ students stand to suffer substantially. Furthermore, given the ease with which overworked classroom practitioners may elect to make assumptions about groups of parents not resembling them in terms of worldview, experience, or social capital (Goodall & Montgomery, 2014; Rudney, 2005), remediating deficit views of Latin@ parental support in education takes on an even more pressing dimension.

The typology of Latin@ parental supports we developed was based on our participating Latinas' educational experiences summarized in Table 10.2. This data indicate that though their parents may not have participated in all of the ways their teachers would have desired, they were exceptionally engaged in their daughters' educations and brought the social capital at their disposal to bear in prompting their daughters to be resilient and to persist in their careers as STEM learners. In providing a culture of high expectations, in which Latin@ parents pushed their daughters to achieve more than they had and to exceed the performance of their age-peers, this study's participants' parents provided accessible and relevant examples against which they could position themselves and futures toward which they could work. In providing emotional supports, the Latina participants' parents trusted their daughters to make responsible and adult decisions, all while contributing to their resilience to withstand external prejudices through freely given advice. Finally, the Latina participants' parents

TABLE 10.2 Typology of Parental Involvement/Engagement

Typology	Supports	Summary
Total PI/E	All three types of support	The parent provides all three types of parental involvement/engagement. Parental support of this typology is the most comprehensive and covers the cognitive, emotional, and school-based needs of the student.
"Warm Demanders"	High expectations plus emotional support	The parent creates an environment where students are given high expectations to succeed, but also emotional support to help reach those expectations. Parental support of this typology provides cognitive and emotional support, but lacks the connection to school-based needs.
"There for You"	Emotional support plus school-related support	The parent is there for their child both emotionally at home and when needed at school. Parental support of this typology provides affective and real-world support, but lacks parent-led drive and high expectations for success.
"Just Do It"	School-related support plus high expectations	The parent expects much of their child, so provides both high expectations and school-related support when needed. Parental support of this typology is present and demanding, but does not provide the needed emotional support.
High Expectations		The parent provides high expectations for their child to outperform themselves (the parent) and the majority (of child's peers).
Emotional Support		The parent creates a home environment that is emotionally supportive of the student's affective needs.
School-Related Support		The parent offers school-based support representative of more traditional ideas of parental involvement.

provided what teachers tend to consider "good parent" involvement, including attending parent–teacher conferences, allowing their daughters to participate in extracurricular STEM related activities, helping with homework, and providing material support.

As scholars concerned with the sociocultural dimensions of science education and with improving the educational experiences of Latina students, promoting a deeper understanding of how Latin@ parents support their children's education is imperative. Promoting a sociocultural understanding of Latin@ parents' involvement in, engagement with, and support of Latin@ children's education through the application of their social capital may serve to redress some of the injustices associated with normativized views of parental involvement and the obstacles these views place in students' pathways to success.

NOTE

1. We use Latin@ as a gender-inclusive term instead of Latino/a, as the latter presupposes a position of male primary importance and female secondary importance. However, we use Latino and Latina when needing to be gender-specific.

REFERENCES

Achieve Inc. (2013). *Next generation science standards: For states, by states.* Retrieved from http://www.nextgenscience.org

Auerbach, E. (1995). Deconstructing the discourse of strengths in family literacy. *Journal of Reading Behavior, 27*(4), 643–661.

Auerbach, S. (2009). Walking the walk: Portraits in leadership for family engagement in urban schools. *School Community Journal, 19*(1), 9–32.

Baquedano-López, P., Alexander, R. A., & Hernandez, S. J. (2013). Equity issues in parental and community involvement in schools: What teachers need to know. *Review of Research in Education, 37*(1), 149–182.

Bourdieu, P. (1977). *Outline of a theory of practice.* Cambridge, England: University of Cambridge Press.

Broadening Participation in STEM education act, United States House of Representatives, 112th Congress, 2nd Sess. (2012).

Clewell, B. C., & Campbell, P. B. (2002). Taking stock: Where we've been, where we are, where we're going. *Journal of Women and Minorities in Science Education, 8*(3/4), 255–284.

College Board. (2010). *National and state summary reports.* Retrieved from https://research.collegeboard.org/programs/ap/data/archived/2010

Cole, D., & Espinoza, A. (2008). Examining the academic success of Latino students in science, technology, engineering, and mathematics (STEM) majors. *Journal of College Student Development, 49*(4), 285–300.

Congress (n.d). H.R.5031–STEM Education Act of 2014. Retrieved from https://www.congress.gov/bill/113th-congress/house-bill/5031/text

Congress Government. (2015). H.R. 1020-STEM education act of 2015. Retrieved from https://www.congress.gov/bill/114th-congress/house-bill/1020/text

Crozier, G. (1998). Parents and schools: Partnership or surveillance? *Journal of Educational Policy, 13*(1), 125–136.

Crozier, G. (2001). Excluding parents: The deracialisation of parental involvement. *Race, Ethnicity and Education, 4*(4), 329–341.

de Carvalho, M. E. (2000). *Rethinking family-school relations: A critique of parental involvement in schooling.* New York, NY: Routledge.

Franz, D. P., Thompson, N. L., Fuller, B., Hare, R. D., Miller, N. C., & Walker, J. (2010). Evaluating mathematics achievement of middle school students in a looping environment. *School Science and Mathematics, 110*(6), 298–308.

Goodall, J., & Montgomery, C. (2014). Parental involvement to parental engagement: A continuum. *Educational Review, 55*(4), 399–410.

Hagedorn, L. S., Chi, W., Cepeda, R. M., & McLain, M. (2007). An investigation of critical mass: The role of Latino representation in the success of urban community college students. *Research in Higher Education, 48*(1), 73–91.

Hagedorn, L. S., & Purnamasari, A. V. (2012). A realistic look at STEM and the community colleges. *Community College Review, 40*(2), 145–164.

Harris, A., & Goodall, J. (2008). Do parents know they matter?: Engaging all parents in learning. *Educational Research, 50*(3), 27–289.

Hoover-Dempsey, K. V., Walker, J. M. T., Sandler, H. M., Whetsel, D., Green, C. L., Wilkins, A. S., & Closson, K. (2005). Why do parents become involved? Research findings and implications. *Elementary School Journal, 106*(2), 105–130.

Horvat, E. M., Weininger, E. B., & Lareau, A. (2003). From social ties to social capital: Class differences in the relations between schools and parent networks. *American Educational Research Journal, 40*(2), 319–351.

Jasis, P. M., & Ordoñez-Jasis, R. (2012). Latino parental involvement: Examining commitment and empowerment in schools. *Urban Education, 47*(1), 65–89.

Kim, Y. (2009). Minority parental involvement and school barriers: Moving the focus away from the deficiencies of parents. *Educational Research Review, 4*(2), 80–102.

Ladson-Billings, G. (1995). But that's just good teaching! The case for culturally relevant pedagogy. *Theory Into Practice, 34*(3), 159–165.

Ladson-Billings, G. (2007). Foreward. In J. Settlage & S. A. Southerland (Eds.), *Teaching science to every child: Using culture as a starting point* (pp. xiii–xix). New York, NY: Routledge.

Lemke, J. L. (2001). Articulating communities: Sociocultural perspectives on science education. *Journal of Research in Science Teaching, 38*(3), 296–316.

Ortiz, R. W., & Ordoñez-Jasis, R. (2005). Leyendo juntos (reading together): New directions for Latino parents' early literacy involvement. *Reading Teacher, 59*(2), 110–121.

Pringle, R. M., Brkich, K. L., Adams, T. L., West-Olatunji, C., & Archer-Banks, D. A. (2012). Factors influencing elementary teachers' positioning of African American girls as science and mathematics learners. *School Science and Mathematics, 112*(4), 217–229.

Rubin, H. J., & Rubin, I. S. (2012). *Qualitative interviewing: The art of hearing data* (3rd ed.). Thousand Oaks, CA: SAGE.

Rudney, G. L. (2005). *Every teacher's guide to working with parents.* Thousand Oaks, CA: Corwin Press.

Sewell, W. H., Jr. (1999). The concept(s) of culture. In V. Bonnell & L. Hunt (Eds.), *Beyond the cultural turn: New directions in the study of society and culture* (pp. 35–61). Oakland: University of California Press.

Smith, L. T. (1999). *Decolonizing methodologies: Research and indigenous peoples.* New York, NY: Zed Books.

Steele, C. M., Spencer, S. J., & Aronson, J. (2002). Contending with group image: The psychology of stereotype and social identity threat. *Advances in Experimental Psychology, 34*, 379–440.

Turney, K., & Kao, G. (2009). Barriers to school involvement: Are immigrant parents disadvantaged? *Journal of Educational Research, 102*(4), 257–271.

U.S. Congress. (2015, October 7). STEM Education Act of 2015. Retrieved from https://www.congress.gov/bill/114th-congress/house

Vincent, C. (1996). *Parents and teachers: Power and participation.* New York, NY: Routledge.

Vygotsky, L. S. (1978). *Mind in society: The development of higher psychological processes.* Cambridge, MA: Harvard University Press.

West-Olatunji, C., Shure, L., Pringle, R. M., Adams, T. L., Baratelli, A.,... Flesner, D. (2008). Increasing mathematics and science achievement among low-income, African American youth using strength-based interventions. *International Journal of Learning, 15*(9), 1–9.

Wilkins, L., Gaskin, J. S., Kuluhiwa, K., & Sodersten, S. (2008, June). *Honoring culture, diversifying the workforce, strengthening science.* Chapter presented at the Women in Engineering ProActive Network (WEPAN) Annual Conference, Saint Louis, Missouri.

Yin, R. K. (2009). *Case study research: Design and method* (5th ed.). Thousand Oaks, CA: SAGE.

CHAPTER 11

PARTICIPATION IN THE ADVANCING OUT-OF-SCHOOL LEARNING IN MATHEMATICS AND ENGINEERING PROJECT

Supporting Middle School Latinas' Bilingual and STEM Identities

Carlos LópezLeiva
Sylvia Celedón-Pattichis
Marios S. Pattichis

This chapter describes Latina[1] middle school girls' participation in mathematics and engineering fields through an integrated curriculum that supports the programming of digital color video and image representations. More specifically, we explore how three bilingual Latina girls developed a sense of comfort, expertise, agency, and belonging to science, technology, engineering, and mathematics (STEM) fields and practices through their participation in the Advancing Out-of-School Learning in Mathematics and Engineering (AOLME) project.

Girls and Women of Color In STEM, pages 183–205
Copyright © 2020 by Information Age Publishing
All rights of reproduction in any form reserved.

BACKGROUND

Current statistics of the STEM workforce describe the underrepresentation of brown and black populations in STEM fields, especially females (Dowd, Malcom, & Macias, 2010; Landivar, 2013; Syed & Chemers, 2011). When analyzing the educational conditions that support these groups of students, a service gap is evident regarding quality and quantity of educational resources (Flores, 2007). This gap often transfers not only into underfunded schools that have limited instructional resources and infrastructure in need of remodeling to provide a more comfortable educational ecology, but this gap also includes an emphasis on low-level content, basic procedures, and remediation in terms of curriculum and instruction. In addition, low student expectations from underprepared teachers, who are most likely to be hired at schools with predominantly brown and Black students, especially Latinas/os. Frequently, these teachers apply pedagogies that present STEM fields disconnected from real-life applications, a situation that translates into low student interest in STEM academics, to the point that high school STEM academics are under-enrolled and are at great risk of closing (Hossain & Robinson, 2012; Rogers, 2009). These low expectations are reflected in students' interest in staying in school. As of 2009, Latinas/os had the highest high-school dropout rates of all demographic groups and the lowest graduation percentages (Chapa & De La Rosa, 2006; Ortiz, Valerio, & Lopez, 2012). The dropout rates directly affect high school graduation and college enrollment. These persistent dropout patterns suggest educational experiences laden with lower expectations for Latina/o students that can, in turn, limit their future opportunities (Ortiz, Valerio, & Lopez, 2012).

The Latina/o youth population has drastically increased in the last few years; the Pew Hispanic Center (2009) reports the United States having a total population of 300.5 million. As of 2010, Hispanics or Latinas/os comprised 16.3% of the U.S. population (U.S. Census Bureau, 2010). In 2012, only 7% of Latinas held women-earned STEM degrees even though they constituted 16% of the female population. As of 2008, the graduation rate for Latinas was 31% compared to 46% for White women. Alarming is the fact that 60% of 12th grade female students see mathematics classes as not engaging and that mathematics as not being useful knowledge to them in the future (NAEP, 2013). Thus, it is not surprising that females are underrepresented in STEM fields (Burke, 2007; Hill, Corbett, & St. Rose, 2010; Lee & Schreiber, 1999; Marra, Peterson, & Britsch, 2008; Thom, 2001) and especially Latinas since only 3% work in STEM fields, while women in general represent 24% of the STEM workforce and 46% of the general workforce (Jackson, 2013). On a more positive note, reports from the National Science Foundation highlight that since the beginning of the new millennium, women have surpassed the number of STEM bachelor degrees received by men; still, this growth has taken place in STEM fields, except in engineering, in which women representation is still very low (NSF, 2007).

Pertinent to our work, also, is access to technology and development of STEM literacy, defined as "the knowledge and understanding of scientific and mathematical concepts and processes required of personal decision making, participation in civic and cultural affairs and economic productivity" (NRC, 2011, p. 5), in which students are "able to function and thrive in our highly technological world" (Vasquez, Sneider, & Comer, 2013, p. 9). Yet, both White and Hispanic children use the Internet at approximately equal rates. The percentages of Internet usage by White and Hispanic children are at 96% and 87% for access anywhere, 91% and 85% at home, 78% and 69% at school, and 59% and 53% at the library (Warschauer & Matuchniak, 2010). Despite these high percentages, access to Internet or computers does not guarantee a thriving development in the technological world, and often this access translates into consumerism. In other words, students become consumers rather than producers of technology, thus undermining one of the major goals in education (Hourcade, Beitler, Cormenzana, & Flores, 2008; Nugroho & Lonsdale, 2010; Perry, 2007). Regarding this issue of producers vs. consumers, the number of computer science degrees in the United States is unevenly distributed. Despite the fact that Hispanic and White populations between 18–24 years represent 17.5% and 61.4% of the population respectively, the distribution of computer science degrees shows a wider gap: 9.8% and 63.1% earn associate degrees, 7.2% and 60.7% earn bachelor's degrees, 4.8% and 55% earn master's degrees, and only 1.2% and 70.3% earn doctoral degrees (Warschauer & Matuchniak, 2010).

STEM Education and Issues With Minority Students and Women

Several studies have attempted to understand these uneven representations in the STEM fields, especially of minority and female students in engineering. Culturally and linguistically diverse students frequently lack access to K–12 engineering education (Katehi, Pearson, & Feder, 2009). Additionally, middle school students in public schools tend to express extremely low levels of interest for participating in STEM related career academics in high school. Instead, they express strong interests in arts, literature, business, and entertainment related careers, and this trend is even stronger for girls (Hossain & Robinson, 2012; Rogers, 2009). This disinterest may be due to the fact that middle school students are "uncertain or not interested in engineering due to a lack of knowledge, inferior perception of science skills, or interest in a different career" (Mooney & Laubach, 2002, p. 317). Furthermore, few engineering education programs exist for the general student population, and these often include low-level curricular materials that portray engineering in unexciting and uninteresting ways (Katehi, Pearson, & Feder, 2009). To complicate this more, most of the engineering outreach community programs have been developed by engineering rather than education people (Johri & Olds, 2011; Litzinger, Hadgraft, Lattuca, & Newstetter, 2011). On the other hand, effective STEM education programs—especially engineering—include inter- or trans-disciplinary approaches (Vasquez, Sneider, & Comer, 2013).

The low participation of girls in STEM fields has been attributed to several different factors. As an example, science and engineering fields have been stereotyped as a male-dominated profession not open or welcoming to women (Burke & Mattis, 2007). Under such conditions, girls tend to lose confidence and spend less effort than boys on confusing/demanding tasks (Dweck, 2007). Moreover, engineering and physical sciences are perceived as uncaring, without social purposes, which lead female students to reject these fields (Baker & Leary, 1995; Eccles, 1994; Jones, Howe, & Rua, 2000). In fact, a study that explored why so few female students enroll in computer science courses at the high school level found through student interviews a series of negative stereotypes about people in this field, such as antisocial geeks, which discouraged students; so a more social and collaborative perception of computer scientists supports these perceptions renovation (Goode, Estrella, & Margolis, 2006).

Additionally, pedagogic approaches also influence career choices. Engineering education, for example, is often based on direct instruction, a strategy that makes girls less motivated to study it, since most prefer a guided-discovery approach (Baker & Leary, 1995; Demetry et al., 2009; Webb, Repenning, & Koh, 2012). Mathematics education studies have also mentioned that the ways of knowing in mathematics represent an issue for women since "separate knowing" is the type of learning (preferred by men) that is prevalent in the field, and which implies that impersonal procedures are used to establish truths and promote rigor, abstraction, deduction, structure, and formality. Contrarily, "connected knowing" is an experience-based approach in which actions and thoughts, intuition, and hypothesizing lead to noticing something already known. These types of conflicting knowledges integrate through a "constructed knowledge" approach that values both intuitions and rules (Becker, 1995; Solomon, 2009).

Underrepresented students and women lack or have limited access to role models, and they do not see successful people in STEM fields that look like them (Evans & Whigham, 1995; Gasbarra & Johnson, 2008). Thus, given the prevailing circumstances of Latina/o students, several programs, like AOLME, have been developed to provide access to STEM information and experiences for middle school students. These approaches are discussed in the following section.

Previous Works Supporting Girls in STEM Fields

Given the trends presented above, providing access into STEM fields to minority students has become a national priority (NRC, 2011). Multiple K–12 outreach programs and activities have emerged to provide science and mathematics experiences to underrepresented students and girls. Some of these are summer science camps that include analytical chemistry experiments, forensic science cases, physical science experiments, engineering classroom activities, inquiry-based activities, and packaged engineering curricula (Bachman, Bischoff, Gallagher, Labroo, & Schaumloffel, 2008; Lee & Schreiber, 1999; McDonald, Sneddon, & Darbeau, 2008; Perrin, 2004; Reid & Feldhaus, 2007; Robbins & Schoenfisch, 2005; Rogers & Portsmore, 2004). For girls, gender-specific active learning environments have been recommended as a means to increase their interest in science and mathematics (Thom, 2001). Careful attention is placed on these environments to support the development of girls' self-confident attitude, which encourages them to take risks and face failure, since this is a crucial part to success in science and mathematics (Dean & Fleckenstein, 2007).

In relation to engineering specifically, the high school and middle school female students that participated in the EngineerGirl program reported being interested in studying engineering in college. The program includes a website where students can browse through a gallery with more than 100 profiles of women working in engineering. These profiles of potential role models describe their personalities and interests. Girls are encouraged to ask questions of the featured female engineers. Annually, there is an essay contest, whose topic is defined yearly. The contest helped girls view engineering more positively (Jenniches & Didion, 2009). Another program that also provided information on engineering and STEM careers was developed at a middle school in the U.S. Midwest. Participants included a section of sixth and eighth grade students who watched 10–15 videos of 8 (5 male and 3 female) STEM professionals. The videos included interviews with the professionals about their responsibilities and activities in their professions. Results from this study reported that watching these videos correlates with an increased interest in STEM fields. Findings also suggested no significant difference in boys' or girls' interest in pursuing a STEM career (Wyss, Heulskamp, & Siebert, 2012).

More experience-based programs also report positive results. One example is the Girls in Engineering, Math and Science (GEMS) outreach program that provided hands-on activities to middle school girls who were immersed in laboratory and field experiences, and interacted with female mentors and role models. Mentors were female undergraduate and graduate students who served as teaching assistants. Middle-school students, who started at Grade 6, were selected as participants for GEMS to improve familiarity and pique student interest in science before eighth grade. The program stimulated interest in science, mathematics and higher education. This experience helped students to realize that in science and technology one does not usually succeed on the first try, and that there is no stigma attached to the failure. GEMS findings indicated that the students enjoyed the activities despite having attended the event due to teacher or parental influence rather than personal interest (Dubetz & Wilson, 2013).

Other programs have provided more extensive STEM experiences. Demetry's Out-Reach Camp program provided a 2-week residential summer camp for seventh grade girls, yearly from 1997–2001. The camp aimed to generate and sustain girls' interest in engineering and technology, motivation in education, and self-confidence. Girls worked with a female middle school teacher and two female high school students on a real-life project-based problem. Results suggest that girls' participation in and understanding of engineering increases through exposure to engineering later in middle school and during high school and extended contact with role models and follow-up participation in engineering (Demetry et al., 2009).

Finally, we include two more programs directly related to computer programming. First, the Storytelling Scratch Club, which was a 6-week program for middle school students in West Philadelphia where 11 students met after school for an hour twice a week. Students learned to program and create their digital stories using the programming language Scratch. Children learned that programming, as storytelling, is a "guess-and-check" venture that requires multiple revisions (Burke & Kafai, 2010). The second includes a program environment, Alice. Alice supports beginning programmers by helping them generate syntactically correct programs. In Alice, running programs are animated, and students can see where they made mistakes in their programs. Twenty-two Girl Scouts in the Pittsburgh area participated in the Alice program. They met for three 4-hour Alice workshops. Results show that Storytelling Alice users had greater engagement with programming. Additionally, girls also showed interest in pursuing a computer science related career in the future. Thus, this approach showed promise in attracting middle school girls into computer science. Nevertheless, there was a prevalence of individual over collaborative work, as students ended up developing individual rather than collective stories (Kelleher, 2006).

THEORETICAL PERSPECTIVE

Our qualitative study is founded on a sociocultural perspective that analyzes the participation of Latina middle school girls in the AOLME project. We focus on participation because we view learning as an experiential and situated process in a specific community of practice (Johri & Olds, 2011; Lave

& Wenger, 1991; Wenger, 1998). "A community of practice is an intrinsic condition for the existence of knowledge…participation…is an epistemological principle of learning" (Lave & Wenger, 1991, p. 98). We understand the AOLME project as a community with practices extended from the engineering and bilingual mathematics education communities applied to the context of programming and processing digital images and video, so we understand that students' participation in this community is facilitating their access to practices connected to greater communities. Computer programming demands conceptual and syntactical knowledge; while both are relevant, we place greater emphasis in the former since it expands beyond the current context and has greater implications for student future applications/careers. This kind of knowledge has been identified as "principled" knowledge, while the syntactical one could be named as "ruled" knowledge. We understand that "a knower has 'principled' knowledge when she shows power to project from what has been learned in the past to appropriate and correct behavior in a variety of new and previously unencountered situations: in a new situation, she knows how to proceed" (Solomon, 2009, p. 180). We also see this conceptual understanding directly connected to the process of reasoning and creating meaning, since "students develop mathematics concepts as they use them discursively to construe meaning" (Schleppegrell, 2007, p. 148). Thus, student conceptual understanding, especially of computer programming, is strengthened through its application with understanding.

In the process of understanding computer programming practices, we believe that social interactions with experts is crucial, so that middle school students make sense of these practices by engaging in these practices supported, or scaffolded through their work with engineering and education undergraduate students (hereafter called facilitators). Scaffolding, however, "does not involve simplifying the task during the period of learning. Instead, it holds the task constant, while simplifying the learner's role through the graduated intervention of the teacher" (Greenfield, 1984, p. 119). Intrinsically to this learning process there is also the development of a sense of belonging and becoming part of that community and its practices (Esmonde, 2009; Litzinger et al., 2011; Martin, 2006).

We view the AOLME project as a bridge for both the STEM communities and the middle school students to meet. Our conceptual assumption, based on the idea that for middle school girls and boys, identity formation process, is a fundamental activity at this age (Stone & Church, 1984). Through this bridging, we hope to witness the development of new identities and practices—mainly engineering and mathematical—in the participant students. New understandings, identities, and practices for the members from the university STEM community were also an expectation (Johri & Olds, 2011; Lave & Wenger, 1991; Wenger, 1998). Following Bishop's (2012) definition, we understand identity as "a dynamic view of self, negotiated in a specific social context and informed by past history, events, personal narratives, experiences, routines, and ways of participating" (p. 38). Further, we understand that the socialized development of an identity not only entails narratives on feelings, attitudes, and beliefs about oneself (Bishop, 2012; Bruner, 1994; Martin, 2006; Wenger, 1998), but also the appropriation of the community discourse practices, namely in AOLME, bilingual (Spanish and English) mathematical and engineering discourses (Chval & Khisty, 2009; Fillmore & Snow, 2000; Gee, 2008; Moschkovich, 2004; Schleppegrell, 2007; Snow, 2008).

PARTICIPATION IN THE ADVANCING OUT-OF-SCHOOL LEARNING IN MATHEMATICS AND ENGINEERING PROJECT

The AOLME project has implemented several programs since 2012. The project's bilingual curriculum includes the programming of digital image and video in ten sessions. The curriculum has been implemented in two contexts or programs: the Mathematics Engineering Summer School (MES^2) and the Mathematics Engineering Club (MEC) developed during the spring semesters. The ALOME project is founded on principles and findings from prior work along with our own experiences in out-of-school settings. First, *The Fifth Dimension* (Cole et al., 2006) and *La Clase Mágica* (Vásquez, 2003) describe that informal and playful atmospheres to support a twofold process: (a) developing an academic agenda and (b) having fun during meaningful activities and interactions with others, wherein roles of teacher and learners are negotiated and intersected. Their results support that students "can learn when they are invested in the goals of a task [they willfully choose] and motivated to participate in challenging activities that include an educational agenda" (Cole et al., 2006, p. 106). So it is not an isolated practice that promotes learning, but the ensemble of practices that support that learning process. Second, research results on out-of-school learning environments also support that these settings play a key role improving the learning of underserved populations (Ferreira, 2001; McClure & Rodriguez, 2007).

Results reported here relate to the application of AOLME Level 1 curriculum in the MEC program. Level 1 includes 12 sessions each implemented once a week during 1½ hours. Level 1 concepts include basic navigational concepts in Linux, introduction to Python programming and functions, black and white, grayscale, color images, binary and hexadecimal numbers, and color video representations. During the last three sessions students work on a final project, which includes the design and programming of a color video. Students come from public middle schools in a large urban

TABLE 11.1			Students Enrolled in AOLME by Gender, Program, & Year								
Year	2012			2013			2014			Totals		Grand Total
Program	F	M	Total	F	M	Total	F	M	Total	F	M	Total
ME-S2	7	13	20	3	17	20				10	30	40
MEC				5	10	15	5	10	15	10	20	30
Grand Total	7	13	20	8	27	35	5	10	15	20	50	70

and rural area of the U.S. Southwest. Most students are bilingual (Spanish and English) Latinas/os that attended a bilingual school. Students formed and worked in teams that they self-selected; they also chose a facilitator to work with. Teams included small groups (3–4 students) that were often gender specific and that were led by an undergraduate student facilitator who was frequently bilingual. Although most of the facilitators were from a Hispanic background, during the 3 years of the project only two of them were female bilingual Latinas in the undergraduate engineering program. They worked during the MEC and MES² programs. However, it was only during the latter semester when we had a group of three bilingual Latina *muchachas* (teenage girls) working with a bilingual female facilitator. Thus, based on the significance of role models from similar gender and racial and linguistic backgrounds (Gasbarra & Johnson, 2008), and the strong performance of this group of *muchachas* in Spring 2014, we decided to explore in detail the interactions and negotiations that this group and their Latina facilitator engaged in to support such learning process and strong STEM identity development. In total, the AOLME project, however, has worked with 70 middle school students (F is females and M is males) distributed as outlined in Table 11.1.

METHODS

Social interactions in this group as well as all work displayed in monitors during all sessions were videotaped. Student interviews and presentations of final projects were also videotaped. Both digital and pencil and paper student work were collected and analyzed. In addition, we administered a mathematics and engineering attitude scale adapted by the AOLME program (the Fennema & Sherman Mathematics Attitudes Scale [FSMAS], 1976). The scale includes twenty items with a 5-point Likert-type response format. The items explore four attitude-related factors: confidence, usefulness, enjoyment, and motivation in mathematics and engineering. As participant observers in this project, we engaged in a qualitative analysis and we compared and contrasted the gathered data sources and examples of student work (Miles & Huberman, 1994) in order to examine how these *muchachas'* participation in AOLME supported their understanding and use of STEM practices and related identities. For this process, all videos were logged and specific segments were transcribed and analyzed. This analysis yielded a series of patterns in similarities, frequency, and correspondence of videotaped interactions and the interviews. These patterns were condensed in emerging themes that were discussed, refined, and agreed upon among the authors. These encompassing themes were triangulated with different data sources, and are presented in the findings through related vignettes. The characteristics of these female (muchachas) focal participants selected for this study are outlined in Table 11.2.

FINDINGS

Findings describe the quality of experiences and transformations that both the facilitator and these Latina students shared in the AOLME project. Based on emerging themes from the analysis of our data, we use selected vignettes to help us describe the context in which bilingual Latina girls participated.

Hybrid Learning: Programming and Personal Interests/ Knowledge

Through our analysis, we came to understand that at AOLME, specifically this group, the process of learning computer programming and mathematics was connected to both the computer programming and mathematics practices and the students' interests and prior knowledge. This connection between students' experiences, interests and computer programming created a development of hybrid goals. These goals were both the program's and the students'. For example, early in the program the *muchachas* learned about how to read, display, and alter digital images. They used pictures taken in the visit to the science museum. They altered this picture by changing the color of an area. For this, they learned how to define variables and change the color of a rectangular area. After typing in Python function calls for the colors and image display, the altered area resulted in an orange square, which then was further resized and colored in different manners by all the girls taking turns. Through this playful process, the *muchachas* showed understanding of the importance of syntax when typing in a Python function call, as well as understanding of how a picture relates to a matrix, and how regions within an image may be altered. Further, they also understood colors as the result of a combination of the Python code. All

TABLE 11.2 Characteristics of Participating Focal Students

Muchachas	Grade	Favorite Courses	Self-Reported Language Skills	Mathematics and Engineering Attitude Score	Self-Reported Knowledge Change Through AOLME	Prior Connections to STEM	Interest in Attending AOLME in Future
Daniela	8th	Mathematics and Science	Biliterate	82/100	Before 0/10 After 10/10	Friends	Yes
Laura	8th	Mathematics	Bilingual/English Dominant	89/100	Before 5/10 After 9/10	AVID Program	Yes
Ligia	8th	Arts	Biliterate	83/100	Before 5/10 After 10/10	2 Siblings in Engineering	Yes

programmed through purposefully designed steps that aligned with the program's and the students' goals.

Likewise, at the end of the program, students created a project through which they applied what they had learned. Students created color video projects. The creation of these projects made this twofold goal much more evident. On the one hand, the videos took the development of stories, which were translated into pictures, and picture creation required girls' knowledge about digital image representation as well as computer programming. The story of the video itself was also a collective creative process and which students took part of willingly. The ideas about the video were discussed thoroughly, so that the final product would be representative of the team. Similarly, the programming required precision and alignment with the programming conventions and discourse.

For example, initially they thought of including a penguin as the protagonist in their video. To design the penguin character, they started using pencil and grid paper. Laura, who was trying to draw it, said: "I don't know how to draw a penguin. At least, let's just do a fish" (moves her left hand up and down), "...a flappy fish!" On the one hand, the number of pixels in the matrix that they selected limited designing a penguin, so designing a fish was more feasible. On the other hand, the idea of the "flappy" character idea emerged from the "flappy bird" game that they were familiar with and which they wanted to imitate in their video. The programming included the character design as well as the story background. The *muchachas* engaged in this generative process of ideas and commands in a nonlinear manner. The video programming and design required simultaneously problem posing and problem solving processes.

The collective problem posing/solving process supported the *muchachas'* collective reasoning and debugging (i.e., process of running programs with the goal of receiving feedback from the computer through the visual images in order to make needed changes in the code). For example, the video characters, the fish, not only needed an appearance, it also needed a way of moving across the background. It needed to "flap" and swim. This requirement that the group found so important for the development of their character required careful attention for the programming of its movement as it was not only a direct horizontal translation of the fish image. It required the fish to move up and down to appear swimming. Our videos were uploaded on YouTube (for more detail watch this video at http://www.youtube.com/watch?v=s2hykSykFLo). During the first 4 seconds of the video, it is evident how the *muchachas* focused on the fish movement. Seemingly effortlessly, this swimming illusion was not an easy task to design. During this time, girls' comments below from an excerpt of the video illustrated the final process when the group successfully programmed this movement:

> **Laura:** "Now, you have to change the coordinates [pixel position in frame] and the color."
> **Daniela:** [9,7] (Daniela and Ligia worked with the keyboard and mouse as Laura guided.)
> **Laura:** "Yeah, now you have to choose the 10 and the 5."
> **Laura:** "So, that one is gonna be 5 and the other can be 6."
> **Ligia and Daniela:** (run the script) "Oh, it worked! Great! It's swimming! Yeah!"
> **Facilitator:** "Yay, looks good! Good job guys!"
> **Ligia:** "Now, we have to push it [the fish] down here" (to get more effect of swimming).
> **Daniela:** "But then, we need to do it a little low because of the flapping."
> **Laura:** "Like go down and then up, up and then down, down, down, and then up, up!"
> **Facilitator:** "And then, we can make a panda haha, just kidding."
> **Laura:** "And then, we can make a bird, a raspberry" (all laugh).

The above interaction portrays the collaboration that the team developed around the video design and programming. They had tried several attempts before the swimming and flapping pattern worked out just the way they wanted. They had just figured out a mathematical pattern that allowed them to move the fish "flapping" through the coordinate system in each video frame they had created. Additionally, the excerpt also portrays that they were motivated during the whole process. As sense of accomplishment, fun, and celebration is depicted through the use of words and jokes made by the *muchachas*, or what we call a hybrid use of discourses from mathematics, computer programming, and their own (Chval & Khisty, 2009; Fillmore & Snow, 2000; Gee, 2008; Moschkovich, 2004; Schleppegrell, 2007; Snow, 2008). The team also experienced a moving back and forth between the application of formal and informal knowledges, of conceptually STEM-based work and fun or recreation in the process of showing what they liked and what they could do. Working in these conditions was not only a participation process in the computer programming practices, it was also an identity development process (Johri & Olds, 2011; Lave & Wenger, 1991; Wenger, 1998).

Consequently, having discovered the pattern to portray a character's flapping movement, the *muchachas* applied this pattern in the rest of the frames to make the fish and the new character, a bear, flap all the way until they meet and fall in love.

All of the examples exemplify actions and decisions that the *muchachas* made in order to use computer programming as an intentional tool to create their video and show in it what they wanted to show. In other words, the *muchachas* started developing a technological and scientific literacy that led them to make purposeful informed decisions and actions applied to a real-life project (Chapa & De La Rosa, 2006; Kesidou & Koppal, 2004). Students also enacted disciplinary agency connected to the STEM subjects integrated in the project as well as their personal or conceptual agency (Boaler, 2006) that allowed them to learn not only on computers, but also about themselves individually, and as a team. This learning is described in the following two sections.

Female Team and Female Engineering Role Model

The facilitator and the *muchachas* developed a strong team relationship. All seemed to feel free to share their opinions and doubts, while the facilitator was always willing to help them in the process. No power dynamics between student–student and student–facilitator could be observed consistently over time. It seems that the intervention of the facilitator was crucial as she was continuously motivating them to try hard, while also challenging them with the AOLME tasks and, when *muchachas* responded to the tasks, the facilitator encouraged them and positively reinforced their achievement. Comments such as, "You guys had it before even having me explain it. So that's pretty awesome, good job"; "We got this guys, we are a team!"; "One thing about engineering is that you can't be afraid to fail, you just have to try." The facilitator—Ana—was a supportive, caring instructor, a friend, and an engineer, a role model that the *muchachas* came to respect and develop a relationship beyond the AOLME context. For example, Laura invited Ana to come and present at another afterschool program that Laura was attending. This invitation took place during work at the AOLME project, described in the following dialogue:

> **Laura:** "...I'm going there [AVID, Advancement Via Individual Determination, program] tomorrow."
> **Facilitator:** "Oh, really?"
> **Laura:** "Yeah, I have to."
> **Facilitator:** "Do you still wanna be an engineer?"
> **Laura:** "Yeah, I still wanna be an engineer."
> **Facilitator:** "Awesome."
> **Laura:** "Yeah."
> **Facilitator:** "What time is your presentation?"
> **Laura:** "It's at 3:30."
> **Facilitator:** "If you want I can be your presenter, I don't know what I have to do but..." (laugh)
> **Laura:** "What type of engineer are you, Ms.?"
> **Facilitator:** "Computer engineer."

> **Laura:** "Computer, we have a group . . . whatever a couple of engineers. Some of them want to be computer, and a couple science engineers."
>
> **Facilitator:** "That's really cool."
>
> **Laura:** "I told my AVID teacher about you teaching us [Ana teaching something] and she said: 'Ask her' [Ana, the Facilitator]."
>
> **Facilitator:** "Yeah, I can!"

The *muchachas* seemed to have encountered in Ana a person that meant something else than an instructor. The fact that Laura had identified Ana as someone whose experiences in engineering were worthwhile sharing with the students in the AVID program indexed Laura's recognition of a potential role model in Ana's studies, interests, and work. In a personal conversation with Ana after the program had ended, she mentioned that as a Latina woman in engineering, she thinks that what happened in her interaction with the *muchachas* meant something very special to her because she remembered that while growing up she did not have opportunities such as AOLME, much less to see and have Latina instructors in engineering. Ana further argued that being able to see someone like you doing things that you like sends a message of thinking that others may also be able to reach such points. We see Ana as a clear role model for this group of *muchachas*. This finding is similar to those of Demetry et al., (2009) and Dubetz and Wilson (2013) in that role models have significant impact in promoting youths' STEM interest development. Ana was not only an instructor, she was a female Latina engineer, who was their inspiring, caring, and fun instructor, who almost seemed like their friend. Again, this blending of traditional separate roles and relationships seemed to have had a positive impact on the students. We see the computer programming teaching and learning of the *muchachas'* team as a challenging, fun, and caring process. This context and relationships seem to have mediated the *muchachas* to figure out a world in which they have a space as girls, Latinas, and students who can be successful (Boaler & Greeno, 2000).

Additionally, the team process was also essential to build these relationships and understandings. Through personal interviews and journal writing, students talked about this collaborative work and its social and academic benefits. In an interview, Daniela mentioned:

> I got along with Laura very well, 'cause me and her, like we never talked or anything before. Then, like we started to know each other on the field trips and everything. También, like we became, yeah, we became closer friends. I just felt like we could, like, brainstorm out and then like we, like, all four of us, Ana, Laura, Ligia, and I, we would just brainstorm random ideas, and like we just . . . , and that is how we did things better.

Furthermore, at the end of the program during the presentation to their families and peers of their video or final project, the *muchachas* also elaborated on how this collaborative process helped them and what it meant to them as illustrated by the following statements:

> **Ligia:** My experience in the program was amazing because I was able to find that this is what I would like to see myself doing in a few years. Also I was able to see how . . . with just basically zeros and ones and letters you can do an image. This program is pretty amazing to see that engineering is not only for men! There is also women! We're only three girls in this . . . oh yea!, four of us in the program that are just women and the rest are just men. So it´s pretty nice to see many people in it, and I got to talk to the people that I have never talked to like at school, and in AOLME we could.
>
> **Laura:** My experience in the AOLME Project, I got to learn a lot that I didn't know about. There were some things that I didn't know even existed. So, it was pretty amazing because I got to work with girls and we understood each other and we had our giggles once in a while (laughs and switches to Spanish). *Mi experiencia fue asombrosa porque aprendí sobre muchas cosas que no sabía y sí me gustó porque fuimos puras muchachas que nos entendíamos y que a veces nos reíamos* (My experience was amazing because I learned many things I didn't know. And I did like it because we were only girls who understood each other and who laughed at times).

The team of *muchachas* clearly emphasized having enjoyed not only learning in a fun way on things that they did not know before, like computer programming, but they also highlighted the fact that they enjoyed working together with only girls. It made them proud of being not only a team of girls, but The Challengers: a team of STEM *muchachas*. When Laura translated her comment into Spanish, she used the term *muchachas*. In our analysis this term became inspiring and descriptive to us so much and for that reason we used it in this chapter.

Stronger Relations With Engineering/STEM Bilingual Identity

The previous sections have already introduced how this group of *muchachas* had started seeing themselves as STEM *muchachas*. We present two more examples that show how they were seeing themselves connected to practices and identities related to engineering. Daniela commented in her group how she had found out that Python, the program they used, could be used with phones also:

> **Daniela:** "It's crazy! I went to a store, I looked at the Python icon. It was actually on the phone and I said: Oh my god! So I can use Python on my phone?"
>
> **Facilitator:** "Yes, you can put our video on your phone."
>
> **Daniela and Laura:** "Ohhh!" (students excited, looking at each other, and smiling)
>
> **Ligia:** "So I could just watch the video I made!"

The *muchachas* learned that what they learned to do is applicable to their lives. Ligia especially took complete authorship of the video they had created. Furthermore, during the interview the *muchachas* mentioned the different concepts they had learned and how it had helped them to develop new relationships with STEM fields, as described by Daniela:

> **Daniela:** "Some people might think it's [mathematics and engineering] boring, 'cause like I guess I don´t know... but when I heard about AOLME, I was like pretty interested, I am like hum..., that is interesting... and then like I signed the form."
>
> **Facilitator (male):** "Did you like computers before?"
>
> **Daniela:** "Not really, I always was intimidated by computers."
>
> **Facilitator:** "What about now?"
>
> **Daniela:** "Not really."
>
> **Facilitator:** "You are not as fearful, you fear more comfortably."

Although Daniela recognized being interested in STEM topics before the program, she also recognized that after having participated in AOLME she feels more comfortable using computers. As students participated in the practice of programming with computers, they also learned to see themselves as fluent, confident users of computers. The AOLME project seems to have provided a context that helped the *muchachas* negotiate their previous narratives of themselves through participating in new practices that socialized them into new attitudes and beliefs about themselves (Bishop, 2012; Martin, 2006; Wenger, 1998).

DISCUSSION/CONCLUDING REMARKS

This study supports the conclusion that bilingual Latina teenage girls can indeed successfully engage in computer programming practices using similar codes to those that engineering college students learn to use. We learned that this process seems successful when there are hybrid goals, so that student engagement is linked to both the fulfillment of students' goals, interests, and knowledge as well as those academic ones of a specific subject field; in other words a relational engagement (Dominguez, LópezLeiva, & Khisty, 2014). Additionally, other computer programming projects have struggled supporting student collaboration even by using storytelling (Kelleher, 2006). We learned that an open and creative process of videos using low programming levels linked to a student-based storytelling process is likely to support genuine collaboration, so that academic learning and playful storytelling support each other (Turner & Celedón-Pattichis, 2011). Of course, all of these elements are better supported through a nurturing environment with caring facilitators and role models (Demetry et al., 2009; Dubetz & Wilson, 2013; Gasbarra & Johnson, 2008). We also learned that the *muchachas* felt supported not only through collaborative work, but also through working in same-gender teams. The *muchachas* asserted having enjoyed this context, but more importantly it seems that it was relevant to them as the engineering field appeared initially male-dominant to them. Thus, a gender-specific team mediated a safer space. Further, nurturing context students also mediate identity negotiations and connections to new fields (Bishop, 2012). Finally, while these results are promising, we wonder about long-term effects of these renovated perspectives and how these could be sustained over time (Demetry et al., 2009), so that the *muchachas'* new goal, dream of becoming engineers may come true.

ACKNOWLEDGMENTS

We are grateful to all the *muchachas*, Daniela, Laura, and Ligia (pseudonyms) in the AOLME program. Similarly, we are grateful to Jessica Morales Flores, José Antonio Lacea Yanguas, and Amanda González for their contributions to this study.

CREDITS

The information used in this article was collected in an after-school program as part of a research project conducted by Drs. Carlos A. LópezLeiva, Sylvia Celedón-Pattichis, and Marios S. Pattichis, principal investigators in the Advancing Out-of-School Learning in Mathematics and Engineering (AOLME) project funded by the University of New Mexico's College of Education. Views expressed here are the authors' and do not reflect the views of the funders.

NOTE

1. In this chapter, we use the terms Hispanics and Latinas/os interchangeably. The term *Hispanics* relates to the Spanish language background and a European influence. The term *Latina/o* relates to a geographical location (Latin America) and a mixture or fusion of American (the entire continent/s) and European backgrounds. Persons from this population group may speak different languages and belong to different racial groups. Still within the United States, there has been a separate statistical analysis for this group.

REFERENCES

Bachman, N., Bischoff, P. J., Gallagher, H., Labroo, S., & Schaumloffel, J. C. (2008). PR2EPS: Preparation, recruitment, retention and excellence in the physical sciences, including engineering: A report on the 2004, 2005 and 2006 science summer camps. *Journal of STEM Education, 9*(1/2), 30–39.

Baker, D., & Leary, R. (1995). Letting girls speak out about science. *Journal of Research in Science Teaching, 32*(1), 3–27.

Becker, J. R. (1995). Women's ways of knowing in mathematics. In G. Kaiser & P. Rogers (Eds.), *Equity in mathematics education: Influences of feminism and culture* (pp. 163–174). London, England: Falmer.

Bishop, J. P. (2012). "She's always been the smart one. I've always been the dumb one": Identities in the mathematics Classroom. *Journal for Research in Mathematics Education, 43*(1), 34–74.

Boaler, J. (2006). Opening our ideas: How a detracked mathematics approach promoted respect, responsibility, and high achievement. *Theory Into Practice, 45*(1), 40–46.

Boaler, J., & Greeno, J. G. (2000). Identity, agency, and knowing in mathematics worlds. In J. Boaler (Ed.), *Multiple perspectives on mathematics teaching and learning* (pp. 171–200). Westport, CT: Ablex.

Bruner, J. (1994). Life as narrative. In A. H. Dyson & C. Genishi (Eds.), *The need for story: Cultural diversity in classroom and community* (pp. 28–37). New York, NY: National Council of Teachers of English.

Burke, R. J. (2007). Women and minorities in STEM: A primer. In R. J. Burke & M. C. Mattis (Eds.), *Women and minorities in science, technology, engineering and mathematics: Upping the numbers* (pp. 3–7). Bodmin, Cornwall: MPG Books.

Burke, R. J., & Mattis, M. C. (2007). *Women and minorities in science, technology, engineering and mathematics: Upping the numbers.* Bodmin, Cornwall: MPG Books.

Burke, Q., & Kafai, Y. B. (2010, June). *Programming & storytelling: Opportunities for learning about coding & composition.* Paper presentation at the 9th Annual International Interaction Designnand Children (IDC) Conference, Universitat Pompeu Fabra, Barcelona, Spain.

Chapa, J., & De La Rosa, B. (2006). The problematic pipeline: Demographic trends and Latino participation in graduate science, technology, engineering, and mathematics programs. *Journal of Hispanic Higher Education, 5*(3), 203–221. https://doi.org/10.1177/1538192706288808

Chval, K., & Khisty, L. L. (2009). Bilingual Latino students, writing and mathematics: A case study of successful teaching and learning. In R. Barwell (Ed.), *Multilingualism mathematics classrooms: Global perspectives* (pp. 128–144). Tonawanda, NY: Multilingual Matters.

Cole, M., & the Distributed Literacy Consortium. (2006). *The fifth dimension: An after-school program built on diversity.* New York, NY: Russell Sage Foundation.

Demetry C., Hubelbank, J. Blaisdell, S., Sontgerath, S., Nicholson, M. E., Rosenthal, E., & Quinn, P. (2009). Supporting young women to enter engineering: Long-term effects of a middle school engineering outreach program for girls. *Journal of Women and Minorities in Science and Engineering, 15*(2), 119–142.

Dean, D. J., & Fleckenstein, A. (2007). Keys to success for women in science. In R. J. Burke & M. C. Mattis (Eds.), *Women and minorities in science, technology, engineering and mathematics: Upping the numbers* (pp. 28–44). Bodmin, Cornwall: MPG Books.

Dominguez, H., LópezLeiva, C. A., & Khisty, L. L. (2014). Relational engagement: Proportional reasoning with bilingual Latino/a students. *Educational Studies in Mathematics, 85*(1), 143–160. https://doi.org/10.1007/s10649-013-9501-7

Dowd, A. C., Malcom, L. E., & Macias, E. E. (2010). *Improving transfer access to stem bachelor's degrees at Hispanic serving institutions through America COMPETES Act.* Los Angeles: University of Southern California.

Dubetz, T., & Wilson, J. A. (2013). Girls in engineering, mathematics and science, GEMS: A science outreach program for middle-school female students. *Journal of STEM Education, 14*(3), 41–47.

Dweck, C. S. (2007). Is math a gift? Beliefs that put females at risk. In S. J. Ceci & W. M. Williams (Eds.), *Why aren't more women in science?* (pp. 47–55). Washington, DC: American Psychological Association.

Eccles, J. S. (1994). Understanding women's educational and occupational choices. *Psychology of Women Quarterly, 18*(4), 585–609.

Esmonde, I. (2009). Ideas and Identities: Supporting equity in cooperative mathematics learning. *Review of Educational Research, 79*(2) 1008–1043.

Evans, M. A., & Whigham, M. (1995). The effect of a role model project upon the attitudes of ninth-grade science students. *Journal of Research in Science Teaching, 32*(2), 195–204.

Fennema, E., & Sherman, J. A. (1976). Fennema-Sherman mathematics attitudes scales: Instruments designed to measure attitudes toward the learning of mathematics by males and females. *Catalog of Selected Documents in Psychology, 6*(1), 31.

Ferreira, M. M. (2001). The effect of an after-school program addressing the gender and minority achievement gaps in science, mathematics, and engineering. *ERS Spectrum, 19*(2), 11–18.

Fillmore, L. W., & Snow, C. (2000). *What teachers need to know about language.* Special Report from the Clearinghouse on Languages and Linguistics. Washington DC: U.S. Department of Education Office of Educational Research and Improvement/ERIC.

Flores, A. (2007). Examining disparities in mathematics education: Achievement gap or opportunity gap? *High School Journal, 91*(1), 29–42.

Gasbarra, P., & Johnson, J. (2008). *Out before the game begins: Hispanic leaders talk about what's needed to bring more Hispanic youngsters into Science, Technology, and Math professions.* New York, NY: Public Agenda.

Gee, J. P. (2008). What is academic language? In A. Rosebery & B. Warren (Eds.), *Teaching science to English language learners* (pp. 57–69). Arlington, VA: NSTA Press.

Goode, J., Estrella, R., & Margolis, J. (2006). Lost in translation: Gender and high school computer science. In W. Apray & J. M. Calhoon (Eds.), *Women and information technology: Research on the reasons for under-representation.* Cambridge, MA: MIT Press.

Greenfield, P. M. (1984). A theory of the teacher in the learning activities of everyday life. In B. Rogoff & J. Lave (Eds.), *Everyday cognition: Its development in social context* (pp. 117–138). Cambridge, MA: Harvard University Press.

Hill, C., Corbett, C., & St. Rose, A. (2010). Women and girls in science, technology, engineering, and mathematics. In *Why so few? Women in science, technology, engineering and mathematics* (pp. 1–28) . Retrieved from http://www.aauw.org/files/2013/02/Why-So-Few-Women-in-Science-Technology-Engineering-and-Mathematics.pdf

Hossain, M., & Robinson, M. G. (2012). How to motivate U.S. students to pursue STEM (Science, Technology, Engineering and Mathematics) careers. *US–China Education Review, A*(4), 442–451.

Hourcade, J. P. , Beitler, D., Cormenzana, F., & Flores, P. (2008). Early OLPC experiences in a rural Uruguayan school. In *CHI '08 extended abstracts on human factors in computing systems* (pp. 2503–2512). Florence, Italy: ACM Press.

Jackson, M. (2013). *Fact sheet: The state of Latinas in the United States.* Washington, DC: Center for American Progress. Retrieved from: http://cdn.americanprogress.org/wp-content/uploads/2013/11/SOW-factsheet-Lat.pdf

Jenniches, S., & Didion, C. (2009). EngineerGirl! A website to interest girls in engineering. *The Bridge: Linking Engineering and Society, 39*(3), 38–44.

Johri, A., & Olds, B. M. (2011). Situated engineering learning: Bridging engineering education research and the learning sciences. *Journal of Engineering Education, 100*(1), 151–185.

Jones, M. G., Howe, A., & Rua, M. J. (2000). Gender differences in students' experiences, interests, and attitudes towards science and scientists. *Science Education, 84*(2), 180–192.

Katchi, L., Pearson, G., & Feder, M. (2009). *Engineering in K–12 education: Understanding the status and improving the prospects.* Washington DC: National Academy of Engineering and National Research Council.

Kelleher, C. (2006). *Motivating programming: Using storytelling to make computer programming attractive to middle school girls* (Unpublished doctoral dissertation). School of Computer Science Carnegie-Mellon University Pittsburgh, PA.

Kesidou, S., & Koppal, M. (2004). Supporting goals-based learning with STEM outreach. *Journal of STEM Education: Innovations and Research, 5*(3/4), 5–16.

Lave, J., & Wenger, E. (1991). *Situated learning: Legitimate peripheral participation.* New York, NY: Cambridge University Press.

Litzinger, T., Hadgraft, R., Lattuca, L., & Newstetter, W. (2011). Engineering education and the development of expertise. *Journal of Engineering Education, 100*(1), 123–150.

Landivar, L. C. (2013). *Disparities in STEM employment by sex, race, and Hispanic origin* (Report number ACS-24). Washington, DC: U.S. Census Bureau.

Lee, N. E., & Schreiber, K. G. (1999). The chemistry outreach program: Women undergraduates presenting chemistry to middle school students. *Journal of Chemical Education, 76*(7), 917–918.

McDonald, P. W., Sneddon, J., & Darbeau, R.W. (2008). The cake caper: A forensics hands-on experience and experiment for grades 4 through 12. *The Chemical Educator, 13*, 117–119.

McClure, P., & Rodriguez, A. (2007). *Factors related to advanced course-taking patterns, persistence in STEM, and the role of out-of-school time programs: A literature review.* Berkley CA: Coalition for Science After School.

Marra, R. M., Peterson, K., & Britsch, B. (2008). Collaboration as a means to building capacity: results and future directions of the national girls' collaborative project. *Journal of Women and Minorities in Science and Engineering, 14*(2), 119–140.

Martin, D. (2006). Mathematics learning and participation as racialized forms of experience: African American parents speak on the struggle for mathematics literacy. *Mathematical Thinking and Learning, 8*(3), 197–229.

Miles, M., & Huberman, A. M. (1994). *Qualitative data analysis* (2nd Ed.). Thousand Oaks, CA: SAGE.

Mooney, M. A., & Laubach, T. A. (2002). Adventure engineering: A design centered, inquiry based approach to middle grade science and mathematics education. *Journal of Engineering Education, 91*(3), 309–318.

Moschkovich, J. N. (2004). Appropriating mathematical_practices: A case study of learning to use and explore functions_through interaction with a tutor. *Educational Studies in_Mathematics, 55*(1), 49–80.

National Assessment of Educational Progress. (2013). *2013 mathematics and reading: Grade 12 assessments.* Retrieved from https://nces.ed.gov/pubsearch/pubsinfo.asp?pubid=2014087

National Research Council. (2011). *A framework for K–12 science education: Practices crosscutting concepts, and core ideas.* Washington, DC: National Academy Press.

National Science Foundation. (2007). *Women, minorities, and persons with disabilities in science and engineering* (NSF 07-315). Arlington, VA: Author.

Nugroho, D., & Lonsdale, M. (2010). *Evaluation of OLPC programs globally: A literature review.* Camberwell, Australia: Australian Council for Educational Research.

Ortiz, C. J., Valerio, M. A., & Lopez, K. (2012). Trends in Hispanic academic achievement: Where do we go from here? *Journal of Hispanic Higher Education, 11*(2), 136–148. https://doi.org/10.1177/1538192712437935

Perrin, M. (2004). Inquiry-based pre-engineering activities for K–4 students. *Journal of STEM Education, 5*(3/4), 29–52.

Perry, T. S. (2007). The laptop crusade. *IEEE Spectrum, 44*(4), 28–33.

Pew Hispanic Center. (2009). *Between two worlds: How young Latinos come of age in America.* Retrieved from http://www.pewhispanic.org/2009/12/11/between-two-worlds-how-young-latinos-come-of-age-in-america/

Reid, K., & Feldhaus, C. (2007). Issues for universities working with K–12 institutions implementing pre-packaged pre-engineering curricula such as Project Lead the Way. *Journal of STEM Education, 8*(3/4), 5–14.

Robbins, M. E., & Schoenfisch, M. H. (2005). An interactive analytical chemistry summer camp for middle school girls. *Journal of Chemical Education, 82*(10), 1486–1488.

Rogers, C., & Portsmore, M. (2004). Bringing engineering to elementary school. *Journal of STEM Education, 5*(3/4), 17–28.

Schleppegrell, M. J. (2007). The linguistic challenges of mathematics teaching and learning: A research review. *Reading & Writing Quarterly, 23*(2), 139–159,

Snow, C. (2008). What is the vocabulary of science? In A. Rosebery & B. Warren (Eds.), *Teaching science to English language learners* (pp. 71–84). Arlington, VA: NSTA Press.

Solomon, Y. (2009). *Mathematical literacy: Developing identities of inclusion.* New York, NY: Routledge.

Stone, L. J., & Church, J. (1984). *Childhood and adolescence: A psychology of the growing person* (5th ed). New York, NY: Random House.

Syed, M., & Chemers, M. M. (2011). Ethnic minorities and women in STEM: Casting a wide net to address a persistent social problem. *Journal of Social Issues, 67*(3), 435–441.

Thom, M., (2001). *Balancing the equation: Where are the women and girls in science, engineering and technology?* New York, NY: Prentice Hall.

Turner, E., & Celedón-Pattichis, S. (2011). Mathematical problem solving among Latina/o kindergartners: An analysis of opportunities to learn. *Journal of Latinos and Education, 10*(2), 146–169.

U.S. Census Bureau. (2010). *Newsroom archive: 2010 census shows America's diversity.* Retrieved from http://www.census.gov/newsroom/releases/archives/2010_census/cb11-cn125.html

Vásquez, O. A. (2003). *La clase mágica: Imagining optimal possibilities in a bilingual community of learners.* Mahwah, NJ: Erlbaum.

Vasquez, J. A., Sneider, C., & Comer, M. (2013). *STEM lesson essentials, grades 3–8: Integrating science, technology, engineering, and mathematics.* Portsmouth, NH: Heinemann.

Warschauer, M., & Matuchniak, T. (2010). New technology and digital worlds: Analyzing evidence of equity in access, use, and outcomes. *Review of Research in Education, 34*(1), 179–225.

Webb, D. C., Repenning, A., & Koh, K. H. (2012). Toward an emergent theory of broadening participation in computer science education. In L. S. King & D. Musicant (Eds.), *SIGCSE '12: Proceedings of the 43rd ACM technical symposium on computer science education* (pp. 173–178). New York, NY.

Wenger, E. (1998). *Communities of practice: Learning, meaning, and identity.* New York, NY: Cambridge University Press.

Wyss, V. L., Heulskamp, D., & Siebert, C. J. (2012). Increasing middle school student interest in STEM careers with videos of scientists. *International Journal of Environmental & Science Education, 7*(4), 501–522.

CHAPTER 12

EXPLORING HOW SCHOOL COUNSELORS POSITION

Low-Income African American Girls As Mathematics and Science Learners: Findings From Year Two Data

Cirecie West-Olatunji
Eunhui Yoon
Lauren Shure
Rose Pringle
Thomasenia Adams

It has been well documented that African American and Latino students experience persistent underachievement in education over the past several decades (Aud et al., 2013). Additionally, test scores in mathematics and science despite evidence that the gender gap has narrowed (Aud et al., 2011; Ross, Scott, & Bruce, 2012). Some educational scholars have asserted that opportunities for African American and other culturally marginalized students are influenced by low-resourced schools (Kozol, 2005), teacher attitudes (McKown & Weinstein, 2008; Murray & Malmgren, 2005;

Girls and Women of Color In STEM, pages 207–228
Copyright © 2020 by Information Age Publishing
All rights of reproduction in any form reserved.

Siddle-Walker, 1992), and school counselor referrals (Harley, Jolivette, Mc-Cormick, & Tice, 2002; Rose, 2007).

For African American girls, in particular, whether or not they are recommended for more challenging coursework in gifted or magnet programs during the middle and high school years (that often include advanced mathematics and science coursework), is dictated by teacher and/or counselor referrals at the elementary school level (Bonner, 2009). In particular, school counselors' referrals for African American girls may be influenced by several factors. First, school counseling scholars have asserted that counselor–trainees exhibit stereotyping and bias in their attitudes toward marginalized students, including culturally diverse, immigrant, female, and LGBT (lesbian, gay, bisexual, and transgender) youth (Constantine & Gushue, 2005; Fisher, Matthews, Robinson Kurpius, & Burke, 2001). Second, while few researchers have explored the relationship between counselors' anxiety about an academic domain (e.g., mathematics or science) and student educational outcomes, several scholars have investigated this issue among teachers in elementary and secondary schools (Effandi, Normalizam, Amalina, & Ayu, 2012; Gunderson, Ramirez, Bellock, & Levine, 2013). Finally, it has been stated that school counselors, themselves, are often marginalized within school settings and experience role confusion as well as lack empowerment within the school setting (Armstrong, MacDonald, & Stillo, 2010; West-Olatunji et al., 2010).

Prior research on student underachievement has explored African American students, (Foster & Peele, 1999; Murrell, 2012), students from low-income families (Amatea & West-Olatunji, 2007), and girls and STEM (science, technology, engineering, and mathematics) education (Dasgupta & Stout, 2014; Kerr & Kurpius, 2004). Using the concept of *positionality* as a framework, the goal of the larger research project was to explore the intersectionality of three constructs: ethnicity, gender, and class. Positionality theory suggests that groups of individuals have given social locations in society based upon power dynamics and social prejudice. This framework helped us to understand how some groups are fixed in their social class and how their potential can be hampered (Sakai, 2012).

In this chapter, the authors disseminate findings from a 3-year longitudinal study funded by the National Science Foundation that investigated socially constructed attitudes and perceptions as they relate to low-income African American primary school girls' science and mathematics achievement. The larger study explored African American girls as they transitioned from elementary to middle school while deconstructing the concept of positionality and its relationship to their science and mathematics learning. In collaboration with teachers, students, counselors, and parents, this longitudinal investigation provided a deeper understanding of low-income African American girls and their engagement in mathematics and science at a critical juncture for girls in the educational pipeline. In this chapter, we report Year 2 outcomes of counselor level data exploring how seasoned school counselors perceived their role in the school setting and conceptualized low-income, African American primary school girls as mathematics and science learners.

We discovered that the participants, after 2 years of observation and professional development: (a) evidenced sufficient cultural awareness and knowledge to meet the needs of the low-income African American school girls at their schools; (b) demonstrated reflexivity, based upon their own experiences with mathematics and science; and (c) showed a tendency to stay in the traditional-passive role even though they were offered some possibility for change. Recommendations include re-emphasizing multicultural competence in school counselor training, sustaining supervision for the school counselors, and developing a pool of master counselors to support other counselors.

REVIEW OF THE LITERATURE

Prior research has explored several key factors related to persistence in STEM education, including: ethnicity (Aud et al., 2013), socioeconomic status (Betancur, Votruba-Drzal, & Schunn, 2018; Tate, 1997), and gender in mathematics and science education (Ross et al., 2012). According to the annual report by the National Center for Education Statistics (Aud et al., 2013), among fourth graders in 2011, African American students achieved an average 26 points less than White students in the mathematics assessment. Additionally, in 2009 and 2011, female students achieved three points less than male students on the mathematics assessment. In 2009, students enrolled in low resourced schools scored 31 points less than their more privileged counterparts on the mathematics assessment (Aud et al., 2011). In 2009, there were big gaps in average scores in science achievement by students' ethnicity and the degree of poverty. For fourth graders, among White students, the average science score was 163, compared to 127 for Black students, the average score was 127. Further, 54% of the students from high resourced schools performed at or above the proficient achievement level, while only 11% of the students show the same level in low resourced schools (Aud et al., 2011).

Furthermore, in the science assessment in 2009, male students received higher results than female students among fourth, eighth, and twelfth graders. Specifically, 35% of male fourth graders showed at or above proficient performance in science, whereas 32% female fourth graders were at or above proficiency (Aud et al., 2011). The NCES annual report presented that, from 1990 to 2003, male students showed advantages in their mathematics assessment results in all ethnicity and SES groups (McGraw, Lubenski, & Struthens, 2006). Also, when Penner and Paret (2008) analyzed the Early Childhood Longitudinal Study-Kindergarten (ECLS-K) class of 1998–1999 data for all ethnic groups, they found that male students were advantaged in mathematics achievement from early onset. The researchers argued that the gender difference in mathematics achievement occurs in early ages; it has to be considered seriously. Researchers have investigated how persistent underachievement by gender, ethnicity, and socioeconomic status (SES) is generated and the factors, such as low-resourced schools, teacher attitudes, and counselor referrals, have influenced this phenomenon.

Low-Resourced Schools

Some researchers have argued that students from low-income families are often placed in low-resourced schools with insufficient funding, larger class sizes, and less capable teachers (Akerlof & Kranton, 2002; Guryan, 2001; Hedges, Laine, & Greenwald, 1994; Rose, 2007). Also, it has been asserted that the schools with the fewest resources enroll the highest percentage of low-income, culturally diverse, and low performing students (Clotfelter, Ladd, Vigdor, & Wheeler, 2006; Lankford, Loeb, & Wyckoff, 2002). Further, teachers at these schools are also the least qualified (Boyd, Lankford, Loeb, Rockoff, & Wyckoff, 2008). Although few studies have investigated the characteristics of school counselors in low-resourced schools, some scholars have asserted that: (a) training for school counselors needs to include additional course requirements that include content related to working with underperforming groups of students and (b) national certification should be a requirement (Amatea & West-Olatunji, 2007; Chata & Loesch, 2007; Wingfield, Reese, & West-Olatunji, 2010). Multicultural education scholars have posited that the obstacles to academic achievement for African American and other culturally marginalized students is, in part, due to the attitudes and expectations of teachers and other school personnel (McKown & Weinstein, 2008).

Teacher Attitudes and STEM Education

Recent studies suggest that underachievement among female students in mathematics and science is diminishing (Kerr & Kurpius, 2004; Ross et al., 2012). However, the confidence and willingness gap by gender seems to continue. Female students show low self-confidence and willingness to: (a) engage in mathematics- and science-based tasks, (b) choose advanced courses in mathematics and science, and (c) pursue careers that require mathematics and science training (Meece & Scantlebury, 2006; Ross et al., 2012).

It has been asserted that teachers have differential expectations and attitudes toward students by ethnicity, SES, and gender (Auwarter & Aruguete, 2008). In particular, African American students have consistently earned significantly lower test scores than their White counterparts not only in mathematics and science but also in all national academic tests (Aud et al., 2011; Jencks & Phillips, 1998). Although some scholars have explained this phenomenon by looking at family influences, it has been found that the underachievement by ethnicity and race increases after the students enter school (Phillips, Brooks-Gunn, Duncan, Klebanov, & Crane, 1998). Also, Maher and Tetreault (1993) found that some groups of students have differential educational experiences (by teachers' and students' ethnicity), even though all the participants were dealing with the same academic content.

School Counselor Referrals

Counselor Bias

Research exploring school counselors' perceptions of culturally diverse students has shown that counselor attitudes demonstrated: (a) bias toward diverse students (Constantine & Gushue, 2005; Fisher et al., 2001), (b) countertransference (Rosenberger & Hayes, 2002), and (c) lack of empowerment within the school setting (Armstrong, MacDonald, & Stillo, 2010; Wingfield et al., 2010).

Shure (2010) studied the chance that school counselors would refer students for advanced and remedial interventions dependent upon the students' culturally influenced behavior styles. She concluded that counselor bias may affect racial/ethnic disproportionality in special education. School counselors' attitudes toward African American students may also be influenced by unconscious reactions, such as countertransference, toward these students. Behaviors associated with countertransference (defined as counselor unconscious reactions to clients' attitudes and behaviors) includes counselor withdrawal, antagonism, or hostility (Van Wagoner, Gelso, Hayes, & Diemer, 1991). Thus, school counselors can fall prey to unbridled, negative reactions to African American students that can aggravate students' marginalization in schools.

Counselor Anxiety

Another unconscious response that school counselors might exhibit relates to their reactions to mathematics and science content matter. Similar to teacher anxiety about academic domains (Effandi et al., 2012; Gunderson et al., 2013), school counselors may experience similar reactions. Thus, school counselors may be reluctant to foster students' interest in mathematics and science because of their own anxieties.

Counselor Marginalization

Finally, scholars have asserted that the history and evolution of school counseling has contributed to confusion about counselors' roles in schools (Wingfield et al., 2010). This role confusion has contributed to school counselors' marginalization in schools. As such, there has been a call for school counselors to become more empowered to serve as advocates for students and parents and specifically give voice to the experiences of marginalized students (West-Olatunji, Shure, & Goodman, 2011). Currently, researchers have begun to explore the relationship between school counselors and students' career choices in mathematics and science (Kerr & Kurpius, 2004; West-Olatunji et al., 2010). In particular, school counselors' differential expectations in relation to African American girls' academic achievement has not been sufficiently explored prior to this longitudinal study.

Positionality as a Theoretical Framework

The concept of positionality, rooted in feminist study, has been considered a useful tool to understand social positioning. The researchers employed this framework for the larger study. We sought to understand how teachers, students, parents, and other personnel: (a) interact and relate to each other, construct their knowledge; (b) identify themselves and each other; and (c) make decisions on educational choices reflected by gender, ethnicity, class, and other politics within the classroom and the school setting (Cooper, 2005; Kwak, 2008; Maher & Tetreault, 1993; Sakai, 2012).

Positionality is defined as how an individual or a group of individuals are socially located in relation to others according to background factors, such as ethnicity, class, and gender, and the meaning associated with these identities (Cooper, 2005; Maher & Tetreault, 1993). Positionality is keenly connected with power configuration (Sakai, 2012) and it is related to extent or accessibility towards power, resources, and privilege to navigate successfully in social structures (Cooper, 2005). Thus, positionality should be doubted, criticized, analyzed, explored, and changed in the network of the community. One group of scholars (West-Olatunji et al., 2010) asserted that counselors can support culturally diverse students in their mathematics and science achievement by understanding students' positionality.

By reviewing previous literature, it was hypothesized that African American girls from low-income environments would be poorly positioned in their mathematics and science learning in three ways: gender, ethnicity, and class. For this reason, we focused on students who were African American, female, and from low-income families as the population of interest. The purpose of this study was to investigate how these practicing primary school counselors positioned low-income African American primary school girls in their mathematics and science learning. In this chapter, we share the findings from the Year 2 school counselor data around the question, "How do school counselors position low-income African American primary school girls as mathematics and science learners?"

METHODS

This study was part of a 3-year ethnographical study investigating positionality patterns of teachers, school counselors, and parents towards low-income African American female students in their mathematics and science learning at three primary schools. The research group consisted of a multiethnic, cross-disciplinary team of faculty members in mathematics, science, and counselor education programs, doctoral, and masters level students. All team members participated in the project design and the data collection and analyses process. For the counselor level data analysis, the research team members were aware of findings from the Year 1 counselor data. As with the Year 1 investigation, critical ethnography was used as a methodological approach. Critical ethnography allows researchers to take active ethical responsibility by framing questions, promoting actions and social change (Madison, 2005), and to consider the impact of researchers' interpretation (Pringle, Brkich, Adams, West-Olatunji, & Archer-Banks, 2012). Critical ethnography is grounded in the assumption that cultural institutions can produce a false consciousness in the power dynamics. This methodological perspective allows researchers to dispute distorted power relationships and social injustice by taking action to improve positive social change (Kincheloe & McLaren, 2000; Madison, 2005; Simon & Dippo, 1986).

Data Sources and Protocols

The data sources consisted of three semi-structured individual interviews approximately 50 minutes long with three seasoned school counselors working in three separate elementary schools located in a small suburban/rural school district in the southeastern region of the United States. Each of the schools has a high proportion of low-income, African American students. School "A" (K–5) enrolled 475 students of which 92% were African American and 96% of the students were eligible for free or reduced lunch. School "B" enrolled 445 students (K–5) of which approximately 79% of students were African American and 90.3% were eligible for free or reduced lunch. School "C" enrolled approximately 700 students wherein 92% of the students were identified as culturally diverse with the major identifying as

African American. Approximately 99% of the students at this school were eligible for free or reduced lunch.

Participants

Research team members recruited the participants via school visits, e-mails, and telephone calls. All the participants agreed to the research with the consent forms and the principals approved the research and the data collection process. Also, the institutional review boards of the host university and the local school board gave their approval.

The first school counselor was a White female with more than 30 years of counseling experience who had been serving in the current school over 10 years. The second counselor was also a White female and had less than 5 years of counseling experience and had been working for the current school for about two years. The third counselor was an African American female, had more than 10 years of experience, and had been working for the current school for 3 years.

Protocols

The interview protocols were guided by results from the Year 1 study conducted in the previous year by the research team (West-Olatunji et al., 2010). The Year 1 study employed a purposeful sample of practicing school counselors employed at low-resourced primary schools. As a critical ethnographical study, we expected the research questions to become more relevant and specific each year as we deepen our understanding of the data through consistent and systematic collection and analysis (Kincheloe & McLaren, 2000). Thus, while we began with the same set of interview questions that were used for the counselors in the first year, we modified the questions in Year 2 based upon the findings in the first year. Additionally, there were no indicators of differences among these professionals in how they conceptualized the factors affecting student achievement and their own advocacy roles. However, the school counseling profession has shown a recent push towards the inclusion of advocacy (Amatea & West-Olatunji, 2007; West-Olatunji et al., 2010).

Analysis

After the audiotaped interviews were transcribed, each research team member read through the script while listening to the session to assess its accuracy and highlighted comments and phrases that were representative of the participants' attitudes and thoughts. They clustered highlighted statements into summary statements and organized them into emerging themes in the data. Following individual analysis of data, the team met to reach consensus to ensure credibility of themes. Commonly viewed themes were organized into a tree structure that indicated relationships among themes and subthemes. Themes that were viewed as outliers were also discussed and juxtaposed with relevant literature to determine whether or not an emergent theme was evident.

FINDINGS

Information generated from the three semi-structured interviews generated 42,364 words, 114 pages, and 270 minutes of audiotaped data. After each research team member individually coded the data set, they formed a consensus group to agree on the most salient themes. These themes were analyzed using NVIVO software (v. 7). While the initial total number of nodes was 55, the researchers merged and categorized those nodes by meanings and hierarchy to develop three overarching themes: *lack of knowledge and awareness, reflexivity,* and *traditional-passive roles.*

The findings from the Year 2 data are similar to those of Year 1 in some ways, but the findings of Year 2 data indicated more specific and negative influences from the counselors. In the Year 1 data, four themes emerged: *awareness and unawareness, counselor role, knowledge construction,* and *reflexivity* (West-Olatunji et al., 2010). Overall, the findings from the Year 2 data was similar to the findings from Year 1 data, but findings from Year 2 data analyses indicated the negative impact of the counselor's positioning more accurately. The themes of awareness and unawareness and knowledge construction were merged into one theme: lack of knowledge and awareness. This theme is specified by three sub-themes: (a) deficit of orientation and view, (b) lack of awareness, and (c) false knowledge.

The theme of reflexivity continued to be a main theme in the Year 2 data and the theme of the counselor's role was changed to *passive and traditional role.* Compared to the findings of Year 1 data, the themes in Year 2 are more focused on the negative influences of the participants' positioning. The descriptions and examples of themes from the Year 2 data follow.

Lack of Knowledge and Awareness

The theme of lack of knowledge and awareness is described as disconnection between theory and practice and limitation of counselors' perceptions toward their own social positioning. It can be surmised that the school counselors are not aware of their possibility to have prejudice about African-American girls and are unaware of the impact of their false knowledge. The theme could be linked to the unawareness from the theme of awareness and unawareness at the Year 1 data and the theme of knowledge construction. However, for Year 2 data, themes focused on false knowledge. The theme is divided into three sub-themes: (a) deficit of orientation and view, (b) lack of awareness, and (c) false knowledge.

Deficit Orientation and View (19 References)

This sub-theme can be described as counselors having wrong or biased perceptions toward African American female students from low-income families. The participants tended to expect that the students would not be able to be high academic achievers in mathematics and science. They didn't expect that African American students' class control would go very well. One counselor stated,

> I also think it has to do with the population here, that if you have clear expectations you do not get out of your seat and you must be quiet, umm it, it's easier to keep control of the classroom, it's just hard to keep control of the classroom when the kids are actually doing things and it's just more difficult so.

Another counselor disclosed, "I'm not saying it's not being done, I know that it is being done, you know, um, but I think it's more of a difficult way to teach in this population, them."

The participants tended to maintain the perception that students' low-income status was a problem or a negative indicator of the students' life rather than believing their task to be to promote the students' strengths or investigating possible support and resources for their students, as described in the following statement by one of the counselors, "And at this school it's 95% free and reduced lunch, that's, um, a difficult thing." Another counselor offered, "That's my theory, I could be wrong, I don't know. I think some of its got to do with poverty."

Moreover, the counselors showed their biased views of the African American students' cultural background. Another counselor stated,

> And we talked about um...how, because I already did it once with one of the classes, they loved it, we talked about how White people are different than Black people; how they're the same and how they're different. One of the kids brought up, you speak differently than I do, I said but can you speak like me, and he goes, "Yeah." And we talked about, um...learning to speak in the, um, where you grow up and learning to make that shift and being able, and I said would you do that in a job interview? I said could you, could you do the other thing in a job interview and he said "I'm not sure." So it's learning to make that shift, again more social skills! And so I've been talking to them about stepping outside of the box, stepping outside of themselves next year and trying to make one friend that's White, Asian, Hispanic, that's, that's different than you. Find somebody that's different than you and get to

know them because you're going to grow as a person . . . and you know, some of them are going to listen and some of them are gonna not and I hope the ones that listen do it because these are the people that are going to change this world for us.

Lack of Awareness (14 References)

The second sub-theme, lack of awareness and knowledge, is described in terms of how counselors do not recognize their own social positioning toward African American students in mathematics and science learning and neglect systemic context of students' lives which can influence students' academic achievement issues. A counselor stated,

> Oh the kids like it, too, cause they don't necessarily wanna hash out, especially not in there, I mean this is their one environment where they don't have to deal with all that stuff. And so they like the idea of being looked at individually for their own actions and their own achievements and not for whatever chaotic thing is going on in their home environment.

This counselor demonstrated that she is not aware of the necessity to deal with students' academic issues with considering the systemic and environmental contexts.

The False Knowledge (12 References)

This sub-theme is described around counselors having wrong knowledge about their students. It also can be described as their lack of awareness of the impact of the wrong knowledge. The sub-theme, false knowledge, spanned various aspects. The participants stated their knowledge related to students' learning, developmental nature, and how they facilitate their low-income African American students' mathematics and science learning. One counselor asserted that, "Um . . . it depends on the kids. Some kids are very open to help, some are, I think, um, it really just depends on the personality of the child. She wants to be a teacher so she thinks it's great. You know." Another stated,

> Because that's what they want to know, you know, do I get to tell everybody about this? Am I going to be able to show this to someone? So I think it's that, I think it's that ability to share their writing and the fact that there's gonna be something about themselves that they can reveal through that. That if we were doing a science experiment or something, yes the experience is there, but there's nothing necessarily that they can share about themselves when they're doing it. And I do think that's a huge part of it, because I probably get that question every time I ask them to do something [they both laugh], the question is, "Are we gonna get to share this when we're finished? Do we get to tell everybody about it?"

Additionally, counselors also tended to demonstrate a biased interpretation towards students' behaviors because of the counselors' wrong or lack of knowledge of African American students' cultural background. This was reflected in one counselor's statement,

> They laugh at other people's misfortune. I don't know why that is. I don't know why... maybe it's the violent cartoons they're watching. I don't know. But we'll, we'll, we have, you know because we're a performing arts school we do plays and a lot of times we'll, they'll be a play. The fifth grade did a play, it was wonderful. And the homeless boy falls and something terrible happens and normally you would go (gasp). Everybody cracked up laughing. It was so funny because he fell and hurt himself. And you know of course being the social anthropologist—They're laughing, why are they laughing? Why are they laughing at somebody else's misfortune? And does it make them feel better about themselves? I don't know. Interesting though.

In addition, one participant seemed to use her lack of knowledge toward African American students as an excuse for not engaging in further contemplation as exemplified in this statement: "Ummm well I don't know because I haven't worked with this population in another setting. So I don't know, umm. I know we do have in terms of the parent's strong women roles models you know and uh (laughs)."

Reflexivity (21 References)

The second main theme, reflexivity, was defined as the participants' personal experiences in math and science education between the school counselor and the student's positioning. It seemed that the counselors' personal experiences in math and science learning influenced their expectations toward students' learning and their attitude to motivate students' learning in these two fields. Counselors stated that they did not like or were not good at mathematics and science. Also, they did not think of a science-related field or medical school as their possible future career. It seemed that counselors might have positioned themselves by gender when they were students. Thus, the self-positioning by gender might have influenced their positioning of any female mathematics and science learners. This is reflected in the following statement,

> Well when I was in physics, I mean, I got the grades I needed because I got them, you know I mean, because I had to get them, um, but I hated every step of it and I never considered myself good at it and I was never natural at it. It was pure forcing force feeding yourself and I found that um, I was excited for the day when I would never have to take a class again in science and then um, a lot of education is like that ah, we force kids to take classes in subject

areas that they won't ever use and that even educators question if they're, if they're useful.

Another counselor stated, "Physics in high school that turned me off in science entirely. I was just like not at all interested, I mean and the only I mean, the concept of gravity, come on did I really need a full course on that?" And, the third counselor stated,

> Interest is huge and you know I don't think that when I was in these classes, I didn't get a big I couldn't make the connection with how I was ever going to use this information . . . yeah, all of them I mean depending on their interest area. I've never focused on math and science or anything in particular.

Passive and Traditional Role (26 References)

The third main theme, passive and traditional role, refers to the participants' tendencies to not want to be actively involved in relationships with students, even though they found something further they could do. The Year 1 data included the theme of counselor role. The researchers perceived that counselors did not include facilitating students' learning as their responsibility. For example, when they perceived their role as an academic advisor, they didn't make further effort to help students overcome environmental barriers or consult with teachers to develop better approaches to instructional practice that might include regarding students' cultural aspects or home background. The counselors tended to stay in narrowly defined roles as academic advisors and not as advocates for the students. Here, the academic advisor role was used as an excuse for not actively advocating for students, not researching community-related support for the students, even when they found something further they could do. This is evidenced by the following statement, "But my primary focus is [pause] this is a school. I'm a school counselor. I'm here to help you academically succeed in school." Another counselor stated,

> Well language too, but definitely math/science, I know my own children had lots of toys to play with and you know they are constantly manipulating things, I think in this culture, the culture, umm you that we have here, umm toys are not a big thing because you know they get in the way, they get messy, get broken umm, you know it's more sitting in front of the TV or you know they have less experience with hands on types of things at home.

The third counselor offered,

> But mostly behavior, because you can have a kid that's interested, we've got this one little girl here, she could be a Supreme Court judge if she wanted to,

seriously. She comes from the most dysfunctional family you've ever met, her behaviors are all over the place, this little girl is so smart, but she also argues with adults, she fights with parents that walk in here, and she's, oh and she's going into sixth grade and I go, "oh what's going to happen with her?," but she's so smart and she'll ask, and um, again relationship. She likes ya, she'll give ya 100%, and so I've been in situations with her where I've had conversations that I'm just blown away by her common sense and intelligence, and she could do it, but I don't think she's got what she needs in terms of the guidance.

The participating school counselors in this study positioned their African American female students as not capable of significant involvement in mathematics and science achievement. Three themes emerged from the Year 2 data that supported this generalization were: lack of knowledge/awareness, reflexivity, and passive and traditional role. The first theme suggested that the school counselors who participated in this study evidenced biases toward their students. The second theme highlighted that school counselors did not remember themselves as capable mathematics and science learners and these attitudes influenced their motivation to support mathematics and science learning for their female students. The third theme suggested that, even though they see themselves as advocates, the counselors stayed in their conventional roles as academic advisors and guidance personnel.

DISCUSSION

The findings from this study suggest that counselors' attitudes may perpetuate stereotypes that maintain the cycle of low involvement in mathematics and science education among low-income African-American female students. This supports prior research exploring school counselor bias and culturally diverse students' achievement, particularly in mathematics and science (Kerr & Kurpius, 2004; West-Olatunji et al., 2010). After more than three decades of multicultural counseling training, school counselors continue to exhibit resistance to achieving multicultural competence. The school counselors who participated in this study seemed to lack awareness and knowledge about their own social positioning. It seems that the lack of knowledge about cultural diversity led them to have insufficient knowledge about how to encourage their students to be more engaged in their mathematics and science education and to connect this learning to their lives. In addition, the participants believed that mathematics and science education is not really needed for their students because the students already had other learning experiences that didn't seem to connect to their potential careers or life.

The counselors also stated that they did not perceive themselves as capable in mathematics and science subject areas. Thus, their inability and disinterest in promoting mathematics and science education in their professional roles seemed to reflect their negative experiences with mathematics and science in their own schooling. Similar to the reflexivity found among teachers, school counselors may also exhibit anxiety about teaching mathematics and other content areas. Moreover, counselors may be experiencing countertransference and reacting to African American students with preconceived notions that promote fear, anger, and irritation at unconscious levels. This reflexivity may also be connected to the counselors' tendencies to assume passive roles and not advocate for their students' mathematics and science learning.

In the findings from Year 1 data, counselors showed their role confusion. It seemed that they were not sure what range of students' issues they would be able to address. And from the Year 2 data, counselors seemed to take on passive roles, even though they recognized that their students needed more support and advocacy. The fact that all three school counselors responded as they did suggested that even more recently educated school counselors are being inculcated into these passive roles. This passive identity may serve as an obstacle to school counselors' assumptions of leadership and advocacy roles within the school setting.

RECOMMENDATIONS

Based on our study and review of the literature, we offer the following recommendations around each of the three themes: lack of knowledge/awareness, reflexivity, and passive/traditional role.

Knowledge and Awareness

We suggest that counselor education programs need to have more focused and evidence-based multicultural training to enhance future counselors' knowledge and awareness towards diverse populations. Counseling candidates' perceptions towards ethnic diversity and gender equity can be significantly predicted by two things: (a) the program's ambiance about cultural sensitivity (Dickson, Jepsen, & Barbee, 2008) and (b) supervisors' instructional focus on multicultural issues are related to supervisees' conceptualization of multicultural counseling strategies (Ladany, Inman, Constantine, & Hofheinz, 1997). Therefore, program administrators need to develop a strategic plan for developing multicultural competence that is data driven and establishes clear outcomes. Each program should assess students' multicultural competence at matriculation and then again during the exit interview process. The university counseling faculty can then modify the curriculum content and professional development activities based upon annual reviews of the multicultural counseling skills inventories. Second, counseling preparation program administrators can audit their programs to assess the multicultural climate to determine what message is being sent to candidates regarding their multicultural counseling competencies. Third, in supervision training, counselor educators need to inform graduate students and community supervisors about the various multicultural supervision approaches to ensure that candidates being supervised are held accountable for their multicultural awareness, knowledge, and skills.

Immersion programs for school counselors are needed to assist them in reconceptualizing the needs and strengths of culturally marginalized students. Outreach experiences can improve school counselors' insight regarding their biases about this population of learners and serve to reduce or prevent the marginalization of diverse students.

Reflexivity

To overcome the negative impact of school counselors' reflexivity, sustained supervision for school counselors is recommended. Supervision is helpful in assisting school counselors to enhance their self-awareness (Glaes, 2010) and to understand the relationship between their own lived experiences and their ability to effectively assist clients in resolving their issues. (Del Moro, 2012). In this case, supervision can assist school counselors to be aware of their self-positioning by gender in their own experience in mathematics and science learning and their hidden preconception towards culturally diverse students. Thus, their reluctances to serve as facilitators of mathematics and science learning for nontraditional and female students. Counselor educators are encouraged to serve as faculty-in-residence at schools to provide on-site supervision for practicing counselors (West-Olatunji et al., 2011). Given that practicing school counselors frequently do not participate in regularly scheduled supervision sessions (Paisley & McMahon, 2001), they could benefit from receiving sustained supervision within the school setting.

Passive Role

Several scholars have articulated the need for school counselors to guide program design and advocacy (Hatch & Bowers, 2002; Herr, 2001), to participate in school reform (Adelman & Taylor, 2002), and to embrace particular institutional roles in the school (Dollarhide, 2003). However, it may be difficult for school counselors to overcome their passive identities to become catalysts of change in school communities. Thus, it may require that counselor educators invest in the retraining and resocialization process for school counselors. Such training should be ongoing from preservice through post-masters placement in a school setting and involve experiential activities, such as live on-site supervision and peer mentoring.

Further, there is a need to identify master counselors who can model more effective roles and interventions for school counselors working in school settings where low-income students predominate (West-Olatunji et al., 2011). Master teachers have been utilized in schools and their improvements, such as increased academic outcomes, augmented engagement, culturally embedded knowledge construction, critical thinking, and interpersonal skill development (Foster, Lewis, & Onafowra, 2003). Given the known benefits from having master teachers in classrooms, it would be of interest to apply a similar approach to counselors in school settings. Thus, master counselors, who are experienced and have a proven record can address the needs of underperforming students. Master counselors can be models to take more effective roles and interventions for their students at the school settings based on their cumulative knowledge about students' populations, the school system, and effective ways of communicating with parents, teachers, and administrators. Therefore, new counselors can ask consultation from the master-counselors when they need to, and then, they can practice with more confidence.

Future Research

Large-scale quantitative studies based on the findings from this research are suggested. One such quantitative research project could be conducted using the emerged themes. The study could be correlational investigating the relationship among school counselors' awareness/knowledge, reflexivity, and role recognition and mathematics and science achievement for African American students in low-resourced primary schools. Such a study would investigate the correlation between the emerged themes from this study and counselor demographics, such as age, years of service, ethnicity, gender, amount and type of professional development training, and year received degree. This study might also explore the correlation between the emerged themes of this study and African American primary school students' achievement in mathematics and science. The study could also examine the correlations among three themes. From the Year 2 data, the researchers hypothesize that the three themes would be positively correlated to one another. The statistical evidence for this assumption about the relationships among these themes can be explored.

In sum, researchers have agreed that school counselors should take a critical role in maximizing students' academic success (Lapan, Gysbers, & Kayson, 2007). They should actively intervene to advocate for their students at both the individual and systemic levels (American School Counselor Association, 2003). However, from the Year 1 data, participating school counselors could not take active roles because they (a) stood between awareness and unawareness, (b) were confused about their counselor role and the way of knowledge construction related to the low-income African American female students population, and (c) were influenced by their own reflexivity. In the Year 2 data, the researchers found similar but more specific themes. School counselors' lack of knowledge and awareness about the population and their own biased perspectives and knowledge, their reflexivity based on their own negative experiences with mathematics and science, as well as their tendency to stay in passive and traditional roles were all factors contributing to their positioning of low-income African American primary school girls. To overcome this positioning, the authors recommend more emphasis on multicultural competence, sustained supervision, and the use of a master counselor model. School counselors are trained to help teachers, students, and parents. By strengthening their multicultural counseling skills, reducing countertransference, and taking leadership roles in school communities, school counselors can become agents of change in STEM education for culturally marginalized students, especially girls in low-resourced schools.

REFERENCES

Adelman, H. S., & Taylor, L. (2002). School counselors and school reform: New directions. *Professional School Counseling, 5*(4), 235–248.

Akerlof, G. A., & Kranton, R. E. (2002). Identity and schooling: Some lessons for the economics of education. *Journal of Economic Literature, 40*(4), 1167–1201.

Amatea, E., & West-Olatunji, C. (2007). Rethinking how school counselors work with families and schools: An ecosystemic approach. In J. Wittmer & M. Clark. (Eds.), *Managing your school counseling program: K–12 Developmental strategies* (3rd ed.; pp. 211–222). Minneapolis, MN: Educational Media.

American School Counselor Association. (2003). The ASCA national model: A framework for school counseling programs. *Professional School Counseling,* 165–168.

Armstrong, S. A., MacDonald, J. H., & Stillo, S. (2010). School counselors and principals: Different perceptions of relationship, leadership, and training. *Journal of School Counseling, 8*(15), 1–27.

Aud, S., Hussar, W., Kena, G., Bianco, K., Frohlich, L., Kemp, J., & Tahan, K. (2011). *The condition of education 2011* (NCES 2011-033). Washington, DC: U.S. Government Printing Office. Retrieved from https://nces.ed.gov/pubs2011/2011033_1.pdf

Aud, S., Wilkinson-Flicker, S., Kristapovich, P., Rathbun, A., Wang, X., & Zhang, J. (2013). *The condition of education 2013* (NCES 2013-037). Washington, DC. Retrieved May 28, 2013 from Author (2010c). (Doctoral dissertation).

Auwarter, A. E., & Aruguete, M. S. (2008). Effects of student gender and socioeconomic status on teacher perceptions. *The Journal of Educational Research, 101*(4), 243–246, 256.

Betancur, L., Votruba-Drzal, E., & Schunn, C. (2018). Socioeconomic gaps in science achievement. *International Journal of STEM Education, 5*(1), 1–25.

Bonner, E. P. (2009). Achieving success with African American learners: A framework for culturally responsive mathematics teaching. *Childhood Education, 86*(1), 2–6.

Boyd, D., Lankford, H., Loeb, S., Rockoff, J., & Wyckoff, J. (2008). The narrowing gap in New York City teacher qualifications and its implications for student achievement in high-poverty schools. *Journal of Policy Analysis and Management, 27*(4), 793–818.

Clotfelter, C., Ladd, H. F., Vigdor, J., & Wheeler, J. (2006). High-poverty schools and the distribution of teachers and principals. *NCL Review, 85*, 1345.

Constantine, M. G., & Gushue, G. V. (2003). School counselors' ethnic tolerance attitudes and racism attitudes as predictors of their multicultural case conceptualization of an immigrant student. *Journal of Counseling & Development, 81*(2), 185–190.

Cooper, C. W. (2005). School choice and the standpoint of African American mothers: Considering the power of positionality. *The Journal of Negro Education, 74*(2), 174–189. Retrieved from http://www.jstor.org/stable/40034542

Dasgupta, N., & Stout, J. G. (2014). Girls and women in science, technology, engineering, and mathematics: STEMing the tide and broadening participation in STEM careers. *Policy Insights from the Behavioral and Brain Sciences, 1*(1), 21–29.

Del Moro, R. (2012). *Cultivating self-awareness in counselors-in-training through group supervision.* Gainesville: University of Florida. Retrieved from https://ufdc.ufl.edu/UFE0044928/00001

Dickson, G. L., Jepsen, D. A., & Barbee, P. W. (2008). Exploring the relationships among multicultural training experiences and attitudes toward diversity among counseling students. *Journal of Multicultural Counseling and Development, 36*(2), 113–126.

Dollarhide, C. T. (2003). School counselors as program leaders: Applying leadership contexts to school counseling. *Professional School Counseling, 6*(5), 304–308. Retrieved from https://www.schoolcounselor.org/asca/media/asca/LeadershipSpecialist/Dollarshide.pdf

Effandi, Z., Normalizam Mohd, Z., Nur Amalina, A., & Ayu, E. (2012). Mathematics anxiety and achievement among secondary school students. *American Journal of Applied Sciences, 9*(11), 1828–1832. https://doi.org/10.3844/ajassp.2012.1828.1832

Fisher, T. A., Matthews, L. G., Robinson Kurpius, S. E., & Burke, K. I. (2001). Counselor preparation. *Counselor Education & Supervision, 41*(1), 3.

Foster, M., Lewis, J., & Onafowora, L. (2003). Anthropology, culture, and research on teaching and learning: Applying what we learned to improve practice. *Teachers College Record, 105*(2), 261.

Foster, M., & Peele, T. (1999). Teaching and learning in the contexts of African American English and culture. *Education and Urban Society, 31*(2), 177–189.

Glaes, J. M. (2010). *Implementing an ASCA-informed school counselor supervision model: A qualitative field-based study* (Doctoral dissertation). Retrieved from ProQuest Dissertations and Theses Database. (503250273)

Gunderson, E. A., Ramirez, G., Beilock, S. L., & Levine, S. C. (2013). Teachers' spatial anxiety relates to 1st- and 2nd-graders' spatial learning. *Mind, Brain & Education, 7*(3), 196–199. https://doi.org/10.1111/mbe.12027

Guryan, J. (2001). *Does money matter? Regression-discontinuity estimates from education finance reform in Massachusetts* (NBER Working Paper No. 8269). Cambridge, MA: National Bureau of Economic Research.

Harley, D. A., Jolivette, K., McCormick, K., & Tice, K. (2002). Race, class, and gender: A constellation of positionalities with implications for counseling. *Journal of multicultural Counseling and Development, 30*(4), 216.

Hatch, T., & Bowers, J. (2002). The block to build on. *ASCA School Counselor, 39*(5), 12–17.

Hedges, L. V., Laine, R., & Greenwald, R. (1994). Does money matter? A meta-analysis of studies of the effects of differential school inputs on student outcomes. *Education Researcher, 23*(3), 5–14.

Herr, E. L. (2001). The impact of national policies, economics, and school reform on comprehensive guidance programs. *Professional School Counseling, 4,* 236–245.

Jencks, C., & Phillips, M. (1998). The Black–White test scope gap: Why it persists and what can be done. *The Brookings Review, 16*(2), 24–27.

Kerr, B., & Kurpius, S. E. (2004). Encouraging talented girls in math and science: Effects of guidance intervention. *High Ability Studies, 15*(1), 85–102.

Kincheloe , J. L., & McLaren , P. L. (2000). Rethinking critical theory and qualitative research. In N. K. Denzin & Y. S. Lincoln (Eds.), *Handbook of qualitative research* (2nd ed.; pp. 279–313). Thousand Oaks, CA: SAGE.

Kozol, J. (2005). Still separate, still unequal. *Harper's Magazine, 311*(1864), 41–54.

Kwak, S. (2008). *Feminist pedagogy: Advent of learning leadership and its meaning.* Seoul, South Korea: Ewha Womans University Press.

Ladany, R., Inman, A. G., Constantine, M. G., & Hofheinz, E. W. (1997). Supervisee multicultural case conceptualization ability and self-reported multicultural competence as functions of supervisee racial identity and supervisor focus. *Journal of Counseling Psychology, 44*(3), 284–293.

Lankford, H., Loeb, S., & Wyckoff, J. (2002). Teacher sorting and the plight of urban schools: A descriptive analysis. *Educational Evaluation and Policy Analysis, 24*(1), 37–62.

Lapan, R. T., Gysbers, N. C., & Kayson, M. A. (2007). *Missouri school counselors benefit all students.* Jefferson City, MO: Missouri Department of Elementary and Secondary Education.

Madison, D. S. (2005). *Critical ethnography : Method, ethics, and performance.* Thousand Oaks, CA: SAGE.

Maher, F. A., & Tetreault, M. K. (1993). Frames of positionality: Constructing meaningful dialogues about gender and race. *Anthropological Quarterly, 66*(3), 118–126. Retrieved from http://www.jstor.org/stable/3317515

McGraw, R., Lubienski, S. T., & Strutchens, M. E. (2006). A closer look at gender in NAEP mathematics achievement and affect data: Intersections with achievement, race/ethnicity, and socioeconomic status, *Journal for Research in Mathematics Education, 37*(2) 129–150.

McKown, C., & Weinstein, R. S. (2008). Teacher expectations, classroom context, and the achievement gap. *Journal of School Psychology, 46*(3), 235–261. http://doi.org.lp.hscl.ufl.edu/10.1016/j.jsp. 2007.05.001

Meece, J. L., & Scantlebury, K. (2006). Gender and schooling: Progress and persistent barriers. In J. Worrle & C. Goodheart (Eds.), Handbook of girls' and women's psychological health (pp. 283–291). New York, NY: Oxford University Press.

Murray, C., & Malmgren, K. (2005). Implementing a teacher–student relationship program in a high-poverty urban school: Effects on social, emotional, and academic adjustment and lessons learned. *Journal of School Psychology, 43*(2), 137–152.

Murrell, P. C., Jr. (2012). *African-centered pedagogy: Developing schools of achievement for African American children.* Albany: State University of New York Press.

Paisley, P. O., & McMahon, H. G. (2001). School counseling for the twenty-first century: Challenges and opportunities. *Professional School Counseling, 5*(2), 106–115.

Penner, A. M., & Paret, M. (2008). Gender differences in mathematics achievement: Exploring the early grades and the extremes. *Social Science Research, 37*(1), 239–253. https://doi.org/10.1016/j.ssresearch.2007.06.012

Phillips, M., Brooks-Gunn, J., Duncan, G., Klebanov, P., & Crane, J. (1998). Does the Black-White test score gap widen after children enter school? In C. Jencks & M. Phillips (Eds.), *The Black-White test score gap* (pp. 229–272). Washington, DC: Brookings Institution Press.

Pringle, R., Brkich, K., Adams, T., West-Olatunji, C., & Archer-Banks, D. (2012). Factors influencing elementary teachers' positioning of African American girls as science and mathematics learners. *School Science and Mathematics, 114*(4), 217–229.

Rose, S. R. (2007). *School counselor perceptions and competencies for closing the achievement gap: Implications for counselor and higher education programs for all educators* (Doctoral dissertation). Retrieved from ProQuest Dissertations and Theses Database. (304847168)

Rosenberger, E. W., & Hayes, J. A. (2002). Origins, consequences, and management of countertransference: A case study. *Journal of Counseling Psychology, 49*(2), 221.

Ross, J. A., Scott, G., & Bruce, C. D. (2012). The gender confidence gap in fractions knowledge: Gender differences in student belief—achievement relationships. *School Science and Mathematics, 112*(5), 278–288. https://doi.org/10.1111/j.1949-8594.2012.00144.x

Sakai, N. (2012). Positions and positionalities: After two decades. *Positions: East Asia Cultures Critique, 20*(1), 67–94.

Shure, L. A. (2010). *The relationship between school counselors' multicultural knowledge and awareness and their likelihood of recommending students for advanced and remedial interventions based upon students' culturally-bound behavioral styles* (Unpublished doctoral dissertation). University of Florida, Gainesville, Florida.

Siddle-Walker, E. V. (1992). Falling asleep and failure among African-American students: Rethinking assumptions about process teaching. *Theory into Practice, 31*(4), 321–327.

Simon, R. I., & Dippo, D. (1986). On critical ethnographic work. *Anthropology & Education Quarterly, 17*(4), 195–202.

Tate, W. F. (1997). Race-ethnicity, SES, gender, and language proficiency trends in mathematics achievement: An update. *Journal for Research in Mathematics Education, 28*(6), 652–679.

Van Wagoner, S. L., Gelso, C. J., Hayes, J. A., & Diemer, R. A. (1991). Countertransference and the reputedly excellent therapist. *Psychotherapy, 28*(3), 411–421.

West-Olatunji, C., Shure, L., & Goodman, R. D. (2011). Use of multicultural supervision with school counselors to enhance cultural competence. *Journal of School Counseling, 9*(16). Retrieved from http://www.jsc.montana.edu/articles/v9n16.pdf

West-Olatunji, C., Shure, L., Pringle, R., Adams, T. L., Lewis, D. R., & Cholewa, B. (2010). Exploring how school counselors position low-income African American girls as mathematics and science learners. *Professional School Counseling, 13*(3), 184–195.

Wingfield, R., Reese, R., & West-Olatunji, C. (2010). Counselors as leaders. *Florida Journal of Educational Administration and Policy, 4*(1), 114–130.

CHAPTER 13

STEM-ING THE TIDE

Women of Color Reimagining Their "Place" Through Sociocultural Action

Aria Razfar
Zayoni Torres

Science, technology, engineering, and mathematics (STEM) fields have been a major focus of U.S. education reform efforts since the 1958 National Defense Education Act (Zhao, 2009). While federal financial support and other K–12 initiatives have followed, there is little evidence that instructional strategies have changed or that students have gained more interest in STEM from such initiatives (Breiner, Harkness, Johnson, & Keehler, 2012). Furthermore, the recruitment and retention of women of color into STEM fields continues to be low (Ong, Wright, Espinosa, & Orfield, 2011). The socialization of students into prescribed gender roles and its relation to STEM is lifelong and transpires in the intricacies of everyday talk (Ochs, 1990). By middle school, students have already formed strong affinities or aversions towards STEM disciplines based on gender and/or race (Hayden, Ouyang, Scinski, Olszewski, & Bielefeldt, 2011; Sadker & Sadker, 1982). Given the prevailing patriarchal and Eurocentric "White" paradigm that

Girls and Women of Color In STEM, pages 229–252
Copyright © 2020 by Information Age Publishing

permeates STEM education, girls and women of color who excel in these fields are in a sense "STEM-ing" the tide and creating a counter narrative to the dominant script. PROJECT,[1] a long-term professional development program for teachers working with English learners (ELs), aims to provide *spaces of reclamation* for teachers of color designing STEM activities in K–8 urban classrooms. Two questions guide this study: (a) How do women of color teachers (WCT)[2] negotiate the tensions of integrating STEM with language and literacy? and (b) How do they reimagine STEM possibilities for themselves and for students of color?

A key proposition in attracting students into STEM careers (i.e., for this study women and girls of color) holds that students "must be provided with more meaningful learning experiences in order to motivate and excite them—learning-experiences that relate directly to the world in which they live" (Dischino, De Laura, Donnelly, Massa, & Hanes, 2011, p. 23). An avenue for providing such experiences stems from ongoing professional development for teachers at the elementary and secondary levels integrating STEM concepts into the classroom (Morrison, Raab, & Ingram, 2009; Nadelson et al., 2013). Our study builds on this tradition, focusing on long-term professional development (PROJECT) to develop reflexive and critical *teacher–researchers*.

In this chapter we examine the ideological and identity struggles of 20 WCT participating in PROJECT. Our goal is to provide an empirically informed approach to developing WCT doing STEM in urban schools. In the remainder of this chapter, we provide the context, conceptual frameworks, global findings, two illustrative case studies, followed by concluding remarks and implications for teacher preparation.

CONTEXT

PROJECT is a long-term professional development program for in-service K–8 teachers working with ELs in predominantly low-income urban neighborhoods in a large Midwestern city (Razfar, 2007, 2011). Teachers are encouraged to collaboratively develop and apply mathematics and science instruction that is linguistically and culturally relevant and in alignment with district and state standards. To date, 42 teachers have successfully completed all requirements of PROJECT. Of the 42 teachers, 95% self-identify as women and 5% self-identify as men, with 38% Latin@, 10% African American, 7% Asian, and 45% White. During this 2½–3-year process, teachers take courses towards an ESL/bilingual endorsement or approval and pursue a master's degree with a focus on mathematics and/or science. Teachers also design and execute three curricular units that draw on students' funds of

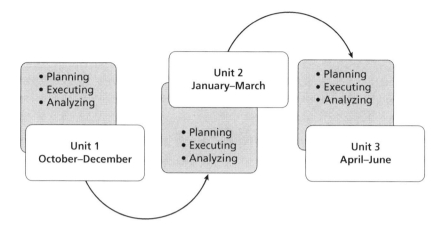

Figure 13.1   Action research timeline.

knowledge (Moll, Amanti, Neff, & Gonzalez, 1992) and integrate mathematics, science, and literacy practices. These funds of knowledge (FoK) include linguistic, cultural, gender, racial, and STEM FoK. The action research timeline of PROJECT is depicted in Figure 13.1.

Teachers collaborate with researchers from the university to plan, execute, and analyze curricular units embedded in the constructs of cultural historical activity theory (CHAT), FoK, third space, multiple languages/discourse, and integrative curriculum. A key outcome of PROJECT is for teachers to appropriate the theoretical underpinnings and utilize researcher tools to develop sustainable teacher–researcher practices once the project has ended (Razfar et al., 2015).

CONCEPTUAL FRAMEWORKS

We took an explicit sociocultural approach to doing action research where we used sociocultural tools of language and learning to empower teachers to become teacher researchers and curriculum designers (Razfar, 2011; Razfar et al., 2015; Wells, 2011). Action research in general assumes that change comes from the ground up rather than top-down, and is an effective form of professional development (Razfar, 2011). More specifically, we adopted a cultural-historical activity theory (CHAT) framework to learning and development which allows for diachronic and synchronic analysis of instructional practices. In this context, language, gender, and racial ideologies were viewed as key mediational tools in the social organization of learning for teachers and students.

Language, Gender, and Racial Ideologies

Our conceptualization of gender and racial identity(s) was grounded in critical and sociocultural, or *sociocritical*, perspectives of identity construction and ideological stance taking (Razfar, 2012). Language ideologies are not only our beliefs and ideas about how language works, but language practices that index widespread systems of belief about language. This includes how language is used to construct ideas about race and gender. Racial and gender ideologies are constructed through language (Hill, 1998, 2008; Philips, 2003; Silverstein, 2003). The discursive construction of gender and race is inscribed with status and differentiation that is historically informed and locally enacted. They are made visible through discourse analysis and critical reflection. Visibility of gendered and racialized discourse is an important precursor to STEM-ing the tide of differentiating and inequitable socialization practices. In our professional development model, participating teachers engaged in critical discussions about the nature of language use, identity, and ideological stance-taking vis-á-vis race, gender, and STEM epistemologies.

Stance-taking are the discursive practices by which speakers take moral and value laden positions in relation to objects in the world. There are numerous ways in which sex or gender is indexed through language use, and every language has its own ways of accomplishing this (Silverstein, 1985). In English, some nouns related to occupation add a suffix "-ress" to index a female worker (e.g., waiter vs. waitress; seamstress, etc.). In Spanish, bound morphemes such as "-a" and "-o" are used at the end of nouns and adjectives to mark femaleness and maleness respectively. While these examples show how linguistic structure can index sex or gender, there are numerous non-referential modes where the speaker's sex or gender can be shown (Silverstein, 2003). Much of the early sociolinguistic literature showed how pronunciation variations, rising intonation, and hypercorrection can be predictable indices of sex or gender (e.g., Winford, 1978). Moreover, these gendered practices were informed by issues of power and status. In some cases, there are vivid examples of how multiple layers of values and identities converge. For example, in Japanese politeness, affixes are used to index feminine social identity (Silverstein, 2003).

Thus, through everyday language, gendered hierarchies and ideologies are co-constructed by interlocutors. In the context of STEM education, dominant gender ideologies become normative and define the "normal, appropriate, and acceptable" ways in which males and females are supposed to act (Spencer, Porche, & Tolman, 2003, p. 1777). Martin (1991) showed how scientific discourse as evidenced by the language used in texts and journals can convey discriminating notions of masculinity and femininity. For example, biological nomenclature such as "eggs" and "sperms" are often depicted in passive (feminine) and active (masculine) states. This type of positioning is often subtle, pervasive, and subconscious.

The study of language in relation to ideological constructions allows for conscious reflection on the way hegemonic cultural systems are rationalized and sustained by both dominant and subordinated actors. While not exactly the same, a similar discursive phenomenon exists with racial ideological constructions and in the case of women of color, there is overlap (Castambis, 1994). Racial ideologies refer to "racially-based frameworks used by actors to explain and justify…the racial status quo" (Bonilla-Silva, 2003, p. 65). Racial ideologies exist along a continuum of eugenic, biological determinism on one end and sociocritical relativism on the other. In practice, people do not occupy fixed ideological positions, in the "ideology" sense of the word. Rather, ideological commitments (or lack thereof) are instantiated in situated practice. Racial ideologies are often inherently multiple, contradictory, and contested both inter-personally and intra-personally. Nevertheless, ideologies as discursive practices are attempts by interlocutors to achieve coherence amongst seemingly divergent ideas, attitudes, and beliefs about people in the world. Racial ideologies (emphasis on practices) can reify the status quo or counter dominant narratives. Similar to gender ideologies, participants can take up neutral stances where race is rendered invisible or a posture of "color-blindness" is assumed. They can also take up a critical stance to explicitly express anti-racist positions and consciously find ways to redress grievances and deconstruct racist myths. Since "everyday language" particularly position women of color in subordinated roles, discourse analysis of talk can help reclaim one's learner and teacher identity (Hill, 2008). For STEM WCT, this reclamation is necessary in order to change the trajectory of their students as well as their teaching.

Reclaiming One's "Place" in STEM Education: Can Girls Do STEM?

Razfar & Rumenapp (2014) speaks to the dynamic nature of identity construction, where individuals are socially positioned and repositioned within and across discursive boundaries. This process often creates an ethos of being *in-between* multiple poles of identity. Anzaldúa (1993) further recognizes this state (i.e., *nepantla*) where identity is relational and exists in relation to some "Other." Gutiérrez (2012) links *nepantla* to the knowledge teachers need to know for teaching within content domains. This space is "an in-between state, that uncertain terrain one crosses when moving from one place to another, when changing from one class, race, or gender position to another, when traveling from the present identity into a new identity" [or the] "liminal state between worlds, between realities, between systems of knowledge" (Anzaldúa, 1993, p. 110). Furthermore, the concept of *nepantla* is an indigenous and asset-based stance on the reclamation and struggles of historically colonized and subjugated populations. Rather than viewing this space as a marginal space, it can be seen as a space of creativity and innovation (Razfar & Rumenapp, 2014). A third space represents a psychological, social, and even physical space where new possibilities for STEM education and other discursive identity(s) emerge (Bhabha, 1994; Razfar, 2013). Within third spaces, static cultural boundaries are stretched and existing categories can be questioned, expanded, and reimagined (Meredith, 1998).

From the onset of PROJECT, it became evident that third space theory would play a vital role for WCT doing STEM education. Throughout PROJECT, WCT's addressed a range of stances towards STEM related vocations and epistemologies. Some teachers resisted integrating STEM with language learning by avoiding delving deeply into STEM aspects of the curriculum. Given PROJECT's expectation that teachers would design activities that integrated STEM with literacy, this became a source of great anxiety for both teachers and the university team. This became a problem we could not ignore and addressed during classroom discussions, focus groups, and study groups. As these teachers opened up about their prior experiences in STEM, and worked with colleagues of various STEM specializations, they were encouraged to engage in these struggles with an end goal of providing equitable learning opportunities for their students. Sandra (African American), Belize (Latina), and Leslie (Asian American) were three teachers of color who exemplified this initial anxiety:

01 **Sandra:** I have always kind of had an aversion to math. And I think it's
02   because of the way they taught it like it was always like "these
03   are the rules and learn this way. This is how you do it. So I
04   never understood it. I never learned it well."
05 **Belize:** I detested math. Like I hated the rules. Memorizing everything. I
06   didn't get it. Plus to make things worse, I have a terrible
07   memory. So that just doesn't work for me.

Sandra and Belize grappled with these tendencies of anxiety and avoidance of subject areas in which they grew aversions towards (Lines 1, 6). Leslie positions her anxiety within the pervasive ideology of Asians as the "model minority" for excelling in STEM (Lines 1–10):

01 **Leslie:** I'm not the typical Asian whose good at math, everyone says
02   you must be good at math because it's stereotypical (making
03   quotes with fingers) "You're Asian you must be good at math."

04   [...] I was a reading specialist and then my professor at
05   North Brooks [pseudonym] said "reading you don't really
06   want to do reading" so I moved to science [...] I told her I
07   hate science and she said "We'll get to like it." I
08   switched over to science. I got my master's in science [...]
09   I am really glad because it has opened up a lot of doors
10   for me.

Leslie was stereotyped as an Asian who is expected to excel in mathematics (Lines 1–3). Furthermore, she was encouraged to switch to a master's degree in science from reading (Lines 5–8). She acknowledged how this move "opened up a lot of doors" for her (Lines 9–10). Continuing on a path of anxiety when it comes to STEM fields impedes teacher and student learning. We quickly recognized that for WCTs to integrate literacy with STEM based on students' FoK requires critical identity and ideological reflection and conscious reclamation of one's STEM identity.

Reclaiming One's "Place": Girls Can Be Engineers

Socialization into STEM identities begins in early childhood (NRC, 2007) and teachers need to access non-school STEM experiences, whether positive or negative (Maltese & Tal, 2010). Kindergarten–8 teachers are uniquely positioned to impact the development of positive and/or negative affinities for STEM (Driver, Leach, Milar, & Scott, 1996). In the following vignette (Lines 1–17), a PROJECT teacher finds an opportunity to reframe dominant gendered ideologies and STEM. In this activity students are discussing how to build a safe playground at their school as part of the action research unit designed by the teacher. Clearly, the teacher has an explicit egalitarian gender ideology (Lines 1–3) and overhears Alex whisper a contrary stance. She prompts him to articulate his stance for the whole class (Lines 4–5):

01 **Teacher:** You're going to do something that grown-ups do as their
02   job. Our turning into engineers.
03 **Class:** Ooh yeah.
04 **Teacher:** I want to say something that I just heard. Alex can you say
05   that just a bit louder?
06 **Alex:** Girls can't be engineers.

The teacher moves to open a dialogue about gender roles and engineering (Lines 7–17):

07	**Teacher:**	He said girls can't be engineers, why do you say that Alex?
08		Who's ever seen a girl engineer? Maybe you've never seen
09		one.
10	**Samantha:**	What's an engineer?
11	**Teacher:**	Okay let's start, what is an engineer? […] Elsa, what's an
12		engineer?
13	**Elsa:**	A person who works.
14	**Teacher:**	I work, am I an engineer?
15	**Elsa:**	Person who builds something.
16	**Teacher:**	Who's seen a guy build something?
17	**Class:**	[raise hands, overlapping responses]

Students continued to provide examples of people they've seen "building something" and what they were building. All examples were of men (i.e., "dad," "uncle," "man") building. The teacher noticed this and elicited counter examples (Lines 18–19):

18	**Teacher:**	Who's ever seen a girl build something or saw a girl
19		outside build something?

As a result of the teacher's question, we observed the potential for anti-sexist discourse and alternative gender ideological stances where boys and girls can see themselves and the "other" as engineers (Lines 20–36):

20	**Samantha:**	I saw a [girl build a house].
21	**Teacher:**	So a girl was helping to build a house, so do you think
22		that girl is an engineer. Okay anyone else? Alejandro?
23	**Alejandro:**	A girl…
24	**Teacher:**	Building what?
25	**Alejandro:**	A house.
26	**Teacher:**	Do you know the girl or was it someone you saw walking by?
27		So you actually saw a girl building a house? So what Alex
28		and Edgar said is very true, lots of people don't see
29		girls engineering things. I agree I mostly see guys
30		building things when I see people outside working on

31		construction, it's usually girls, I mean, usually boys, but
32		as we said there are girls too. So we are going to be both
33		boys and girls engineers. So this is a question just for
34		the girls, girls ready? Do you think you are smart enough
35		to be engineers like boys?
36	**Class:**	Yes.

The historical inertia of static gender and racial ideological stances in combination with reductive STEM ideologies can be attributed to teachers' own STEM socialization. Without professional development and critical reflection, most teachers tend to enact discursive practices that are rooted in their own experiences (Deemer, 2004; Llinares & Krainer, 2006). This often results in discrete views of STEM fields and dominant gender/racial identities. These ideologies can present a challenge for teachers adopting an integrative approach to STEM as well as empowering new gender and racial practices. Many WCT in PROJECT expressed deficit stances about themselves as capable STEM learners and teachers. They often traced it back to their experiences in elementary or secondary school. In Lines 1–9, Belize interrogated her own mathematics identity and ideological stances:

01	**Belize:**	And so it wasn't until high school that math kind of got a
02		little better. Where I had teachers, "No, Belize, you really
03		are good at this." And I was like "Are you kidding me?"
04		And so they really pushed me and pushed me and I am like in
05		senior year, I took precalculus. […] We had a teacher that
06		was very formulaic. This is how it is. This is how it is.
07		This is how it is. Follow the formula. Follow the formula.
08		I was like "I don't even know what formula you are
09		talking about."

Despite positive reinforcement "No, Belize, you really are good at this" (Lines 2–3), Belize struggled with self-efficacy and her mathematics identity (Line 3). While she does not invoke racial and gender factors, it is clear that reductive ideologies of STEM mediated her "formulaic" experience. Teachers who have reductive stances toward STEM tend to avoid teaching STEM (Appleton, 2003) and may transfer dislike towards these fields to students (Deemer, 2004). Dischino et al. (2011) stress that one of the reasons for the declining enrollment of students [particularly women of color] in STEM programs is that students often become disinterested because of the way these domains are taught in the traditional classroom. STEM disciplines continue to be taught in silos (Nadelson et al., 2003) and fail to relate to students' lives in solving real-world problems as the modern conception of STEM suggests (Labov, Reid, & Yamamoto, 2010).

METHODS AND DATA SOURCES

Becoming Teacher Researchers

We conceptualized teacher development in terms of a cultural-historical view of learning. To highlight the shifts and struggles of teachers throughout the action research process, we focused on STEM identities (Table 13.1 and Figure 13.2), gender ideological stances (Table 13.2 and Figure 13.3), and racial ideological stances (Table 13.3 and Figure 13.4). Given teacher learning was the appropriation of new teacher identities over time, we classified the development of teachers according to shifts from resistance (*R*) and procedural (*P*) to ethnographic inquiry (*EI*) and ultimately teacher researcher (*TR*). The path toward becoming a *TR* exhibited a spiral and

TABLE 13.1 Typology of Teacher STEM Identities

Identities	Frequency (*N* = 20) Total Shifts = 60	Definition	Example
Resistant (R)	4	Explicitly avoids integrating disciplinary knowledge.	For example, a teacher may plan to integrate STEM concepts, but in practice it never transpires.
Resistant/ Procedural (R/P)	5	Shifting between resistant and procedural identities.	Within a single unit, a teacher moves between these two positions.
Procedural (P)	24	Simply goes along with integrating subject domains. Maintains teacher-centered approach.	"it is a lot easier to know what it is you are gonna be teaching them because all of a sudden you are prepared and you may anticipate some issues, but when you don't know about the math and you are learning with them, it's a real challenge."
Procedural/ Ethnographic Inquiry (P/EI)	1	Shifting between procedural and ethnographic inquiry identities.	Within a single unit, a teacher moves between these two positions.

(continued)

TABLE 13.1 Typology of Teacher STEM Identities (continued)			
Identities	Frequency (*N* = 20) Total Shifts = 60	Definition	Example
Ethnographic Inquiry (EI)	10	Aligns with FoK and able to integrate content in somewhat meaningful way. Struggles to allow students to be knowledge holders.	"I feel very intimidated about the sciences [...] its not my best subject [...] so after doing the units and integrating them [...] it was not as intimidating as having to teach this science class and this subject for me it was much more comfortable and I believe that's how they felt too."
Ethnographic Inquiry/Teacher Researcher (EI/TR)	5	Shifting between ethnographic inquiry and teacher researcher identities.	Within a single unit, a teacher moves between these two positions.
Teacher-Researcher (TR)	11	Appropriated at least one construct of the project and utilizes research tools to meaningfully draw on students' FoK and integrate curriculum. Okay with novice role in relation to content domains.	"So that's where that started to come up, but it just wasn't planned like I would normally plan a structured lesson for children. It really depended on the problems we were working on at that time."

bidirectional model of development consistent with a sociocultural lens. In Table 13.1, we provide a typology of this classification for WCT of PROJECT.

A *R* teacher identity refers to explicitly avoiding integrating disciplinary knowledge. For example, a teacher may plan to integrate STEM concepts, but in practice it never transpires. A *P* identity refers to superficial integration of STEM concepts, while maintaining a teacher-centered approach. For example, a teacher may integrate STEM concepts in a way where she maintains control "it is a lot easier to know what it is you are gonna be teaching them because all of a sudden you are prepared and you may anticipate some issues." An *EI* identity suggests that a teacher aligns with FoK but is unable to integrate STEM concepts in culturally relevant ways and struggles with ideological positioning. For example, a teacher may connect with students' FoK but is unable to identify STEM funds. A *TR* refers to teachers appropriating at least one major construct of PROJECT, utilizing the research tools to draw on students' FoK, and successfully integrates STEM concepts. Here the teacher is unafraid to take a learner role. For example, a teacher allows for the organic unfolding of STEM concepts based

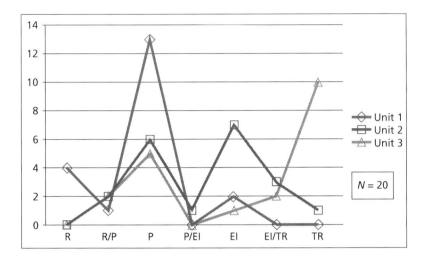

Figure 13.2 STEM identity(s).

on students' FoK and the negotiated trajectory, "It really depended on the problems we were working on at that time." Figure 13.2 depicts the shifts of WCT STEM identity from Unit 1, Unit 2, and Unit 3.

A few noteworthy shifts include a significant number of teachers ($n = 13$) aligning with a *P* identity during Unit 1, to a significant number of teachers ($n = 7$) aligning with an *EI* identity in Unit 2, and a large number of teachers ($n = 10$) aligning with a *TR* identity during Unit 3.

Shifting Gender and Racial Ideological Stances

As WCT teachers traverse the path of becoming *TR*, they continuously negotiate multiple ideological stances with respect to gender and race. The research team identified 60 episodes across the data corpus where gender and racial ideological stances were explicitly invoked. These were episodes where multiple coders independently agreed on the presence of gender and racial ideological stances. Table 13.2 provides a typology based on gender (*G*) ideological stances (adapted from Streitmatter, 1994)—either in alignment with a deficit (*D*), deficit/neutral (*D/N*), neutral (*N*), neutral/egalitarian (*N/E*), egalitarian (*E*), egalitarian/anti-sexist (*E/AS*), and/or anti-sexist (*AS*). *D* ideological stances refer to a focus on what one lacks based on gender. For example, a teacher might focus on a negative aspect of boys or girls, "mischievous little boy." *N* stances refer to not recognizing

TABLE 13.2 Coding Typology of Gender Ideological Stances

Stance	Frequency (N = 20)	Definition	Example
Gender (G)	60	Socially constructed form of sex (i.e., attributes assigned to sex).	Any mention/addressing of female, male, girl, boy, and associated roles or lack thereof.
Deficit (D)	1	Focus on what one lacks based on gender.	"There was just always the same mischievous little boy, the same Anna, trying to run things."
Deficit/Neutral (D/N)	0	Shifting between deficit and neutral stances.	Within a single unit, a teacher moves between these two positions.
Neutral (N)	12	Gender as not a factor.	"We had issues of more or less not getting along, but none of the male female thing, no gender, no changing over time."
Neutral/ Egalitarian (N/E)	13	Shifting between neutral and egalitarian stances.	Within a single unit, a teacher moves between these two positions.
Egalitarian (E)	29	Equal treatment based on gender, although lack of debunking misconceptions.	"I was sitting with this group of boys [...] I knew that they were interested in superheroes and some of the cartoons. [...] All the girls in my class this year are very into princesses, into all the Disney characters."
Egalitarian/Anti-Sexist (E/AS)	1	Shifting between egalitarian and anti-sexist stances.	Within a single unit, a teacher moves between these two positions.
Anti-Sexist (AS)	4	Actively push for gender equity and debunking misconceptions.	"I opted to move students around in the group because in unit 2 the boys stuck together and the girls stuck together."

gender as a factor. For example, a teacher may demonstrate a lack of recognition that gender plays a dynamic role in interactions "no gender, no changing over time." An *E* stance refers to the equal treatment of gender, although at the same time the failure to debunk misconceptions. For example, a teacher may treat gender equally, although reaffirm traditional gender roles by not addressing such issues as "boys interested in superheroes" and "girls interested in princesses." Lastly, an *AS* stance actively pushes for gender equity and addresses misconceptions of gendered groups. For example, a teacher may do something different in the classroom in order to address gendered divisions or participation, "I opted to move students around in the group because in Unit 2 the boys stuck together and the girls stuck together." Figure 13.3 depicts the shifts of WCT from Unit 1, Unit 2, and Unit 3 based on *G* ideological stances.

A few noteworthy shifts include a significant number of teachers (*n* = 10) aligning with *N/E* ideological stances during Unit 1, to a significant number of teachers (*n* = 11 and 13) aligning with *E* stances in Units 2 and 3, and a number of teachers (*n* = 4) aligning with an *AS* stance during Unit 3. Table 13.3 provides a typology based on race (*R*) ideological stances (adapted from Streitmatter, 1994)—either in alignment with a deficit (*D*), deficit/neutral (*D/N*), neutral (*N*), neutral/egalitarian (*N/E*), egalitarian (*E*), egalitarian/anti-racist (*E/AR*), and/or anti-racist (*AR*).

D ideological stances refer to a focus on what one lacks based on race. For example, a teacher may point to race as a reason for a deficit in a student or family "but what kind of children are they raising." A *N* stance refers to not recognizing race as a factor. For example, a teacher may not consider students' racial identification when drawing on FoK or for curricular choices. An *E* stance refers to the equal treatment of race, although at the same time the failure to debunk misconceptions. For example, race may come up in classroom discussions or interactions, but any conflicts or misconceptions are not addressed. Lastly, an *AR* stance actively pushes for racial equity and addresses misconceptions of racial groups. For example, a teacher may have an overrepresentation of materials that reflect students' realities and when conflicts and misconceptions come up, actively addresses them. Figure 13.4 depicts the shifts of WCT from Unit 1, Unit 2, and Unit 3 based on

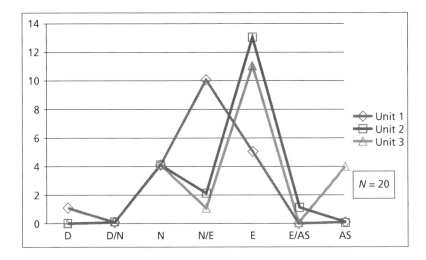

Figure 13.3 G ideological stances.

TABLE 13.3 Coding Typology of Racial Ideological Stances			
Stance	Frequency (*N* = 20)	Definition	Example
Race (R)	60	Social concept used to categorize humans into large populations.	Any mention/addressing of race/ethnicity or lack thereof.
Deficit (D)	6	Focus on what one lacks based on race.	"I did home visits and found that most don't clean-up or have chores. The parents and grandparents do everything for these kids. They just want them to go to school, but what kind of children are they raising when they don't have to fend for themselves."
Deficit/Neutral (D/N)	2	Shifting between deficit and neutral stances.	Within a single unit, a teacher moves between these two positions.
Neutral (N)	23	Race as not a factor.	For example not acknowledging any racial/ethnic identification of students in drawing on FoK or in curricular units.
Neutral/ Egalitarian (N/E)	1	Shifting between neutral and egalitarian stances.	Within a single unit, a teacher moves between these two positions.
Egalitarian (E)	24	Equal treatment based on race, although lack of debunking misconceptions.	"And for instance like I remember Anthony in one of the activities he's like saying 'I don't mean to, you know, be mean, but I don't like White people. When I see em.'"
Egalitarian/Anti-Racist (E/AR)	2	Shifting between egalitarian and anti-racist stances.	Within a single unit, a teacher moves between these two positions.
Anti-Racist (AR)	2	Actively push for racial equity and debunking misconceptions.	"Those misconceptions found their way into mine as well with White and rich […] so for Unit 3 […] we brought it back to the community […] I wanted to somehow have them see themselves. Like how do you play into these social justice issues and what's going on in your community and what's fair and not fair. And kinda like their misconceptions and what role you play."

R ideological stances. A few noteworthy shifts include a significant number of teachers (*n* = 11) aligning with a *N* stance during Unit 1, to a significant number of teachers (*n* = 9 and 10) aligning with an *E* stance in Units 2 and 3, and a couple of teachers (*n* = 2) aligning with an *AR* stance during Unit 3.

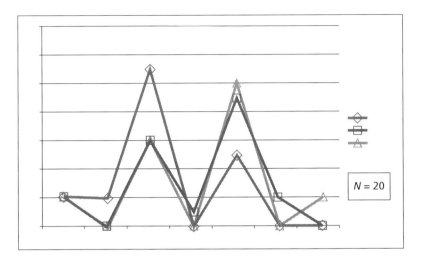

Figure 13.4 R ideological stances.

In order to concretize the above global findings, we focus on two case studies—Belize and Kamala—in the following sections. These cases were chosen since these two teachers demonstrated significant shifts in terms of all identities/ideologies (i.e., STEM identity, gender and racial ideologies) from the execution of Unit 1 to Unit 3. We attempt to move towards a focus on two fundamental questions: What do people mean? and How do values, beliefs, social, and institutional relations of power mediate meaning? (Razfar, 2012). Belize identifies as Latina and a dual-language (Spanish–English) speaker. At the time of the study, she had been teaching for 5 years and was a third grade general education teacher. The demographics of the school was 38% Asian, 32% Hispanic, 18% African American, 8% White, 4% Other with 38.1% ELs and 87.3% low-income. Kamala identifies as Pakistani and a dual-language (Urdu–English) speaker. At the time of the study, she had been teaching for 12 years and was a sixth/seventh grade language arts/reading teacher. According to district reports, the demographics of the school were 89.6% Hispanic, 7.5% African American, 1.5% White, 0.9% Asian with 28.7% ELs and 91.6% low-income.

OVERCOMING STEM ANXIETY

Belize found herself facing her anxiety towards mathematics and science head on through the integration of mathematical and scientific practices in her units:

01	**Belize:**	[…] Math kind of scared me because they were going in a
02		direction where I wasn't familiar or even comfortable with
03		cause, I will be honest, I am really good up to third grade
04		math and after that I am kind of dense about it. But, I
05		gave it a try. I gave my best shot. But yeah, it was a
06		little intimidating to not know because it is a lot easier
07		to know what it is you are gonna be teaching them because
08		all of a sudden you are prepared and you may anticipate
09		some issues or whatever but when you don't know about the
10		math and you are learning with them, it's a real challenge.
11		It's a real challenge.

Belize initially was afraid of delving into the mathematics in her curricular unit (Lines 1–4). She attempted to integrate mathematics (Line 4–5), although acknowledged it was a challenge (Lines 10–11). Through these constant reflections on students developing mathematical and scientific practices as they learn language, Belize was also developing certain orientations as a teacher and learner.

01	**Belize:**	I think for me, it's less intimidating knowing that it
02		can be a dual learning experience between student and
03		teacher. Like I mean I have already told my kids like I am
04		not the only teacher in this classroom. Like I don't know
05		everything. But at the same time, I always felt like I
06		didn't need to know more than they did so that I can guide
07		them through like math and stuff. So, like math has always
08		been really intimidating for me. But, now, knowing like
09		what kinds of questions you could ask them and what kinds
10		of, you know? You can kind of go through all of them
11		together and not be the "know it all" teacher I guess.

By Unit 2, Belize continued to speak to how intimidating mathematics has been (Line 7). By breaking down her guard to allow the experience to be a "dual learning experience" (Line 2), she was able to shift her role from a "know it all teacher" (Line 11).

Belize spoke about these shifts in the classroom as well as with students. Belize focused on the grouping and organizing of learning as it fostered role shifting. During a unit drawing on students' FoK of smoking and its effects on the community, students worked in groups to share the data they collected in alignment with this theme. In her individual report, Belize provided an example demonstrating her awareness of the dynamics of gender as inhibiting full student participation:

01   In [Unit 3] I decided to keep the same group from Unit 2. However, I
02   opted to move students around in the group because in Unit 2 the boys
03   stuck together and the girls stuck together. And, the nature of the
04   group seemed to be more pair work than it was group work. I switched
05   students around and this time, it seemed that the shifts in
06   participation, modality, roles, and identities were evident in the group
07   dynamics. During Unit 3, two students demonstrated leadership roles.
08   Julia took a more active leadership role. [excerpt individual report]

Belize in reflecting on her values and relations acknowledged that certain grouping practices resulted in "boys [sticking] together and girls [sticking] together" (Line 3), where the dynamic was mainly "pair work" (Line 4) rather than "group work" (Line 5). Since her goal was to facilitate the process of students taking on different roles within the group, she noticed that reorganizing the groups, and thus the learning, allowed for "two students [to demonstrate] leadership roles" (Line 8). One student in particular who took an "active leadership role" (Line 9) was Julia. This student had previously rarely participated. This relates to Brown, Reveles, and Kelly (2005), as they discuss how the success or failure of becoming a member of a discourse community may center on how students are provided with opportunities to position themselves with respect to the subject matter, discourse practices, other members of the community, and so forth. By reorganizing students because they "stuck to" similar gendered groups, Belize provided for more equitable opportunities for students to develop more positive dispositions towards the content and the dynamic roles within a group.

Speaking Mathematics

For Kamala, Unit 1 became the initial phase of drawing on students' FoK and building relationships with students. Kamala found it difficult viewing mathematics as integrated with literacy development. She mentioned that mathematics is a "language that I can't speak." Brown and McNamara (2011) identify this fear of mathematics and the need to move beyond mathematics as "just scary numbers" (p. 95). Kamala initially designed an integrative curricular unit incorporating mathematics and science ideas. For example, in drawing on the community knowledge of substance abuse, she planned to incorporate Maya Angelou's poems to discuss her message of survival (excerpt curriculum plan), and draw on substance abuse data (excerpt curriculum plan) and materials reflecting the effects of substance abuse on the body and brain (excerpt curriculum plan). However, after reflecting on and analyzing her practice and values, stated, "I don't know where it went." Kamala documented this struggle recognizing that she had difficulty stepping out of that "reading teacher identity":

01 You can definitely incorporate a lot of math into reading and vice
02 versa. I know you can. I think more where I fall short, is how. Like
03 I don't know how. I see math differently than a lot of you guys
04 see it because you guys are more mathematicians. I can see bringing in
05 in the [inaudible] era, analyzing the data, African Americans struggles
06 how many statistics. There's so much math there, just so much math.
07 As the transcript shows, I admitted that I did not know how and
08 described the others in my cohort as "more mathematicians." After
09 analyzing the three units, there seemed to be a shift in teacher
10 discourse. I had a difficult time viewing myself as more than
11 just the "reading teacher." [Kamala's Action Report]

Through discourse analysis, Kamala understood her negative orientation towards mathematics (Lines 7–9). At the same time, she was able to point to mathematical practices that can be incorporated (Lines 5–6), while also pointing to race, which eventually became common for her to incorporate in her lessons (Line 5).

By Unit 2, Kamala demonstrated an ideological shift in terms of mathematics and science content integration with literacy. She worked with students through the mathematics and stated, "Now, I was seeing the math and science in everything." Her approach to an integrated curriculum also allowed for resonating themes of gender and race to come to the fore. For example, during a unit on "The Great Depression and the Cost of Living," students determined if they would be able to survive off of the current state minimum wage. She stated (Lines 1–14):

01 **Kamala:** I think for Unit 2 both had a lot to say. I think there was
02 a lot of gender stereotypes going on. Especially when we
03 were doing the . . . what can you afford in the 1920s. The

04	division of labor. Especially if a boy and girl was grouped
05	together on purpose. Well you're going to stay home because
06	one person is going to work. So I'm going to make the
07	money. The boy would make the money. And, I think some
08	things were said, "Oh we can't afford that." So somebody's,
09	Nicholas said. Um, uh to his partner and he brought it up
10	to Melody, which they were dating at the time ironically.
11	And he's like "you know, you need to go out and get a job. I
12	can't make all the money." It was interesting how they
13	decided that he was going to go work and he decided that he
14	was going to be the one to get that $5 a day job.

Kamala acknowledged how the lesson allowed for traditional and stereotypical gendered roles to come up (Lines 2–4). She pointed to these specific examples in the classroom (Lines 5–12). By establishing how problematic these gendered interactions are, she demonstrated her own stances by building awareness of the gendered dynamics within the larger community.

The structure of her activities also allowed for students to discuss misconceptions. For example, during a unit on poverty and misconceptions, students engaged in a discussion that led to the following reflection (Lines 1–15):

01	**Kamala:**	I think their perception is that, well Mexicans are not,
02		um, Mexicans are not poor, we don't see them, there are
03		mostly Black people out there. So when you saw the data
04		that says that there's a rise in the Mexican population,
05		um, uh, uh I think 2% each year, I forgot what the data
06		was, and the students wrote down, "Wow I can't believe
07		that." It was a/it was a good discussion that we had, um,
08		because I think it helped them to understand that it's us
09		that are sitting here. It's my people, it's your people,
10		it's their people, and they didn't really see that. They
11		associate Black with poor. They associate Mexican with
12		working. They associate White with rich. That's their
13		association. They associate Asians with, you know, [smart,
14		educated] and rich and rich if you talk about rich and poor
15		I feel like.

Kamala noticed that students had a misconception of who is rich "Whites" (Line 12), who is poor "Blacks" (Line 11), who is smart/educated

"Asians" (Line 13–14), and where their community falls within that continuum (Lines 1–2 and 11–12). The lessons to follow within the same unit were students discussing what they believed the word "misconceptions" mean and grappling with their own misconceptions about race and class.

CONCLUSION AND IMPLICATIONS

This chapter presents how 20 WCT working closely with university researchers collectively reimagined their gender, racial, language, and STEM ideological stances through action research. As they learned to become researchers of their own practice, they designed integrated STEM activities with literacy in order to create *culturally sustaining* pedagogy for their students (Paris, 2012). PROJECT, by design, structured spaces of possibility for WCT to explore the *in-between* places in order to mediate learning through the third space, or *nepantla*. For WCT doing STEM, this is a necessary reclamation. The cases of Belize and Kamala demonstrated this necessity, however complex, in order to recast prior negative experiences with STEM as constituted by dominant racial and gender ideologies.

The sociocultural embedded approach to action research presented here aims to not only build teachers' STEM expertise, but to develop WCT doing STEM through the complex and stressful in-between spaces that are mediated by deficit views of race and gender in relation to STEM. Implications include (a) more approaches to teacher professional development facilitating the process of WCT engaging in action research in an authentic and collaborative way, (b) designed activities that challenge teachers to move toward integrating STEM content with students' FoK, and (c) the need to create spaces where issues of STEM, gender, and race are critically discussed through discourse analysis and a language ideologies framework.

NOTES

1. All names are pseudonyms.
2. By women of color teachers (WCT) we refer to non-white, underrepresented women.

REFERENCES

Anzaldúa, G. (1993). Border arte: Nepantla el lugar de la frontera [Border art: Nepantla the place of the border]. In Centro Cultural de la Raza (Ed.), *La frontera/The border. Art about the Mexico/United States border experience* (pp. 107–114). San Diego, CA: Museum of Contemporary Art.

Appleton, K. (2003). How do beginning primary school teachers cope with science? Toward an understanding of science teaching practice. *Research in Science Education, 33*(1), 1–25.

Bhabha, H. K. (1994). *The location of culture.* London, England: Routledge.

Breiner, J. M., Harkness, S. S., Johnson, C. C., & Kehler, C. M. (2012). What is STEM? A discussion about conceptions of STEM in education and partnerships. *School Science and Mathematics, 112*(1), 3–11.

Brown, B. A., Reveles, J. M., & Kelly, G. J. (2005). Scientific literacy and discursive identity: A theoretical framework for understanding science learning. *Science Education, 89*(5), 779–802.

Brown, T., & McNamara, O. (2011). *Becoming a mathematics teacher: Identity and identifications.* Dordrecht, Netherlands: Springer.

Bonilla-Silva, E. (2003). Racial attitudes or racial ideology? An alternative paradigm for examining actors' racial views. *Journal of Political Ideologies, 8*(1), 63–82.

Castambis, S. (1994). The path to math: Gender and racial-ethnic differences in mathematics participation from middle school to high school. *Sociology of Education, 67*(3), 199–215.

Deemer, S. (2004). Classroom goal orientation in high school classrooms: Revealing links between teacher beliefs and classroom environments. *Educational Research, 46*(1), 73–90.

Dischino, M., De Laura, J. A., Donnelly, J., Massa, N. M., & Hanes, F. (2011). Increasing the STEM pipeline through problem-based learning. *Technology Interface International Journal, 1*(12), 21–29.

Driver, R., Leach, J., Milar, R., & Scott, P. (1996). *Young people's images of science.* Buckingham, England: Open University Press.

Hayden, K., Ouyang, Y., Scinski, L., Olszewski, B., & Bielefeldt, T. (2011). Increasing student interest and attitudes in STEM: Professional development and activities to engage and inspire learners. *Contemporary Issues in Technology and Teacher Education, 11*(1), 47–69.

Hill, J. H. (2008). *The everyday language of white racism.* Oxford, England: Wiley-Blackwell.

Hill, J. H. (1998). Language, race, and white public space. *American Anthropologist, 100*(3), 680–689.

Gutiérrez, R. (2012). Embracing *nepantla*: Rethinking "knowledge" and its use in mathematics teaching. *REDIMAT–Journal of Research in Mathematics Education, 1*(1), 29–56.

Labov, J. B., Reid, A. H., & Yamamoto, K. R. (2010). Integrated biology and undergraduate science education: a new biology education for the twenty first century? *CBE Life Science Education, 9*(1), 10–16.

Llinares, S., & Krainer, K. (2006). Mathematics (student) teachers and teacher educators as learners. In A. Gutierrez & P. Boero (Eds.), *Handbook of research on the psychology of mathematics education* (pp. 429–459). Rotterdam, Netherlands: Sense.

Maltese, A. V., & Tai, R. H. (2010). Eyeballs in the fridge: Sources of early interest in science. *International Journal of Science Education, 32*(5), 669–685.

Martin, E. (1991). The egg and the sperm: How science has constructed a romance based on stereotypical male-female roles. *Journal of Women in Culture and Society, 16*(3), 485–501.

Meredith, P. (1998, July). *Hybridity in the third space: Rethinking bi-cultural politics in Aotearoa/New Zealand*. Paper presented at the Te Oru Rangahau Maori Research and Development Conference, Massey University, Palmerston North, New Zealand.

Moll, L. C., Amanti, C., Neff, D., & Gonzalez, N. (1992). Funds of knowledge for teaching: Using a qualitative approach to connect homes and classrooms. *Theory into Practice, 31*(2), 132–141.

Morrison, J. A., Raab, F., & Ingram, D. (2009). Factors influencing elementary and secondary teachers' view on the nature of science. *Journal of Research in Science Teaching, 46*(4), 384–403.

Nadelson, L. S., Callahan, J., Pyke, P., Hay, A., Dance, M., & Pfiester, J. (2013). Teacher STEM perception and preparation: Inquiry-based STEM professional development for elementary teachers. *The Journal of Educational Research, 106*(2), 157–168.

Ochs, E. (1990). Indexicality and socialization. In J. Stigler, R. Shweder, & G. Herdt (Eds.), *Cultural psychology: Essays on comparative human development* (pp. 287–308). New York, NY: Cambridge University Press.

Ong, M., Wright, C., Espinosa, L. L., & Orfield, G. (2011). Inside the double bind: A synthesis of empirical research on undergraduate and graduate women of color in science, technology, engineering, and mathematics. *Harvard Educational Review, 81*(2), 172–208.

Paris, D. (2012). Culturally sustaining pedagogy: A needed change in stance, terminology, and practice. *Education Researcher, 41*(3), 93–97.

Philips, S. (2003). The power of gender ideologies in discourse. In J. Holmes & M. Meyerhoff (Eds.), *The handbook of language and gender* (pp. 252–276). Oxford, England: Blackwell.

Razfar, A. (2007). *Transforming literacy, science, and math through action research (LSciMAct)*. Grant funded by U.S. Department of Education.

Razfar, A. (2011). Action research in urban schools: Empowerment, transformation, and challenges. *Teacher Education Quarterly, 38*(4), 25–44.

Razfar, A. (2012). Discoursing mathematically: Using discourse analysis to develop a sociocritical perspective of mathematics education. *The Mathematics Educator, 22*(1), 39–62.

Razfar, A. (2013). Multilingual mathematics: Learning through contested spaces of meaning making. *International Multilingual Research Journal, 7*(3), 175–196.

Razfar, A., & Rumenapp, J.C. (2013). *Applying linguistics in the classroom: A sociocultural approach*. New York, NY: Routledge.

Razfar, A., Troiano, B., Nasir, A., Yang, E., Rumenapp, J.C., & Torres, Z. (2015). Teachers' language ideologies in classroom practices: Using English learners' linguistic capital to socially reorganize learning. In P. Smith (Ed.), *Handbook of research on cross-cultural approaches to language and literacy development* (pp. 261–298). Hershey, PA: IGI Global.

Sadker, M. P., & Sadker, D. M. (1982). *Sex equity handbook for schools*. New York, NY: Longman.

Silverstein, M. (1985). Language and the culture of gender: At the intersection of structure, usage, and ideology. In E. Mertz & R. J. Parmentier (Eds.), *Semiotic mediation* (pp. 219–259). Orlando, FL: Academic Press.

Silverstein, M. (2003). *Indexical order and the dialectics of sociolinguistic life. Language and Communication, 23*(3), 193–229.

Spencer, R., Porche, M. V., & Tolman, D. L. (2003). We've come a long way—maybe: New challenges for gender equity in education. *Teachers College Record, 105*(9), 1774–1807.

Streitmatter, J. (1994). *Toward gender equity in the classroom: Everyday teachers' beliefs and practices.* Albany: State University of New York Press.

Wells, G. (2011). Integrating CHAT and action research. *Mind, Culture, and Activity, 18*(2), 161–180.

Winford, D. (1978). *Hypercorrection in the process of decreolization: The case of Trinidadian English.* Cambridge, England: Cambridge University Press.

Zhao, Y. (2009). *Catching up or leading the way: American education in the age of globalization.* Alexandria, VA: ASCD.

ABOUT THE EDITORS

Dr. Barbara Polnick is a full professor in the Department of Educational Leadership at Sam Houston State University, Huntsville, Texas. Her involvement in STEM, specifically mathematics, spans over 40 years. From high school mathematics teacher, mathematics and curriculum specialist, curriculum director, and now professor at Sam Houston State University, she has focused much of her work on improving teaching and learning in mathematics, as it relates to gender, leadership, and early childhood. Her expertise lies in writing and evaluating grants, leading school improvement initiatives, and curriculum alignment. Author of 47 publications (peer-reviewed articles, book chapters, textbook), she has delivered over 60 national presentations. She holds an EdD in educational administration from Texas A&M University and a master's in reading from Sam Houston State University. She is past chair of the Research on Women and Education (RWE) AERA SIG, currently serving on the RWE Executive Committee, and recipient of the RWE Information Age Author Legacy Award. Dr. Polnick is an especially proud recipient of the Texas A&M University College of Education and Human Development Outstanding Alumni Award.

Dr. Beverly J. Irby is a professor and associate dean of Academic Affairs at the College of Education and Human Development at Texas A&M University. Dr. Irby is also the director of the Educational Leadership Research Center. Her primary research interests center on issues of social responsibility, including bilingual and English as a second language education, science-infused literacy and literacy-infused science, administrative structures, curriculum, instructional strategies, and women's and girls' issues.

Girls and Women of Color In STEM, pages 253–255
Copyright © 2020 by Information Age Publishing
All rights of reproduction in any form reserved.

She is the author of more than 200 referred articles, chapters, books, and curricular materials for Spanish-speaking children. She is the series editor for Research on Women and Education (RWE). She has had in excess of $20,000,000 in grants. She was awarded in 2009, the Texas State University System—Regent's Professor. Dr. Irby has extensive experiences working with undergraduate students in the past 25+ years, and many of these students are underrepresented including first-generation college students, ethnic and economically challenged students, who have obtained doctorates and received research/teaching awards under her mentorship. Dr. Irby is the editor of the *Mentoring and Tutoring: Partnership in Learning* journal.

Dr. Julia Ballenger is a professor in the Department of Educational Leadership at A&M University-Commerce. Julia's work with STEM-related research, specifically as it relates to the intersection of gender, race, and ethnicity spans over 15 years. Julia has conducted research on issues related to the disproportionate representation of undergraduate females and people of color in STEM-related majors and graduates of STEM-related fields in comprehensive universities. In addition, Julia has conducted research on women of color in STEM-related fields navigating the workforce. Other areas of research include mentoring female leaders in higher education, leadership for social justice, school improvement, and efficacy of principal preparation programs on school principals' leadership. Author of over 50 peer-reviewed publications (articles, book chapters, books), she has delivered over 100 regional, state, and national presentations. She holds a PhD in educational administration from The University of Texas in Austin and a master's in psychology and elementary education from A&M University-Commerce (formerly East Texas State University). Julia serves on the executive board of the Research on Women and Education (RWE) Special Interest Group (SIG), of the American Educational Research Association (former president, program chair, and currently the treasurer) and on the executive board of the Action Research SIG (AERA-program chair). Julia is a recent recipient of the RWE Information Age Author Legacy Award.

Dr. Nahed Abdelrahman, PhD, graduated from the educational administration at the Department of Educational Administration and Human Resources. Her research interests center on education policy and principal preparation. She was selected as a Barbara Jackson Scholar from (2015–2017) and EAHR Graduate Student Achievement Award in 2016. She authored and co-authored several publications related to education policy such as *Dominant Trends in the Evolution of K–12 Education Policy in the United States, Arab Spring and Teacher Professional Development in Egypt, Hybrid Learning: Perspectives of Higher Education Faculty, A Website Analysis of Mentoring Programs for Latina Faculty at the 25 Top-Ranked National Universities,* and *Women and STEM: A Systematic Literature Review of Dissertation in Two De-*

cades (1994–2014). She presented her research in prestigious conferences including but not limited to the American Educational Research Association (AERA), University Council for Educational Administration (UCEA), the National Council for Professors of Educational Administration (NC-PEA), Research on Women and Education (RWE), and the Universality of Global Education Issues Conference. She plays leadership roles in higher education as she serves as the president of Graduate Representative Advisory Board (GRAB), and the chair of the Awards Committee of the Graduate and Professional Student Council (GPSC) at Texas A&M University, and a member in the appeals panel at TAMU. She currently serves as the assistant editor of the *Mentoring and Tutoring Journal, Advancing Women in Leadership, Education Law and Policy Brief Journal,* and *Dual Language Research and Practice Journal.*

ABOUT THE CONTRIBUTORS

Thomasenia Lott Adams is professor of mathematics education in the College of Education at the University of Florida (UF). She serves as the college's associate dean for research and faculty development. Her scholarship has been supported by being a co-principal investigator for an interdisciplinary research project funded by the National Science Foundation to study girls' positionality in mathematics and science as they transition to middle school. Dr. Adams has written 10 books and more than 50 journal articles related to teaching and learning mathematics. One of her recent books, *Making Sense of Teaching Mathematics, Grades 3–5*, received the 2018 Teacher's Choice Award. She is an associate editor of the National Council of Teachers of Mathematics' journal, *Mathematics Teacher: Learning and Teaching, PreK–12*. In addition, Dr. Adams is the mathematics program officer for the UF Lastinger Center for Learning.

Gillian Bayne is associate professor of science education at Lehman College of the City University of New York (CUNY) with a dual appointment in the Urban Education Department at CUNY's Graduate Center. She has over 25 years of science education experience, which has helped to deepen not only her passion for the science content, but equally important, the ethical underpinnings of its pedagogical enactment. Dr. Bayne's research is grounded in sociocultural theory, and encompasses addressing STEM equity issues within marginalized communities locally, nationally, and internationally. Her current book project details the personal and professional trajectories of underrepresented scientists of color.

Girls and Women of Color In STEM, pages 257–264
Copyright © 2020 by Information Age Publishing
All rights of reproduction in any form reserved.

Theodorea Regina Berry, EdD, is associate professor of curriculum studies and director of African American studies at The University of Texas at San Antonio. She focuses her scholarship on the critical examination of race, ethnicity, and gender for teaching and teacher education and the lived experiences of women of color as preservice teachers and teacher educators. Her teaching and research interests are qualitative research methodologies, curriculum theory, and critical race theory/critical race feminism.

Sarah Blanchard is a doctoral candidate in the Department of Sociology at the University of Texas at Austin. Her work examines how structural, relational, and social-psychological aspects of schools shape the transition to college at the intersection of gender and race/ethnicity with a focus on STEM. Recent publications have appeared in *Social Science Research, Demography*, and the *Journal of Pre-College Engineering Education.*

Katie Brkich is associate professor of early childhood science education in Georgia Southern University's College of Education. Her current areas of scholarship interest are reconceptualizing success in STEM fields, increasing underrepresented populations' access to quality STEM education, and justice-oriented preservice and in-service elementary school teacher education. She has numerous peer-reviewed publications in national and international science education journals, with audiences ranging from the science education researcher to the classroom practitioner.

Belinda Bustos Flores is chair and professor for the Department of Bicultural-Bilingual Studies at The University of Texas, San Antonio. Her research focuses on teacher development including self-concept, ethnic identity, efficacy, beliefs, teacher recruitment/retention, and high stakes testing. Flores is lead editor for *Teacher Preparation for Bilingual Populations: Educar para transformer* and for *Generating Transworld Pedagogy: Reimagining La Clase Magica.* Dr. Flores was recently selected as the recipient of the 2015 Hispanic Research issues SIG Elementary, Secondary, and Postsecondary Award.

Sylvia Celedón-Pattichis is senior associate dean for research and community engagement in the College of Education and professor in the Department of Language, Literacy, and Sociocultural Studies. Her research interests include linguistic and cultural influences on the teaching and learning of mathematics, especially with emergent bilinguals; preparing teachers to work with culturally and linguistically diverse students; equity in mathematics education; and integrating mathematics education with other fields.

Lorena Claeys is executive director and research associate for the Academy of Teacher Excellence in the College of Education and Human Development at The University of Texas at San Antonio. Her research focuses on teacher recruitment, preparation, retention, and teachers' motivation to teach culturally and linguistically diverse students; including school–community–university collaborative partnerships.

Mayra L. Cordero is currently assistant professor at PK Yonge, the University of Florida Lab School teaching sixth grade science for 7 years. As a participant of the NSF U-FUTuRES project she has been leading a transformation in middle school science education through the implementation of an inquiry-based science curriculum. Her research interests include supporting science learning of African American middle school girls, inquiry-based science practices, and technology integration in the science classroom.

Andrea S. Foster, PhD, is currently a professor of science education at Sam Houston State University in Huntsville, TX. She has been involved in K–16 STEM education for more than 30 years. She is a former Presidential Awardee for Excellence in science and mathematics teaching and has earned numerous awards for her teaching, service, and scholarship at all levels.

Alejandro José Gallard Martínez is professor and Goizueta Distinguished Chair at Georgia Southern University's College of Education and the director of the Georgia Center for Education Renewal. The platform for his research is to explore equity and social justice in education in general and in science education specifically. His frameworks include global perspectives on differences, otherness, polyphony of voices, and meaning making that reflects categories used to situate people in social life.

Teresa Jimarez is a retired professor from the University of Texas Pan American, Brownsville, TX. Her research includes preparing science teachers for diverse classrooms and Latino girls in science.

Charlease Kelly-Jackson, EdD, is an associate professor of science education in the Department of Elementary and Early Childhood Education at Kennesaw State University. Dr. Kelly-Jackson's research focuses on teacher professional development and STEM education, specifically diversity and equity issues around women and underrepresented minorities in these disciplines. As a STEM faculty fellow at Kennesaw State's A.T.O.M.S. Center, Kelly-Jackson is a resource to schools seeking STEM professional development and/or outreach collaborations.

Natalie S. King is a doctoral candidate in curriculum and instruction, specializing in science education at the University of Florida. Natalie's research agenda focuses on K–12 STEM education with an emphasis on the middle grades, advancing African American girls in STEM, informal science education programs, and the role of curriculum in fostering equity in science teaching and learning. Natalie's passion fueled her development of Fostering Opportunities and Cultivating Upstanding Students (FOCUS)—a community-based informal STEM program.

Patricia J. Larke is professor in the Department of Teaching, Learning, and Culture, Texas A&M University, College Station, TX. Her research areas are educational issues of African American girls, educating instructors to work with diverse populations, educational needs of students of color, and more recently, integrating culturally responsive practices in driver education. She is the author of over 100 publications and co-editor of two books.

Yeping Li is professor in the Department of Teaching, Learning, and Culture. His research interests are curriculum studies in school mathematics, international education, STEM education, and teacher education. He is the author of 100 publications including nine books.

Carlos A. LópezLeiva is assistant professor in the Department of Language, Literacy, and Sociocultural Studies at the University of New Mexico, whose research concerns how the social dimension of learning mediates Latina/o students' identities as bilingual doers of mathematics. For this purpose, LópezLeiva promotes and studies the integration of mathematics with other fields (e.g., engineering, science, literature), mathematization and modeling processes, as well as the learning and teaching of mathematics in formal and informal settings.

Carol T. Mitchell, PhD, is professor emeritus of science education at the University of Nebraska-Omaha. Her research focused on systemic reform in math and science education, culturally relevant pedagogy and increasing the participation and achievement in math and science by underrepresented students. She conducted two science/mathematics institutes in Lesotho, Africa for students and teachers and has co-authored a book *Hard to Teach Science Concepts—Elementary* (NSTA Press), several journal articles, and nine book chapters. She served as co-principal investigator for several NSF and NIH grants.

Karisma Morton is a doctoral candidate in STEM Education at the University of Texas at Austin. Informed by her experience as a high school math teacher in a predominantly minority district, her research focuses on exploring the factors that contribute to racial/ethnic inequalities in STEM education, with a particular focus on the intersection of race/ethnicity and gender.

Marios Pattichis is associate chair and professor in the Department of Electrical and Computer Engineering at the University of New Mexico. His research interests include digital image and video processing, biomedical image and video analysis, computer architecture for image and video processing, and engineering education.

Wesley Pitts is an associate professor of science education in the Department of Middle and High School Education, School of Education, Lehman College, CUNY. Dr. Pitts also holds a joint appointment in the PhD program in the Urban Education Program at the CUNY Graduate Center. His research uses frameworks from cultural sociology to investigate how encounters in urban secondary and postsecondary education settings and science teacher preparation programs create success in science education.

Rose Pringle is an associate professor in science education at the University of Florida. Her research focuses on interrelated themes within science teacher education: pre-service teachers' positionality as science learners, science-specific pedagogies of both pre- and in-service science teachers, and translation of these practices into equitable inquiry-based science experiences. Currently, she is exploring partnerships with scientists in developing science curriculum for middle school teachers within the context of a comprehensive science teachers' professional development.

Aria Razfar, PhD, is professor of literacy, language, and culture at the University of Illinois at Chicago and an affiliate with Linguistics and the Learning Sciences Research Institute. Professor Razfar's research has been published widely in premier academic journals including *Applying Linguistics in Classrooms: A Sociocultural Perspective* (Routledge, 2014). His work has been funded by NSF and the U.S. DOE. He was the University of Illinois at Chicago's Researcher of the Year for the social sciences.

Natalie M. K. Ridgewell is a doctoral candidate in the School of Teaching and Learning at the University of Florida. Her areas of concentration are in curriculum, teaching, and teacher education; and schools, society, and culture. Natalie's research agenda includes (a) the scholarly development of curriculum, pedagogy, teacher education, and educational leadership, as well as (b) effective pedagogy that enhances both future and current teachers' ability to meet the high demands of school environments.

Catherine Riegle-Crumb, PhD, is associate professor of STEM education and sociology at The University of Texas at Austin. She also holds appointments as the associate director for research at the Center for STEM Education, and as a faculty research associate at the Population Research Center. Her current NSF-funded research investigates how both social and academic factors shape inequality the STEM trajectories of students from secondary school through college and beyond.

ReAnna S. Roby, (Mississippi native), is a postdoctoral research associate at Michigan State University in the Department of Teacher Education. She obtained a PhD in interdisciplinary learning and teaching (curriculum and instruction) from The University of Texas at San Antonio, a master's in curriculum and instruction from Washington State University, and a bachelor's in chemistry from Alcorn State University. Currently, she works on separate NSF funded projects geared toward transformation in STEM education and teacher education. As a first-generation scholar, Roby's background as a Black Southern woman in science greatly informs her service, research, and teaching—praxis. Roby's scholarship employs critical race feminism, curriculum theory, and critical qualitative methodologies to explore the ways in which the narratives of minoritized people, with special attention to Black women and girls, in STEM (formally and informally) could be used to reconceptualize STEM curriculum.

Kathryn Scantlebury, PhD, is a professor in the Department of Chemistry and Biochemistry and director of secondary education in the College of Arts & Sciences at the University of Delaware. Her research interests focus on feminist and gender issues in STEM education in preservice teacher education and teachers' professional development.

Lee Shumow is a Distinguished Teaching Professor in educational psychology at Northern Illinois University. She has utilized both observational methods and the experience sampling method (ESM) in numerous studies. Shumow has published articles on students' motivation and learning in science and mathematics. With Dr. Jennifer Schmidt, she is an author of a recent book for middle and high school science teachers based on research findings that provides important practical information and resources to science teachers.

Lauren Shure, PhD, is an associate professor of counseling at Barry University. Dr. Shure holds a BS in psychology, MEd and EdS in marriage and family counseling, and PhD in counselor education with a specialization in clinical mental health counseling from the University of Florida. Before joining the Barry Counseling Program, she planned and coordinated research and evaluation on the PBIS Indiana project, a statewide network of culturally responsive positive behavior intervention and support programs (CR-PBIS) in K–12 schools. She is a licensed mental health counselor in Florida. Her professional interests include multicultural training and supervision, as well as issues of educational equity.

Amelia Squires Tangeman graduated with a BS in elementary education from Creighton University in 2010, and a MS in elementary education with a concentration in STEM education from the University of Nebraska at Omaha (UNO) in 2015. Since 2014, she has worked as the STEM outreach coordinator at UNO. She is the project director of the UNO Eureka!-STEM summer program, and serves on multiple committees and boards related to STEM Outreach in the Community.

Alma D. Stevenson is associate professor of literacy at Georgia Southern University. Her research explores sociocultural perspectives on literacy, literacy in science, and the role of language and literacy in culture, identity, and academic achievement. She is particularly interested in the role of home languages and cultures as sources of affective support and positive identity formation in historically underserved minorities. Her research looks to construct empowering curricula and pedagogies that advocate for social justice.

Zayoni N. Torres received her PhD in curriculum and instruction, with a concentration in gender and women's studies, from the University of Illinois at Chicago (UIC). She is a former project coordinator for the English Learning through Math, Science, and Action Research (ELMSA) project at UIC and a former research fellow for the Center for the Mathematics Education of Latinos/as (CEMELA). She currently works for the Arizona Department of Child Safety. Her research interests include sociocultural and feminist perspectives to explore the teaching of mathematics and science literacy for English learners.

Teresa A. Wasonga is a Fulbright scholar and Presidential Engagement Professor of Educational Leadership at Northern Illinois University. Her research is focused on educational leadership and the empowerment of girls, specifically in Kenya where she has co-founded an innovative all girls' boarding school with a focus on indigent students. She has published in several journals including *Journal of East African Studies, Journal of School Leadership, International Journal of Educational Management*, and *Leadership and Policy in Schools*.

Beth Wassell, PhD, is a professor in the Department of Language, Literacy, and Sociocultural Education at Rowan University in Glassboro, NJ. Her research focuses on the experiences and achievement of English language learner (ELL) students in STEM contexts, the roles of families of ELL students, and teaching for and about social justice in K–12 schools and teacher education.

Gwendolyn Webb-Hasan is associate professor in the Department of Educational Administration and Human Resources at Texas A&M University, College Station, TX. Her research interests include culturally responsive (a) leadership, (b) pedagogy, (c) classroom management, and (d) special education interventions as a result of disproportionate representation, in socially just and equitable contexts. Her primary focus is on the school empowerment among African American learners in PreK–16 settings and their families.

Cirecie West-Olatunji, PhD, is associate professor of counseling in the Division of Education & Counseling at Xavier University of Louisiana. Her research focuses on the role of cultural identity in the psychological, emotional, and educational development of marginalized students. She is Co-PI on the National Science Foundation investigating socially constructed attitudes and perceptions of African American primary school girls in science and mathematics.

Eunhui Yoon, PhD is an independent researcher in Gainesville, FL. Dr. Yoon specializes in bullying within the school context and research methodologies.

Jamaal R. Young, PhD, focuses his attention on culturally responsive mathematics teaching, particularly related to the educational needs of African American children, multicultural STEM project based learning, preparation of preservice mathematics teachers to work with diverse learners, and literature synthesis and meta-analysis methodology. Dr. Young currently seeks to examine the instructional factors that contribute to the success of children of color in STEM content areas.

Jemimah L. Young, PhD, is an assistant professor of multicultural and urban education at the University of North Texas. Her research interests include the academic achievement of Black Girls, achievement gap research, in addition culturally responsive pedagogy—particularly in STEM. She implores critical lens and mixed methods research to investigate the impact of learning for marginalized groups.

Made in the USA
Monee, IL
24 October 2020

45969369R00155